A TALE *of*
TWO COLONIES

A TALE *of*
TWO COLONIES

What Really Happened in Virginia and Bermuda?

VIRGINIA BERNHARD

University of Missouri Press
Columbia

Copyright © 2011 by
The Curators of the University of Missouri
University of Missouri Press, Columbia, Missouri 65211
Printed and bound in the United States of America
All rights reserved
First paperback printing, 2017

Cataloging-in-Publication data available from the Library of Congress.
ISBN: 978-0-8262-2145-2 (paperback : alk. paper)

∞™ This paper meets the requirements of the
American National Standard for Permanence of Paper
for Printed Library Materials, Z39.48, 1984.

Typefaces: Castellar and Minion

CONTENTS

MAPS

ACKNOWLEDGMENTS

This book would not have been possible without my Bermuda friends and colleagues, especially the late Archie Hallett, whose work on early Bermuda formed the basis for my own and whose friendship encouraged me until his death in 2003. Archie's wife, Clara (Keggie), a scholar in her own right, shared her expertise and her hospitality. Others whose aid was invaluable were Edward C. Harris, director of the Bermuda Maritime Museum (now the National Museum of Bermuda); John Adams and Karla Hayward at the Bermuda Archives; and the staffs of the Archives and the Bermuda Library. The late Cecil Dismont, former mayor of Hamilton, and his family, especially his wife, Lee, were gracious hosts on my many visits to Bermuda.

I am grateful to a host of other friends and colleagues who offered advice, read parts of the manuscript, commented on earlier papers and articles, and helped to shape the final product. Alden Vaughan was extraordinarily helpful, Larry Gragg, likewise. John Boles, Elaine Crane, Sheila Skemp, Michael Jarvis, and Clarence Matthews offered both encouragement and perceptive criticisms. William Kelso, Sara Bearss, and Brent Tarter shared their knowledge of early Virginia.

To my coworkers in the History Department at the University of St. Thomas, especially Irving Kelter, Joseph McFadden, Lee Williames, and Tom Crow, who heard more about early Bermuda and Virginia than they wanted to know, my thanks.

To my son, Paul, whose map skills were invaluable, and to his sisters, Catherine and Anne, who listened patiently, many thanks. To my husband, Jim, who was endlessly supportive and juggled his own writing projects to read mine, I owe more than words can say.

I am indebted to Clair Willcox, Sara Davis, Daren Dean, and Beth Chandler at the University of Missouri Press, and especially to Annette Wenda, my indefatigable copy editor.

A TALE *of*
TWO COLONIES

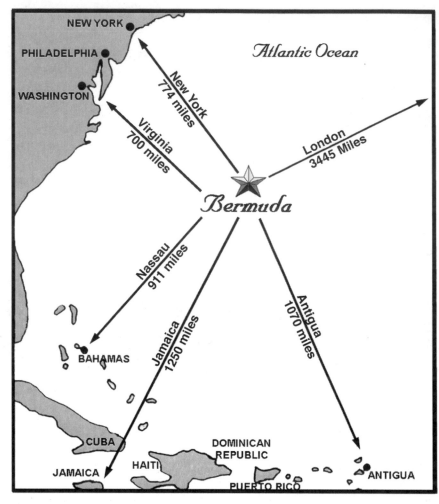

Map of the Atlantic Ocean, with Virginia and Bermuda. *Courtesy Paul Bernhard.*

INTRODUCTION

Y EARS BEFORE THE *Mayflower* set sail, English colonists in the New World confronted Native peoples and set the stage for savagery and slavery. In the early 1600s a series of disasters, miscalculations, and intrigues—each with unintended consequences and unanswered questions—changed the history of the New World and left a legacy that shaped attitudes toward race and culture in America for four hundred years. This book explores seventeenth-century narratives, letters, public records, and the recent work of historians and archaeologists to compel us to look again at what we know—and what we may never know—about America's beginnings.

In the past few years, colonial historians have begun to widen the focus of their studies to a larger perspective: the transatlantic world. It is no longer enough to examine the history of a particular colony, or, indeed, the history of the United States, within its narrow boundaries on the map. As the globe shrinks due to modern technology and communications, its history enlarges. Earlier generations were content to know America's history as the narrative of European (mostly English) settlers who came to the New World in search of freedom and a better life. Often omitted from this narrative were the histories of Native Americans who were forced off their lands and of Africans who were brought to the new land against their will. Overlooked as well were the histories of other nations whose aims and actions were inextricably bound up—and sometimes in conflict—with those of the English. The history of colonial America is not as simple as it used to be.

Besides learning to paint on a larger canvas, colonialists must deal with a perennial problem: evidence. Whereas historians of later periods are faced with the task of selecting from a wealth of evidence—documents, newspapers, journals, photographs, films, and audio recordings—colonial historians have the opposite problem: too little material. They must seize upon every scrap of evidence they can find, constructing their histories from shards and shreds, pieces of a vast jigsaw puzzle whose borders are missing and whose images are unclear. Often a single source—the writings of Capt. John Smith, for instance—must be parsed and stretched to fill in gaps in what happened, or what may have happened, in the past. The same is true for William Strachey's narrative of the *Sea Venture*'s shipwreck on Bermuda. Smith's 1608 pamphlet, *A True Relation of such occurrences and accidents of note as hath happened in Virginia,* was the first published account about England's newest colony. How truthful was he? Scholars disagree. But Smith's writings, especially his monumental *Generall Historie of Virginia, New-England, and the Summer Isles* (1624), are the basis of what we know about early Virginia. There are a handful of accounts by Smith's contemporaries, some of whom were his enemies. The earliest records of the Virginia Company have been lost. Existing documents must be compared and analyzed, their writers' circumstances studied and set against those of other writers. For example, George Percy, who wrote a narrative of the 1610 "Starving Time" in Virginia, intensely disliked John Smith and hoped to discredit his leadership as well as his writings.

In making sense of what happened four hundred years ago, documents and their authors are only parts of the puzzle. Audiences must be considered: in an age of widespread illiteracy (about one-third of the people in England in the early 1600s could read), how was information spread? As we shall see, hearsay and rumors about early Virginia and Bermuda flew like arrows, and sometimes inflicted wounds. Historians face other problems: maps have damaged edges or faded lines; journals and letters are partly illegible or have missing pages. And there are the absent voices: Indians and Africans. Their histories must be extracted from the traces they left on the land and from the writings of Europeans who observed them. In the end, some sort of narrative emerges—but how close is it to what really happened?

This history of early Virginia and Bermuda is a tale of events and actions that produced unintended consequences. A hurricane struck the largest fleet that England ever sent to Virginia and wrecked the flagship *Sea Venture* on Bermuda. In Virginia a mysterious, near-fatal accident incapacitated John Smith, and he had to return to England. In London the joint-stock enterprise known as the Virginia Company, mistakenly assuming that the *Sea Venture* expedition had reached its destination, sent no more supplies. Greed and chicanery—and an Indian uprising in Virginia—brought about the collapse of the Virginia Company and a lasting enmity between English and Indians. Africans captured from the Spanish slave ships were first acquired as laborers, not slaves, in both Bermuda and Virginia. Slavery did not exist under English law, but a chain of related events brought Africans to England's colonies, and in a few years, slavery would take root—creating a racial divide in America that lingered for four hundred years.

This book aims not merely to reconstruct a somewhat familiar narrative, for that has already been done. Historians Lorri Glover and Daniel Blake Smith spin a fast-paced story in *The Shipwreck That Saved Jamestown: The "Sea Venture" Castaways and the Fate of America,* as does Hobson Woodward in *A Brave Vessel: The True Tale of the Castaways Who Rescued Jamestown and Inspired Shakespeare's "The Tempest."* Kieran Doherty's *"Sea Venture": Shipwreck, Survival, and the Salvation of the First English Colony in the New World* is for a "young adult" audience.[1] The titles of these works aptly describe their contents. But *A Tale of Two Colonies: What Really Happened in Virginia and Bermuda?* carries the story into the 1620s and invites its readers to consider the fragments of evidence—both written and archaeological—upon which that record is based. Some parts of it, such as the founding of the Jamestown settlement, have been endlessly examined, but the links between Virginia and Bermuda, such as the arrival of the first Africans, remain largely unconnected.

Bermuda, one of the most remote islands in the world, lay unknown until 1505 and uninhabited for more than a century after that. Its reputation as the "Isle of Devils" came from the tales sailors told each other about hidden reefs that spelled death to ships that sailed too close to the land and about infernal cries (later found to be the calls of Bermuda's cahow birds) that emanated from the islands at night. In ports on both sides of the Atlantic, seamen told fearsome stories that constituted Bermuda's first history. Some Spanish mariners and one Englishman who explored parts of the islands wrote accounts of what they saw and did. With these reports, Bermuda's written history began.

In 1609 the *Sea Venture,* bound for Virginia, was shipwrecked on Bermuda. Castaways' journals describe the hurricane at sea and murders and mutinies on land. One such account is said to have inspired Shakespeare's work *The Tempest.* Among the Bermuda castaways, murders were committed, but no graves have been found. Authority was challenged, but the reasons remain unclear. Years later scholars still disagree on the evidence.

Meanwhile, inside a tiny fort at Jamestown, colonists struggled to stay alive. John Smith fought to keep order, battling both English and Indians. When he left, desperate colonists ate lizards, rats, and human flesh. Surviving accounts of the "Starving Time" differ, as do modern scholars' theories. But some evidence is pathetically persuasive: archaeologists have turned up pitiful remnants of colonists' diets—and their graves.

By May 1610 the Bermuda castaways had built two small ships and set sail for Virginia. When they arrived, they found Jamestown's people in the last stages of starvation. The castaways shared what little food they had (recently excavated bones of Bermuda's native cahow birds testify to that), but it was not enough. There was nothing to do but abandon the colony. The leaders, both military and civilian, the Virginia Company, and the members of the rescue expedition all produced different versions of this story.

The Virginia Company poured thousands of pounds sterling and hundreds of colonists into Jamestown, but failed to make a profit. Bermuda, with no native population and a balmy climate, looked much more promising. It became England's second New World colony in 1612. Promotional literature for both colonies made them seem idyllic.

Spain, fearful of English raids on its treasure-laden galleons from the New World, plotted to destroy both Virginia and Bermuda. English informers and Spanish diplomats in London and Spanish spies in Virginia fed various versions of the truth to Spain's King Philip III.

Factions split the Virginia Company. Conflicting reports of conditions in Virginia exacerbated an unpleasant situation. Contraband Africans captured from Spanish ships by English privateers were put to work in both Bermuda and Virginia, and a cover-up of the captures ensued. The official records of the Virginia Company from 1606 to 1619 disappeared and have never been found.

After four centuries, much of what really happened in early Bermuda and Virginia is still part of a vast transatlantic puzzle, subject to scholarly debate. This book examines a few pieces of that puzzle, in hopes that the parts may shed new light on the whole.

A Note on the Sources

In editing the seventeenth-century narratives and other documents for a modern audience, archaic spelling and punctuation have been altered as necessary for clarity's sake, but the original texts have been preserved as much as possible. Under the Julian (Old Style) calendar, the new year began on March 25. To avoid confusion, dates between January 1 and March 25 have been converted to use January 1 as the beginning of the new year. England did not convert to the Gregorian (New Style) calendar until 1752.

1

THE WRECK OF THE *SEA VENTURE*

IN THE TEEMING, brawling, bustling London of the early 1600s, more than two hundred thousand people lived and worked. It was the fastest-growing city in Europe and a major world port. On the wide Thames River, small boats went up and down, oars moving like the legs of water bugs, and east of London Bridge, dozens of large ships rode at anchor. Warehouses full of spices and silks, pottery and bronze, and other exotic foreign goods lined the riverbanks. This was the heyday of the great trading companies: The Levant Company traded in rugs, wine, and fruits from the Mediterranean. The Muscovy Company brought furs and wax from Russia. Sable and seal fur made cloak linings and trimmed robes and gowns; beaver pelts went into felt for hats. Wax, melted and usually imprinted with a signet ring or stamp, sealed letters and lent importance to documents. Thousands of pounds of sealing wax were used in England every year. The largest and richest of the trading companies, the Exxon-Mobil of its day, was the East India Company. Chartered in 1600, it had a monopoly on trade with India, bringing spices, silks, and cotton cloth from exotic places like Madras and Bombay. In 1608 Sir Thomas Smith, one of that company's directors, was about to become the guiding force of the Virginia Company. As the company's treasurer, he was organizing the largest expedition England had yet sent to the New World.[1]

On a chilly day in March 1608, Don Pedro de Zuñiga, Spain's ambassador to the Court of St. James's, sat hunched over a desk in his house at Highgate. He had been living in London for three years, but he still missed the warm sunshine of his homeland. The ambassador was finishing a laborious task, writing a letter in code to his sovereign in Madrid. When it was done, he blotted the ink carefully with sand, folded the paper, and sealed it. The imprint of his signet ring in the soft red wax would ensure that his letter was handled carefully. It was an urgent message, but he did not expect an immediate reply. Diplomatic exchanges between London and Madrid often took as long as three months. Zuñiga wrote to King Philip III that the English were sending eight hundred men to Virginia, and, the ambassador said, "it seems to me necessary to intercept them on the way."[2]

Spain had good reason to be concerned. By the mid-1500s Spanish fleets of up to seventy ships were transporting hundreds of tons of gold and silver from Mexico and Peru every year. Masters of these galleons sailing home from the West Indies followed the coast of North America to latitude 33 degrees. Then they headed eastward toward a landmark in the vast Atlantic, Bermuda. Even though it was a tiny, uninhabited island in the middle of nowhere, Bermuda served as a guide for convoys of Spanish galleons crossing the Atlantic. This tiny island, twenty-four square miles in size, was about to be inhabited, with unintended consequences. But Virginia was already inhabited, and the English there were in a prime position to prey on the Spanish treasure fleets.

The latest English expedition to Virginia was not due to depart until the next year. The flagship *Sea Venture* and the rest of the large fleet would not sail until May 1609. How had Zuñiga come by this information? King James I had not yet signed the Virginia Company's new charter, and the company had not yet made public its grand plan. But the Spanish ambassador had his sources.

Don Pedro de Zuñiga, the first resident Spanish ambassador to England, was a member of what has been called the most efficient and talented diplomatic corps in Europe. When Spain and England signed a peace treaty in 1604, Spain's Philip III chose his ambassador carefully. Zuñiga had been Philip III's chief huntsman, and Philip, knowing James I's fondness for hunting, sent his favorite huntsman as ambassador, along with six "beautifully outfitted horses" as a present to the English king.[3] Zuñiga soon became a hunting companion of James I. The shrewd ambassador also maintained a secret, handsomely paid network of seven "pensioners of Spain," that is, English spies. Among them were the brilliant but unscrupulous Henry Howard, Earl of Northampton and member of the Privy Council; the devious courtier and secretary of state, Robert Cecil, Earl of Salisbury; and a Mrs. Drummond, "first lady of Queen Anne's bedchamber."[4] Today all that remains of Zuñiga's—and his successors'—intrigues is a paper trail of letters in the Spanish archives. Written in diplomatic cipher, the letters document Spain's constant clandestine efforts to destroy England's outposts in Virginia—and, later, in Bermuda.

American historians knew nothing of this correspondence until Alexander Brown published *The Genesis of the United States* in 1890. Brown discovered the collection of letters in the Spanish archives in Seville and persuaded a scholar named Maximilian Schele de Vere at the University of Virginia to translate them. That meant deciphering about fifty thousand words of archaic Spanish. De Vere did it, but not without grumbling. "There is no punctuation," he said, "no stop, no mark of interrogation, no sign to judge where a sentence begins or ends. Then, there are no accents . . . and accents are fully as important as letters in Spanish. Finally, the copyist was evidently not as careful as he might have been; some words are repeated, some manifestly omitted, and some are probably given wrong." That was De Vere's opinion, but Irene A. Wright, who worked with the same documents in Seville in the 1920s, said that "De Vere's statement of the difficulties of translation is greatly exaggerated."[5] The Colorado-born Wright, who explored Mexico in 1895 at age sixteen with three hundred dollars in gold coins sewn into her skirt for spending money, was an intrepid scholar of Spanish history. While she was working in the Spanish archives, she met Henry Wilkinson, who was working on his history of Bermuda. He despaired of finding anything useful in the archives, which were not indexed. But Wright searched, and she discovered that in 1611 King Philip III had ordered his officials to prepare a summary of "all that was known about Bermuda." This lucky find was, said Wilkinson, "the most satisfactory of documents." Thanks to the perseverance of Alexander Brown, Maximilian de Vere, Irene Wright, and Henry Wilkinson, documents of Spain's surveillance of England's New World colonies became accessible outside Seville. The documents prove, as Brown said, that in the seventeenth century, "Spanish spies were everywhere."[6] Had they been more successful, this book might be written in Spanish instead of English.

Protestant England and Catholic Spain had long been enemies, and though they made peace in 1604, trust was not part of the treaty. In 1605 a group of English Catholics tried to blow up the Houses of Parliament in the "Gunpowder Plot" of November 5. By chance, the cache of powder barrels in the cellar underneath the House of Lords was discovered in time, but the fears of Catholic conspiracies continued. Spain was not involved in the Gunpowder Plot, and Ambassador Zuñiga did his best to quell English suspicions. The Spanish, in turn, had their own reasons to distrust the English. The ignominy of Spanish Armada's defeat at the hands of the English in 1588 still rankled. Besides that, English "sea dogs" like Francis Drake and others had been plundering Spain's New World treasures since the 1570s, and such memories died hard. Now, if the English got a foothold in Virginia, what was to keep them from using it to prey on treasure-laden Spanish ships from the West Indies? Philip III had been worried about the Virginia venture since the beginning, when James I issued letters patent to the newly formed Virginia Company in 1606. By January 1607 Ambassador Zuñiga had written a long letter to his king, summarizing the plans for colonizing Virginia. He had heard that the English planned to send two ships each month until they had "two thousand men" in their new colony.[7] Not exactly. Sometimes Zuñiga's sources were wrong, but the ambassador kept his king informed as best he could.

Philip III, Spain's sandy-haired, foppish young monarch, who had come to his throne in 1598 at age twenty, was far from inexperienced in matters of state. When the heir to the Spanish throne was only fifteen, his father, Philip II, had made him sit in on daily meetings of the Council of State to learn about foreign affairs.[8] In June 1607 the young king had written to Zuñiga of his fears of the Protestant English "establishing their kind of religion there." Furthermore, said Philip, "It has appeared right to prevent these plans and purposes of the English by all available means . . . and to ascertain the root of this matter . . . whether it progresses; who aids them and by what means." The Spanish king instructed Zuñiga to express his royal concern that King James would allow his subjects "to try and disturb the seas, coasts, and lands of the Indies." A few weeks later Zuñiga reported his conversation with England's king on this matter: James I declared, said Zuñiga, that "no advantage from it all came to him, and that if his subjects went where they ought not to go, and were punished for it, neither he nor they could complain."[9] The king of England had shrugged off all responsibility for what went on in Virginia. This was not a comforting thought for the king of Spain.

Spanish galleons laden with silver and gold from Mexico and Peru followed the Gulf Stream up the Atlantic coast—sailing within easy range of Virginia-based attackers in Chesapeake Bay. Now England's James I, the darkly serious, thoughtful scholar, was washing his hands of the hundred-odd men and boys in Virginia. What they did would be on their own heads, and he was not to blame. England and Spain were, after all, at peace. But Philip III was surrounded by advisers who urged him to do "whatever was necessary to drive out the people who are in Virginia . . . [and] not to let anyone hear what is being done."[10]

The Spanish were not the only ones keeping secrets: in London the members of the Privy Council and the Virginia Company kept to themselves all information they received about England's colonial ventures abroad, and they imposed a strict censorship on the fledgling Jamestown settlement. But Zuñiga had his London informers, and from them he gathered that "the main thing they [the English in Virginia] find to do in that place is to fortify themselves and to sail as pirates from there."[11] In coded letters and confidential documents, Spanish officials would worry about English pirates for the next fifteen years.

One of the bearers of secrets for the English was Capt. Christopher Newport, who landed the first colonists at Jamestown in April 1607. He had made the crossing from England to Virginia twice more in 1608, each time bringing letters and reports—all of which the Virginia Company classified as top secret.[12] Places of settlement, numbers of colonists and natives, descriptions of the land, and locations of harbors and rivers were closely guarded. No wonder the Spanish were suspicious. Had the English found gold? Silver? Maps were kept under lock and key, and none were to be made public without approval of the royal Privy Council or the Virginia Company Council.

In the late summer of 1608, this wall of censorship and secrecy was about to be breached. In August a pamphlet for sale at a bookseller's stand in St. Paul's churchyard soon became the talk of London. This little forty-four-page book was the first printed report of what had happened to England's new colony in far-off Virginia. Thanks to Captain Newport and his sailors, rumors had been flying all year: Indian attacks, grisly deaths, quarrels among the colonists. Now *A True Relation of such occurrences and accidents of note as hath happened in Virginia*, written by a colonist named John Smith, claimed to set the record straight. The young officer's tale of disaster and derring-do made for sensational reading, and those who could not read could hear about it in London's taverns and on the streets. Smith told of "discontented humours" among the colony's leaders and "such famine and sickness, that the living were scarce able to bury the dead." Indians were by turns curious and hostile. They admired Smith's compass, but killed a colonist "with 20 or 30 arrows in him."[13] This was not exactly the kind of thing to attract new investors and colonists, which is what the Virginia Company desperately needed. *A True Relation* was true enough, but who had made it public?

John Smith had never intended his report—much less the map he sent with it—to be published. But he did send them—or something like them—to another adventurer. Henry Hudson, the English navigator and explorer, referred to "letters and charts which one Captain Smith had sent him from Virginia." Hudson was hoping to discover the Northwest Passage, a waterway through North America to the Far East, and make his fortune. In 1608 he could not get funding from London backers for his explorations, so he signed a contract with the Dutch instead. In September 1609 Hudson explored what is now New York, sailed up the river that is named for him, and claimed the area for the Netherlands. The English were furious. They tried to confiscate Hudson's reports and logbooks, but he managed to keep them for his Dutch employers.[14]

If John Smith's information about Virginia reached Henry Hudson, it also reached someone who rushed it into print for a London audience. Therein lies a mystery. Smith's *Relation* arrived in London as a forty-page letter he addressed to someone now known only as "Kinde Sir." Smith had given it to a ship captain, Francis Nelson, whose ship, *Phoenix*, had left Virginia on June 2. The identity of the person to whom Nelson delivered the letter is unknown. The other part of the mystery is the map: a rough map of Virginia, thought to have been drawn by Smith, was included with his letter. Somehow this map, which contains the first known sketch of the fort at Jamestown (a site unknown to archaeologists until 1994), as well as details of Virginia's rivers and harbors fell into the hands of Don Pedro de Zuñiga. He traced it, or had it traced, and sent the copy to Philip III. Who smuggled the map to Zuñiga? No one knows. The tracing, now known as the Smith-Zuñiga map, was discovered in the Spanish archives nearly three centuries later.[15] The original map has disappeared.

Spanish officials were worried. On August 21 the Council of State advised King Philip that "this matter of Virginia is not to be remedied by negotiation, but by force, punishing those who have gone there." By September the king of Spain knew about the *True Relation* and possessed a map showing the exact location of the Jamestown fort. He wrote to Zuñiga on September 23 urging him to send more papers about Virginia

Barren Island

so that he "might the better come to a decision as to what ought to be done." What Zuñiga sent him is not known, but by November the ambassador wrote with great urgency, "It is very important, Your Majesty should command that an end be put to those things done in Virginia. . . . [T]hey propose (as I understand) to send as many as 1500 men there; and they hope that 12,000 will be gotten together there in time."[16] No wonder the Spanish were uneasy.

Zuñiga would watch and wait as the "Virginia Adventurers," as the investors were called, signed on to a new plan to expand England's fragile colony. Some people still half-believed the lines in a popular satirical play—*Eastward Ho!*—in which a sea captain says about Virginia, "I tell thee, Gold is more plentiful there than Copper is with us. . . . [A]ll their Dripping Pans, and their Chamber pots are pure Gold." In 1607 the Virginia Company had sent a goldsmith, just in case. Hopes were high. Virginia enthusiast Sir Walter Cope wrote to the Earl of Salisbury in August that "we are fallen upon a lande, that promises more than the Lande of promisse: Instead of milk we find pearle, & gold Instead of honey." Capt. Christopher Newport had brought back from Virginia "but a barrell full of the earth, but there seems a kingdome full of the ore." Ambassador Zuñiga wrote to King Philip that he had seen "a letter written by a gentleman who is over there in Virginia, to another friend of his, who is known to me, and has shown it to me. He says that from Captain Newport, who is the bearer of it, he will learn in detail how matters are there, and that all he can say is that there has been found a moderate mine of silver and that the best part of England cannot be compared with that country."[17] But the gold was fool's gold, the silver was only a rumor, and so far all that had come from Virginia were some cedar timbers and sassafras roots.

Virginia Company investors desperately needed to show a profit. They must have ground their teeth as they totted up their losses in hundreds of pounds sterling. Not only were they losing money, but the colonists at Jamestown were also losing their lives. Three hundred two men and two women ("Mistress Forrest and Ann Burras her maide") had been sent there so far, but only "about two hundred" people were alive in the spring of 1609.[18] Diseases, such as dysentery, the "bloody flux," and malaria, and Indian arrows were filling rows of hastily dug graves at Jamestown. The colonists tried to keep the deaths secret from the Indians, as instructed by the Virginia Company: "Above all things Do not advertize the killing of any of your men. . . . [Y]ou Shall Do well also not to Let them See or know of Your Sick men." Under the company's first charter, as an observer wrote some years later, "that plantation went rather backwards than forwards."[19] Despite such setbacks, a new charter and the *Sea Venture* expedition were expected to turn things around.

As the winter and spring of 1609 passed, important-looking men in velvet and fur with plumes in their hats came and went at Sir Thomas Smith's imposing house in Philpot Lane, a short walk from the Thames River. Smith, born in Weston Hanger, Kent, in 1558, was now one of the most powerful, as well as one of the richest, men in London. His portrait shows a dapper-looking man of slender build with a crayon-thin mustache; a close-trimmed beard; heavy, dark eyebrows; and a serene gaze. He might well be serene, considering his accomplishments thus far: now fifty-one, after the deaths of two wives, he had married Sara Blount, the daughter of a prosperous London mercer (cloth merchant), and at last he had a family, three sons and a daughter. He had been sheriff of London and ambassador to Russia, and he was a leading member of the Merchant Adventurers, Muscovy Company, Levant Company, and East India Company. Sir Thomas Smith was also the treasurer (the equivalent of the modern chief executive officer, or CEO) of the Virginia Company, and to save both the company and its fragile settlement on the banks of the James River, he was organizing an enormous (and enormously expensive) expedition to Virginia. He was also a master at propaganda.[20]

In the spring of 1609, promotional tracts published by the Virginia Company and sermons preached by sympathetic clergymen had all London talking about the new Virginia project. The company's first publication, *Nova Britannia: Offering Most Excellent Fruites by Planting in Virginia,* promised, "And as for the generall sort that shall goe to bee planters, bee they never so poore, so they be honest, and painefull [industrious], the place will make them rich." The author was Robert Johnson, a wealthy London merchant and Virginia Company shareholder, who also happened to be Sir Thomas Smith's son-in-law. Said he, "The second thing to make this Plantation is money, to be raised among the adventurers, wherein the sooner and more deeply men engage themselves, their charge will be the shorter, and their gain the greater." But the Reverend William Crashaw, a distinguished London clergyman and dogged supporter of the Virginia project, preached a sermon before the Virginia Company Council, cautioning the investors against expecting a quick return: "Private ends," he warned them, "have been the bane of many excellent exploits." The desire for profit, said the reverend, was to blame for Virginia's present woes: "one fly hath corrupted the whole box of ointment." The Reverend William Symonds, pastor of St. Savior's, at Southwark, was another diligent supporter of the Virginia project. His sermons and those from other London pulpits trumpeted England's duty to colonize and to carry the gospel across the ocean (and, incidentally, to compete with Spain's legions of Roman Catholic priests in the business of conversion). The Virginia Company needed all the help—material and spiritual—that it could muster.[21] This new expedition to Jamestown must not fail. Ambassador Zuñiga was hard-pressed to keep the stream of details flowing from London to Madrid. On March 5, 1609, he sent word to Philip III that new plans were afoot to recruit a fresh batch of colonists for Virginia. "All workmen" who agreed to sign on were being promised "houses to live in, vegetable-gardens and orchards, and also food and clothing at the expense of the Company."[22] He enclosed a copy of a Virginia Company broadside promising instant prosperity to all who signed on. Zuñiga also wrote to Philip that he had heard of a scheme involving one Baron Thomas Arundel, who had wanted to take a shipload of colonists to Virginia, but despite Arundel's connections (his wife's brother was Sir Henry Wriothesley, the Earl of Southampton, a shareholder in the Virginia Company), he had been denied permission because he was "suspected of being a Catholic." (He was.) Now, said Zuñiga, the disaffected Arundel wanted to change sides and strike a blow against Virginia for Spain. Arundel hatched a plan to sail to the Canaries or Puerto Rico, pick up a Spaniard chosen by King Philip, and take the recruited spy to Virginia, where the Spaniard could survey the "sites occupied by the English, and the fortifications they have," and then report to Philip "how those people can be removed without recourse to arms." But Arundel could not raise enough money, and so his plot never materialized. Zuñiga's sources also told him that "Baron de la Warte [Warr]" has been appointed governor of Virginia, and that soon after Gates's expedition, De La Warr "is to sail with 600 or 700 men . . . and some women." Zuñiga had heard that "all the pirates who are out of this kingdom will be pardoned by the King [James I] if they resort there, and the place is so perfect (as they say) for piratical excursions that Your Majesty will not be able to bring silver from the Indies without finding a very great obstacle there."[23]

A month later Zuñiga wrote again of his fears of Virginia's growing power. His letter of April 1, 1609, warned King Philip that the English "are pushing forward with establishing themselves in Virginia." It seemed to Zuñiga that the situation was growing more serious, since "Baron de Lawarre and Captain Gacht [Lord De La Warr and Sir Thomas Gates] will take a big instalment of people, more than I reported; because they are waiting for those whom the [Dutch] Rebels are discharging [English soldiers who had been fighting in the Netherlands] to send them there." Spain's long war with the Dutch ended March 30, 1609, and the ambassador feared that this would free English mercenaries for service in Virginia—perhaps against Spain's New World colonies. On April 12, Zuñiga had more news: he had heard that the Jamestown settlers were abandoning the place where they first settled "because it is unhealthy and many have died there, and farther down the river they had found a good place." The ambassador urged immediate action. "Your Majesty will appreciate how important this is for your royal interests, and so I hope [you] will quickly command the extirpation of these insolents."[24]

While King Philip pondered his next move, the Virginia Company went forward with its new charter, signed and sealed by King James I on May 23. Now the company had a larger grant of land in North America that stretched from what is now Long Island, New York, to Cape Fear, North Carolina—and westward "from sea to sea." No one knew where the western sea was, but so much land was intoxicating to Londoners. Never mind the tales of hostile Indians and hardship in Virginia: investors could hardly wait to sign on for their shares. The list of shareholders totals 659 people, plus 56 "city companies," or craftsmen's guilds: grocers, goldsmiths, haberdashers, ironmongers, vintners, coopers, white bakers, brown bakers, upholsterers, and musicians. Besides these there were 21 peers, 96 knights, 11 "doctors, ministers, etc.," 53 captains, 28 esquires, 58 gentlemen, 110 merchants, and 282 not classified.[25]

The company's latest reports of Virginia's abundance recruited ordinary folks (the "not classified") with promises of "soil more fertile than can be well express'd," "wood of all kinds, and that the fairest, yea, and best that ever any of us (traveler or workman) ever saw," not to mention "multitudes of fish" and "crabs rather better in taste than ours, one able to suffice four men."[26]

One person could invest in the company for £12.10 and get a portion of Virginia land after surveys were made. In present U.S. dollars, £12.10 would be about $3,164—a sizable sum, then or now. But people who could not afford to pay could sign on to work for the company for five to seven years and eventually earn their acreage. In England, only wealthy people owned land. In America, land so plentiful it defied imagination offered wealth for all. Who could resist?

One who took up the Virginia Company's offer was William Strachey, who had to borrow money to do it.[27] Born in 1572 in the town of Saffron Walden in Essex, forty-eight miles from London, Strachey, his family's eldest son, went to Emmanuel College in Cambridge at age sixteen, married at age twenty-three, and studied law at Gray's Inn in London. He did not take a degree or practice law, but in the early 1600s young Strachey moved in London theater and literary circles, wrote some verses, and probably knew Shakespeare. He lived well, but by 1606 he was short of cash.

With a wife and two sons to support, he took a position as the secretary of the English ambassador to Turkey in Constantinople. Unfortunately, Strachey and his employer did not see eye to eye, and Strachey was fired after a year. Now, at age thirty-seven, he was back in London and out of a job. He borrowed £30 from a goldsmith, bought two shares in the Virginia Company for £25, and signed on to sail aboard the *Sea Venture* in 1609.[28] More than a year later, William Strachey's account of that ship's fateful voyage would reach London, with consequences he never expected.[29]

The *Sea Venture* was the Virginia Company's pride and joy: a newly built three-hundred-ton flagship. Designed as a merchant ship, it had been specially fitted to carry a large number of passengers and their provisions. With it would go six other ships—the *Diamond, Falcon, Blessing, Lion, Unity,* and *Swallow*—and two pinnaces (smaller square-rigged vessels with decks), the *Virginia* and one whose name does not appear in the records. In all they would carry six hundred colonists. There is some disagreement as to details: According to one Virginia Company letter, it was sending "8. ships and a pinnace . . . with 600 men." A later Virginia Company tract stated that it had sent "the better part of five hundred men." Zuñiga wrote to Philip III that the English were sending "400 or

500 men and 100 women."[30] The Spanish ambassador was the only one who paid attention to the number of women, not because he possessed a modern concern for gender ratios, but because the king of Spain needed to know how many able-bodied men England was adding to its colony in America.

Commanding Virginia's able-bodied men—and women—was their new deputy governor, Lt.-Gen. Sir Thomas Gates. He was leaving his wife and three daughters at home. Gates had been chosen to take charge of the Virginia colony temporarily until the appointed governor, Capt.-Gen. Thomas West, the third Baron De La Warr (for whom the river and the state of Delaware are named, though he never saw them), could settle his affairs in England. Gates, a stern-looking, craggy-faced man with deep-set, burning eyes and a Cyrano-like nose, was then about fifty. He had a background that made him an ideal choice to take command in Virginia. Born around 1559 in the town of Colyford, Devonshire, in England's west country, Gates had made the military his career and seen a great deal of the world. As a young man he had fought against the Spanish in the Netherlands, when English soldiers helped the Dutch break free of Spanish control. While still in his twenties, Lieutenant Gates had sailed with Francis Drake to raid Spanish towns and ships in the Caribbean. In 1586 he was with Drake's fleet on the coast of what is now North Carolina, where the dispirited remnants of Raleigh's failed settlement had demanded to be taken home to England. Gates had dealt with discouraged colonists before now, and he was determined to see those at Jamestown succeed. By 1596 he was Sir Thomas Gates, knighted by Queen Elizabeth. Ten years later Gates was one of the first to petition King James I for a grant in 1606 to colonize Virginia. Now, in 1609, he was taking a leave of absence from his military duties in the Netherlands in order to go to Virginia. He was also taking with him some of the soldiers who had served under him in the Netherlands. On this voyage, as acting governor, Gates, with the title "lieutenant-general," would be responsible for six hundred people—but so would Sir George Somers, the admiral of the nine-vessel fleet. Both the lieutenant-general and the admiral were accustomed to giving orders— and being obeyed.[31]

No one in the Virginia Company had given much thought to how authority in the two command positions would be divided. The fleet's commander, fifty-five-year-old Adm. Sir George Somers, had a reputation for mercurial changes of mood and an explosive temper. He was said to be "a lamb on the land, so patient that few could anger him," but at sea he was a different man, "(as if entering a ship he had assumed a new nature) a lion at sea, so passionate that few could please him."[32] How he and Thomas Gates would share power remained to be seen. Born in 1554 in the seaport town of Lyme Regis, Dorset, Somers took to the sea at an early age. By the 1590s he was a seasoned mariner with many Atlantic crossings and the commands of four ships to his credit. On land he took up politics and was elected to Parliament in 1603. He was knighted that same year. In 1605 he was elected mayor of Lyme Regis, and in 1606, like Thomas Gates, he was a major player in the formation of the Virginia Company. He had also contributed two of the smaller ships—the *Swallow* and the pinnace *Virginia*—to the 1609 expedition, and he may have mortgaged some of his property to outfit the *Sea Venture*. His portrait shows him as a dark-haired man of vigorous middle age, with a faintly quizzical expression and a trace of a smile under his mustache.

The expedition's two leaders crossed swords from the very beginning. Somers, the admiral of the fleet, did not come to London for what must have been a momentous occasion, the departure of seven of the ships. The majestic flagship *Sea Venture* and its consorts, the *Diamond, Falcon, Blessing, Lion, Unity,* and one of the pinnaces, all set sail from Woolwich, on the south side of the Thames, on May 15. Crowds of London's ever-curious spectators lined the river's banks and cheered as the seven ships, sails billowing, flags flying, glided past them on that spring afternoon. Meanwhile, the admiral of the fleet waited, probably at home in Lyme Regis with his wife, Joanna, while the ships made their way along the south coast of England to Plymouth, a distance of about two hundred miles. When they arrived five days later, on May 20, Somers joined them there with his own additions to the fleet: the *Swallow*, which had his nephew Matthew Somers aboard as master, and the pinnace *Virginia*.[33]

When the *Sea Venture*'s trumpeter played the customary salute for a ship's commander as Adm. Sir George Somers marched up the gangplank, Lieutenant-General Gates, who had been with the flagship since it left London, must have felt somewhat slighted. Perhaps he said so. But Admiral Somers was the commander, not only of the *Sea Venture* but also of the entire fleet. There is no record of the words spoken between the two leaders that day. Bystanders recalled only that "some question of precedence" arose between Gates, the deputy-governor of Virginia, and Somers, the admiral of the fleet.[34] Perhaps they argued about who would oversee the final provisioning of the fleet at Plymouth wharf. That was an enormous undertaking for nine ships and six hundred people: the loading of hundreds of bushels of meal, peas, and oats; barrels of vinegar, oil, cider, wine, and aqua vitae (the seventeenth-century's version of brandy); beer; cheese; salted beef; dried codfish; and ship's biscuits, as well as pots, kettles, dishes, spoons, axes, hoes, hammers, nails, saws, shovels, and the like—not to mention muskets, lead shot, and gunpowder. All of this loading took ten or twelve days, until June 2. Someone had to be in command and to watch and confer with the other ships' masters as supplies were loaded aboard. Tempers flared. Hot words flew. For a while it was doubtful if Gates and Somers would sail on the same ship. At the last minute they grudgingly resolved their differences and agreed to sail together on the *Sea Venture*. Their mutual dislike would flare up again later.

When the fleet finally left Plymouth Sound, the *Sea Venture* carried another seasoned commander, the one-armed forty-nine-year-old Capt. Christopher Newport. The son of a shipmaster at Harwich, Newport had been at sea since he was nineteen, and he had already sailed three times to Virginia. He had been in "sole charge and command" of the 1607 expedition to Virginia until its three small ships reached land. Then a quarrelsome council (including Capt. John Smith) appointed by the Virginia Company had taken over. Newport commanded the company's supply ships, sailing again to Virginia in 1608 and 1609. The *Sea Venture* would be Newport's fourth voyage, but this time he was not in charge. That was not from lack of experience. Captain of a ship at age thirty, he had been a privateer for English merchants, paid to plunder the Spanish on sea and land. In 1590 he had lost his right arm in a sea battle, trying to capture two Mexican treasure ships. In 1595, having been twice a widower, he married Elizabeth Glanfield, whose father was a prosperous London goldsmith. A year later, with two of his wife's relatives and three other partners, Newport had a share in his own privateering vessel, the *Neptune,* raiding Spanish towns and ships and raking in profits in Spanish silver, gold, and pearls. In 1605 he brought back "two young Crocodiles and a wild Boar from Hispaniola," which he "presented alive unto his Majesty."[35] James I's comments are not recorded. Newport was never knighted, but he was a wealthy man. He invested four hundred pounds in the Virginia Company. On this voyage, Newport was given the title of vice-admiral.

The fleet set sail on Friday, June 2, 1609, as William Strachey wrote when he began his journal, "late in the evening."[36] In those days it was the custom when a ship set sail for all aboard to say a prayer for a safe voyage. As the nine vessels let fall their mainsails and waited for the wind to fill them, there was a young clergyman on the *Sea Venture* to offer prayers for the whole company. The Reverend Richard Buck, age twenty-seven, had left his wife and daughter safe at home, but he aimed to send for them as soon as he was settled in Virginia. Perhaps the young clergyman's prayers were answered at first with calm seas. The three-hundred-ton *Sea Venture*, with its mighty spread of sails, towed the smallest of the fleet, a twenty-ton pinnace, so that it could keep up with the others. For the next six weeks the weather was so fine that from June 2 to July 23 the nine ships were able to keep, as Strachey said, "in friendly consort together not a whole watch at any time, loosing sight each of other."[37] When they were a few days out, Lieutenant-General Gates, who was not about to let Admiral Somers usurp his role as the "sole and absolute" governor of Virginia, called a consultation with all the ship captains, masters, and pilots. With Somers's approval, and probably on his recommendation, the fleet would follow a different course from the customary one. Instead of making a stop at the Canary Islands in the accepted route for a trans-atlantic crossing, they would set a different course, "run southerly unto the tropic, and from thence bear away west." But Gates ordered that if the ships should become separated, as well they might, they were to "steer away for the West Indies," make for the island of Barbuda, and wait there seven days for the rest of the fleet.[38]

Vice-Admiral Newport was an astute observer as the fleet sailed the shorter, more direct route across the Atlantic. Strachey reported that they "found the winde to this course indeede as friendly, as in the judgment of all Sea-men, it is upon a more direct line." Besides, Adm. Sir George Somers, "a gentleman of approved assurednesse, and ready knowledge in Sea-faring actions, having often carried command," chose this route because he had sailed it before. The voyage had done well so far: in fifty-one days they had sailed nearly three thousand miles.[39]

By July 23 Vice-Admiral Newport reckoned that the little fleet was only seven or eight days from the coast of Virginia. They were so near their destination that Lieutenant-General Gates countermanded the sealed orders he had given to the fleet's ship captains about what to do if a storm should separate them. Now they were so near their destination that they were not to rendezvous in the West Indies as originally ordered, but were to "make with all speed for Virginia."[40] That, as it happened, was a fateful decision with unintended consequences.

July 23 was their last day of good weather. Day after day, watch after watch, the ships had kept together. A shipboard "watch" was four hours, or eight turns of the half-hour sandglass. Changes of the watch were often marked with Psalms and prayers and the reviewing of "watchwords." At night with the sky and seas pitch-black around them, ships sailing in consort used secret watchwords, or agreed-upon code words, shouted across the dark water to identify each other. A strange ship in their midst would be immediately known. Pirates were but one of the many dangers at sea. A pirate ship could attack a vessel, but a storm could swallow it whole.

Sunday, July 23, had been a cloudy day, but that night the wind began to howl. By daybreak on Monday the foul weather that had been "preparing for no lesse all the blacke night before" showed itself, as Strachey remembered, with "cloudes gathering thicke upon us, and the windes singing, and whistling most unusually."[41] But the little fleet was still together, and passengers aboard the ships carried on that morning as usual, eating a breakfast of porridge or ship's biscuit and salted beef, pork, or codfish. Ship's biscuit was a staple of shipboard larders. Sometimes called hardtack, it was a four-inch-square biscuit made of flour, salt, and water. Washed down with a little beer, it was palatable enough. There was a ration of a gallon of beer per person, but it was "small beer," with about 2.5 percent alcohol. Even children drank it. Water was not considered a safe beverage in those days, but no one could say why. Rivers, streams, and wells were often contaminated by animal and human waste, but bacteria had not yet been discovered, so no one was the wiser.

Beer was plentiful, but privacy was in short supply aboard the ships. Formality was left ashore, as makeshift curtains screened beds, chests, and chamber pots in the crowded belowdecks spaces. Life belowdecks was smelly and cramped, but above on the main deck on this summer voyage the sea air blew fresh and clean, if not always cool. On the high poop deck at the ship's stern was the "great cabin," private quarters for the ship's captain. On the *Sea Venture,* Admiral Somers would have had first claim to this space, but he may have shared it with Vice-Admiral Newport and Lieutenant-General Gates. Sailors slept on narrow wooden bunks or rope hammocks slung between decks. Hammocks were a relatively new addition aboard ships. Columbus had first seen them used by the Indians in San Salvador, and in 1596 the English navy made them standard for its crews. Passengers bedded down in the belowdecks spaces like the *Sea Venture*'s converted gun room, which had been specially outfitted for them. The passenger accommodations were tolerable, but far from comfortable. Men, women, and children slept on canvas mattresses filled with straw. For some, there may have been shallow, boxlike bunks. Mattresses collected sweat and lice, chamber pots stank and sloshed, and personal cleanliness, for sailors as well as passengers, was hard to maintain.

Most sailors came aboard with only the clothes on their backs. These outfits, usually a hooded shirt and loose trousers of coarse wool, were seldom if ever washed (though they were often doused with seawater in rough weather). The idea of a change of clothing for sailors was not standard practice until the 1620s, when the English navy adopted it "for the preservation of health as to avoid nasty beastliness to which many of the men are subject by continued wearing of one suit of clothes."[42] Body lice, common from the Middle Ages to the seventeenth century, often came aboard with their owners, and, thanks to the close quarters and poor sanitation aboard ship, one man's lice soon became another's.

Even for passengers, lice were common, and changes of clothing were few. Most laundry would have to wait until landfall. Bathing was impossible, but no one minded. For most people in the seventeenth century, immersing the entire body in water to wash it was not only unheard of but also considered unhealthy. Shipboard hygiene was a bucket of seawater now and then. For men, the ship's toilet, or "head," was a small enclosure (downwind, for obvious reasons) at the bow of the vessel. It was always near the waterline, so that the waves could wash through it. Women and children used chamber pots in the belowdecks spaces.

Dirty water, urine, and other wastes drained down through the hatches and collected in the bilge, the very bottom of the ship, below the hold. The crew pumped it out from time to time with a bilge pump, a long, wooden tubelike contraption with a plunger and leather valves that sucked water from the bilge and spewed it overboard. Foul-smelling bilge water was a part of seaboard life.

For when that we shall go to bedde,
The pump was nigh our beddes hede;
A man were as good as dede
As smell thereof the stynk.[43]

Some ships had only one pump, but the state-of-the-art *Sea Venture* had three. They were about to be worked nonstop.

On Tuesday morning, July 25, as Strachey wrote:

> A dreadfull storm and hideous began to blow from out the North-east, which swelling, and roaring as it were by fits, some houres with more violence than others, at length did beate all light from heaven: which like an hell of darknesse turned black upon us, so much the more fuller of horror . . . as to overrunne the troubled, and overmastered senses of all . . . the terrible cries, and murmurs of the windes, and distraction of our Company, as who was most armed, and best prepared, was not a little shaken.[44]

So strong was the wind that the *Sea Venture* was obliged to cast off the pinnace it had been towing astern. A mariner named Michael Philes was the commander. He and his crew and their vessel were never seen again.[45] Strachey does not mention when they lost contact with the other ships. But the winds were so fierce that even the hardiest, most experienced seamen aboard the *Sea Venture* feared for their lives: "Death comes not so sudden nor apparant . . . (to men especially even then in health and perfect habitudes of body) as at Sea."[46]

And then a further calamity struck: the *Sea Venture* began to leak. It was a brand-new vessel, and its timbers may not have been well set. "And the Ship In every joynt almost, having spewed out her Oakum, before we were aware, (a casualty more desperate than any other that a Voyage by Sea draweth with it) was growne five foote suddenly deepe with water above her ballast, and we almost drowned within, whilest we sat looking when to perish from above. This imparting no lesse terrour then danger, ranne through the whole Ship with much fright and amazement, started and turned the blood."

Shouts of alarm rang through the ship from stem to stern in a relay of panic. Soon everyone aboard, frantic crew and passengers alike, joined in a desperate search for the source of the leaks: "There might be seene Master, Masters Mate, Boate-Swaine, Quarter Master, Coopers, Carpenters, and who not, with candels in their hands, creeping along the ribs viewing the sides, searching every corner, and listening in every place, if they could hear the water runne."

As the long night of leak hunting wore on, "many a weeping leake was this way found, and hastily stopt." Then water began flowing through the spaces between the timbers in the gun room. There were no guns here; the *Sea Venture* was armed, but its twenty-four guns were positioned on the main deck. The gun room had been fitted to accommodate passengers. Someone, perhaps one of the passengers, thought of stuffing the cracks in the gun room's walls with strips of salt beef ("I know not how many peeces," said Strachey). But even with the gun-room leak temporarily stopped, the water in the *Sea Venture*'s hold kept rising. "The Leake, (if it were but one) which drunke in our greatest Seas, and took in our destruction fastest, could not then be found, nor ever was, by any labour, counsell, or search."

Hours passed, and the water poured in. Weary crew members with blistered, bleeding hands kept working the *Sea Venture*'s three pumps, but they could not make the water level go down. At one point the pumps began spewing out ship's biscuits, whole and in pieces. Desperate shouts summoned the ship's carpenter, who rushed to the bread room, where ten thousand pounds of ship's biscuits were stored. He ripped out planks everywhere, but could find no leak. Said Strachey, "To me, this Leakage appeared as a wound given to men that were before dead." Death seemed as close as the next big wave, and it seemed to Strachey "beyond my reason, why we should labour to preserve life; yet we did."

That labor turned out to be muscle power by every male passenger on board, by order of Lieutenant-General Gates. In this desperate situation he divided the men into three groups and assigned them to three parts of the ship: forecastle, "waist" or middle, and "bittacle" or compass room at the stern. The men were each to take turns working the pumps and bailing. Each man was to pump or bail for one hour and then rest for an hour. As Strachey put it, "Then men might be seen to labour I may well say, for life." And the *Sea Venture*'s officers took their turns elbow to elbow with the others. "The better sort, even our Governour and Admirall themselves, not refusing their turne, and to spell each the other, to give example." Heavy labor may have cooled some of the tension that simmered between them.

There were gentlemen aboard the *Sea Venture* who were unused to working with their hands, but they fell to work beside the others. Christopher Newport, who had only one arm, was probably exempted. Gates and Somers were the only ones with titles, but there were a good many gentlemen of the "better sort." Some of them were younger sons going to Virginia because they stood no chance to inherit their families' lands. English laws of primogeniture and entail gave a family's holdings intact to the eldest son. Robert Rich, for example, was the younger brother of Sir Nathaniel Rich and the first cousin of Sir Robert Rich, who in a few years would become the second Earl of Warwick. Like many a young gentleman of good family, the younger Rich could expect to inherit nothing. Now in his early twenties, single and healthy, he aimed to make his fortune in Virginia. He had about ten years to live.

Some of the "better sort" would leave written records of their adventures. One was a merchant from Lyme Regis named Silvanus Jourdain. He probably knew Lyme Regis's former mayor Sir George Somers. Jourdain, like Strachey, had literary skills and later wrote and published his own version of what happened to the *Sea Venture*.[47] When John Smith wrote his *Generall Historie* in the early 1620s and described the 1609 voyage, he gave credit to Jourdain, Strachey, and two other passengers, a "Mr. Henry Shelly" and a "Master John Ewens." The last two also had tales to tell about the *Sea Venture*'s disastrous voyage, but their written accounts, if they produced any, have been lost.[48]

Another passenger with a literary bent was Ralph Hamor. He was the eldest son of a wealthy director of the East India Company. Young Hamor expected to inherit a substantial fortune from his father, and in 1615 he did. He invested most of it in the Virginia Company. Perhaps Hamor, nineteen or twenty when he boarded the *Sea Venture*, was going to Virginia just for the fun of it. Years later he wrote a promotional tract for the Virginia colony. So did Capt. William Pierce, a young officer in Gates's service aboard the *Sea Venture*. Pierce eventually became a prosperous Virginia planter. Now his wife, Joan, and four-year-old daughter, Jane, were going with him to Virginia, but they were sailing on the *Blessing*. There was not room enough on the *Sea Venture* for officers' wives and children. Joan and Jane must have been much in Pierce's thoughts as he pumped and bailed. God only knew where the other six ships were. Pierce shared his fears with Capt. George Yeardley, whose wife, Temperance, was on the *Falcon*. Both men were in their early twenties, and both were career soldiers, serving under Thomas Gates. Lieutenant-General Gates had chosen Yeardley to serve as his personal bodyguard. But in this crisis both the bodyguard and the man he guarded put in their times at bucket and pump.

So did John Rolfe, who had just turned twenty-four in May. The only surviving son of a family in Heacham, Norfolk, he had married just the year before, and his young wife was sailing with him on the *Sea Venture*. Like everyone else, they hoped to find their fortunes in Virginia. But now all Rolfe could do was heave buckets of water up through the hatches and take his turn at the pump handle. Before his adventures ended, a widowed John Rolfe would marry Pocahontas and become part of a legend. After her death, Rolfe would marry a third time. That wife was then sailing aboard the *Blessing:* she was four-year-old Jane Pierce.

For John Rolfe and all the gentlemen-turned-laborers, dressed in heavy doublets with full-cut sleeves, billowing breeches of wool serge, knitted hose, and linen shirts, clothing made the backbreaking, drenching labor even harder. Their inferiors had no such problem. "The common sort stripped naked, as men in Galleys, the easier both to hold out, and to shrinke from under the salt water, which continually leapt in among them, kept their eyes waking, and their thoughts and hands working, with tired bodies, and wasted spirits."[49] There were two young men aboard the *Sea Venture* who would not have found it peculiar to labor naked: Namontack and Matchumps were Indians from Virginia, where they were accustomed to wearing nothing but breech cloths. Captain Newport had brought them to London the year before. They had learned some English and had been objects of much curiosity, and now they were eager to return home. Matchumps would murder Namontack within the year.

The "better sort" of the *Sea Venture*'s men kept their clothes on, the better to preserve their rank and dignity—but they worked. These 140 men worked their shifts, "destitute of outward comfort, and desperate of any deliverance . . . yet by labour to keepe each other from drowning, albeit each one drowned whilest he laboured."

Strachey calculated the volume of water they were taking out of the foundering ship. With buckets and "barricoes," or casks that held six or eight gallons apiece, the men dumped water overboard at the rate of twelve hundred barricoes every hour. Depending on the gallon size of the barrico, that would be between seventy-two and ninety-six hundred gallons per hour. As for the *Sea Venture*'s three pumps, Strachey figured that with at least four thousand strokes at each pump during a watch, "every eight houres we quitted one hundred tons of water."

Despite this bone-wearying, backbreaking labor, no man shirked. "Whether it were the feare of death in so great a storme, or that it pleased God to be gracious unto us, there was not a passenger, gentleman, or other, after hee beganne to stirre and labour, but was able to relieve his fellow, and make good his course: And it is most true, such as in all their life times had never done [an] hours work before . . . were able twice forty eight houreds together to toil with the best."

Day and night the wind never let up. It became "not only more terrible, but more constant, fury added to fury." And added to the wind was a further trial, "the sickness it lays upon the body, being so unsufferable": seasickness. Many who had overcome their initial queasiness after so many days of smooth sailing now found themselves "most loathsomely" wracked by nausea. Even seasoned sailors may succumb to seasickness in a hurricane. Many of the passengers, especially the women, had never been on so long a sea voyage, much less weathered such a storm. No one ate; no one slept; no one could go on deck. And belowdecks was the water, ever rising, and now mixed with human waste and vomit. Mattresses floated in it. Chests and trunks and barrels bobbed about in it. For the passengers there was no way to escape it. The men, at least, had their work shifts, but the women could do nothing but shiver and huddle together in their sodden skirts and petticoats and try to comfort each other as the ship pitched and yawed.

The women aboard the *Sea Venture* were mostly gentlemen's or craftsmen's wives, bound for Virginia with their husbands. A few were maidservants traveling with their employers. How many were there? Strachey counted the "whole company" as "140 men, besides women," and later spoke of "all our men, women, and children, about the number of one hundred and fifty."[50] Only a handful of women appear by name in his narrative: Elizabeth Persons, a serving girl, stayed close to her mistress, known only as "Mistress Horton." Elizabeth Jones, another servant girl, was traveling alone. She was fifteen years old. There was Edward Eason's wife, not much older, and John Rolfe's bride. There were children aboard the *Sea Venture,* but their number and gender are unknown. Young Mrs. Rolfe was six weeks pregnant.

The force of the winds, Strachey said, "made us look one upon the other with troubled hearts, and panting bosomes: our clamours drowned in the windes, and the windes in thunder. Prayers might well be in the heart and lips, but drowned in the outcries of the Officers." But for the passengers clinging to each other in the dark and fetid hold, "nothing heard that could give comfort, nothing seene that might incourage hope."

The *Sea Venture* was fighting for its life with its sails furled, as ships were often forced to do in storms. Even raising a small part of the fore-sail to steer the ship was futile: "Six and sometimes eight men were not enough to hold the whipstaffe in the steerage, and the tiller below in the Gunner roome." The whipstaff was a stout stick, or staff, attached to the ship's tiller belowdecks. In order to steer the ship, the helmsman had to see the sails, so he stood in the "steerage" and used the whipstaff to move the tiller below. But now the tiller was of no use in a storm like this:

> In which, the Sea swelled above the Clouds, and gave battel unto Heaven. It could not be said to raine, the waters like whole Rivers did flood in the air. . . . Here the glut of water (as is throttling the winde ere while) was no sooner a little emptied and qualified, but instantly the windes (as having gotten their mouthes now free, and at liberty) spake more loud, and grew more tumultuous, and malignant. . . . Windes and Seas were as mad, as fury and rage could make them. . . . [T]here was not a moment in which the sudden splitting, or instant over-setting of the Shippe was not expected.
>
> Once so huge a Sea brake upon the poope and the quarter, upon us, as it covered our Shippe from stearne to stemme, like a garment of a vast cloud, it filled her brimme full for a while within, from the hatches up to the sparre deck. This source or confluence of water was so violent, as it rusht and carried the Helm-man from the Helme, and wrested the whipstaffe out of his hand, which so flew from side to side, that when he would have seized the same again, it so tossed him from Star-boord to Lar-boord, as it was Gods mercy it had not split him: It so beat him from his hold, and so bruised him, as a fresh man hazarding by in chance fell faire with it and by maine strength bearing somewhat up, made good his place, and with much clamour incouraged and called upon others: who gave her now up, rent in pieces and absolutely lost.[51]

This same wave caught Thomas Gates belowdecks at the capstan, where he was "both by his speech and authoritie heartening every man unto his labour." The force and volume of the water swept him and those about him, including Strachey, off their feet, "beating together with our breaths all thoughts from our bosome, else, then that wee were now sinking. For my part, I thought her alreadie in the bottom of the Sea." Even Lieutenant-General Gates was ready to give up. Strachey heard him say that "all his ambition was but to climbe up above hatches to die in *Aperto coelo* [open air], and in the company of his old friends." The huge wave "so stun'd the ship in her full pace, that shee stirred no more, than if she had beene caught in a net."

Until now the wind had been driving the *Sea Venture* forward at a rapid speed: even "without bearing one inch of sail, even then she was making her way nine or ten leagues [twenty-seven or thirty miles] in a watch." Navigation was impossible: "During all this time, the heavens look'd so black upon us, that it was not possible the elevation of the Pole [North Star, or Polaris] might be observed: nor a Starre by night, not Sunne beame by day was to be seene." To keep the *Sea Venture* upright, Sir George Somers lashed himself to the mast on the high poop deck, where he could see and call out orders to those below as the wind shifted. He had been without sleep and food for three days,

On the third night, a Thursday, in the midst of all the darkness, there occurred an extraordinary event, and no one knew what to make of it. Somers saw it first, and Strachey described it: "An apparition of a little round light, like a faint Starre, trembling, and streaming along with a sparkeling blaze, halfe the height upon the Maine Mast, and shooting sometimes from Shroud to Shroud, tempting to settle as it were upon any of the foure Shrouds: and for three or foure houres together, or rather more, halfe the night it kept with us, running sometimes along the Maineyard to the very end, and then returning." Somers shouted for all who could to come and look, and they watched the strange light until nearly morning, when it disappeared.

What they had seen was a phenomenon known as Saint Elmo's fire. Strachey knew of it, writing that this "Sea-fire" was called "Saint Elmo" by the Spanish. It occurs during thunderstorms and is, in the simplest terms, an electric flame caused by ionization of the air. It can dance off the masts of ships and even the horns of cattle.

On whether the apparition aboard the *Sea Venture* boded good or ill, the superstitious sailors could not agree.

> But it did not light us any whit the more to our knowne way, who ran now (as doe hoodwinked men) at all adventures, sometimes North, and North-east, then North and by West, and in an instant againe varying two or three points, and sometimes halfe the Compasse. East and by South we steered away as much as we could to beare upright, which was no small carefulnesse nor paine to do, albeit we much unrigged our Ship, threw over-boord much luggage, many a Trunke and Chest (in which I suffered no meane losse) and staved many a Butt of Beere, Hogsheads of Oyle, Cider, Wine, and Vinegar, and heaved away all our Ordnance on the Starboord side, and had now purposed to cut downe the Maine Mast, the more to lighten her, for we were much spent, and our men so weary, as their strengths together failed them, with their hearts having travailed now from Tuesday till Friday morning, day and night, without either sleepe or foode; for the leakage taking up all the hold, we could neither come by Beere nor fresh water; fire we could keepe none in the Cookeroom to dress any meate, and carefulnesse, griefe, and our turne at the Pumpe or Bucket, were sufficient to hold sleepe from our eyes.[52]

In his account of the storm, passenger Silvanus Jourdain recalled that "some of them having some good and comfortable waters in the ship fetcht them and drunke one to the other, taking their last leave one of the other." They might as well get drunk. Some of them, said Jourdain, "were fallen asleepe in corners, and wheresoever they chanced first to sit or lie." From Tuesday noon to Friday noon they "bailed and pumped two thousand tons." They were long past exhaustion, yet they kept working. By Friday, said Strachey, "it wanted little, but that there had been a generall determination, to have shut up hatches, and commending our sinfull soules to God, committed the Shippe to the mercy of the Sea: surely, that night, we must have done it, and that night had we then perished."[53]

But before noon on Friday, July 27, the sky began to clear, and Sir George Somers sighted land. Seen from a distance of fifteen miles, or, as mariners then would have measured it, five leagues, Bermuda (latitude 32' 20") lies on the watery horizon like a small, thin sea creature, or, as one mariner described it, "a small island and not very high, having a ridge in the middle, and a vast quantity of land and sea birds. It is in 33 [degrees of latitude], and always covered with clouds." At first, the *Sea Venture* passengers could barely see it: a low ridge of land that seemed to float on the distant horizon. But it was land. "Every man bustled up," as Jourdain remembered, "and gathered his strength and feeble spirits together."⁵⁴

Joy at the sight of land nearly caused them not to reach it. As John Smith wrote in his *Generall Historie,* "This unlooked for welcome newes . . . hurrieth them all above hatches . . . forsaking that taske which imported no lesse than their lives, they gave so dangerous advantage to their greedy enemy the salt water, which still entred at the large breaches of their poore wooden castle, as that in gaping after life, they had well-nigh swallowed their death." But they spread "all the saile they could" and made for the islands.⁵⁵

Soon the ecstatic *Sea Venture* company could see the trees waving on the faraway shore. Somers ordered the helmsman to "bear up" and change the course to leeward to escape the wind. That put the *Sea Venture's* bow toward the eastern end of the land. They were approaching what is now called St. George's Island, Bermuda. As they rounded it the boatswain standing near the bow heaved his lead weight overboard to take a sounding. Thirteen fathoms, or seventy-eight feet, of water lay beneath them. By a stroke of good luck they had entered a deep channel known on modern maps as "Sea Venture Channel."

As they would soon discover, Bermuda was ringed by hidden coral reefs, and as Strachey wrote later, "It is impossible without great and perfect knowledge, and search first made of them to bring in a bable Boat, so much as of ten Tun without apparent ruine, albeit within there are many faire harbours for the greatest English Ship. . . . There is only one side that admits so much as hope of safetie by many a league, on which (as before described) it pleased God to bring us, wee had not come one man of us else ashoare, as the weather was." In a little while the water's depth was seven fathoms, then four, as they drew closer and closer to the land. At long last, the seas were growing calmer, and as Strachey wrote, there was "somewhat smooth water." They were now on the leeward side of St. George's Island in about twenty-four feet of water. With no hope of saving the fast-sinking *Sea Venture* by dropping anchor, Somers decided to run it in as close to land as possible. He did just that, bringing the ship,

Strachey thought, "within three quarters of a mile of shore." Suddenly, the bow scraped across an underwater coral reef and wedged itself between two rocks. The *Sea Venture* stuck fast. After three days and nights of tossing, its great oaken hulk now rested calmly in the lapping waves.[56] Parts of it would stay there for the next 350 years, until Edmund Downing, a descendant of George Yeardley, discovered some of the timbers and ballast stones while he was scuba diving in 1958.[57]

When they felt their ship's hull scrape against the reef, the exhausted company could scarcely believe it. But they were not able to rest: the leaking *Sea Venture*'s time above water was limited. It was now afternoon, and before dark they had to get themselves and their few remaining possessions ashore. They readied the *Sea Venture*'s longboat and skiff, two small boats they had never thought to need again. Lieutenant-General Gates gave rapid orders and made a trip ashore in the first boat. When it touched the sandy beach, he leaped jubilantly onto the dry land, waved his arms, and shouted, "Gates's Bay!" That was the first place-name in Bermuda, and the small bay is still called that today. Gathering their last reserves of strength, the rest of the *Sea Venture*'s company made their way ashore, boatload after boatload rowed by men whose backs, arms, and shoulders had already been taxed beyond endurance. At last, as Strachey said, "By the mercy of God unto us, making out our boats, we had ere night brought all our men, women, and children, about the number of one hundred and fifty, safe into the island."

But were they safe? The island they had come upon was Bermuda, the Isle of Devils: "We found it to be the dangerous and dreaded island or rather islands of the Bermuda, so terrible to all that ever touched on them, and such tempests, thunders, and other fearful objects are seen and heard about them, that they be called commonly, *The Devils Islands* and are feared and avoided of all sea travelers alive, above any other place in the world."

And no one in the world knew they were there.

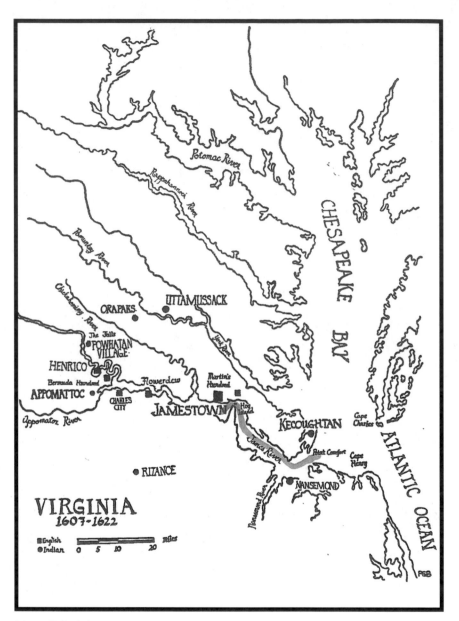

Map of Virginia, 1607–1622. *Courtesy Paul Bernhard.*

2

BAD BLOOD AT JAMESTOWN

BY JULY 1609, when the *Sea Venture* survivors clambered ashore on a Bermuda beach, conditions for the Virginia colonists had gone from bad (as John Smith had reported in his *True Relation* in 1608) to worse. Smith was still in Virginia, but he would not be there long. For two and a half years in Virginia, some of the English who had come with him and the Indians who were already there had plotted to bring him down. Before he left Jamestown in October 1609, they nearly succeeded. But Smith made it back to England safely, with the terrible news that the *Sea Venture* was lost. John Smith never returned to Virginia, but he put what he knew of its history and what others told him into a work that ensured his place in the literature of early America. His *Generall Historie of Virginia, New-England, and the Summer Isles,* published in 1624, is one of the foundation stones of seventeenth-century history. A. L. Rowse, one of the most distinguished scholars of Elizabethan England, called it "the first classic of English America."[1] Without John Smith's writings, much of the history of early Virginia and Bermuda would remain unknown. He was part of that history from the beginning.

On December 10, 1606, the names of seven men were put into a sealed box on a ship bound for Virginia. One of the names was John Smith's. In that bleak English winter, three small ships carrying the first colonists to Virginia were about to set sail, and aboard the flagship *Susan Constant* was John Smith, along with the box containing the seven names. Smith, young (he was twenty-six) and adventurous (he had traveled over much of Europe), was eager to see America. He and six other men had been handpicked by the Virginia Company to be the governing council of England's new colony. No one on the voyage knew who had been chosen, and the box was not to be opened until everyone was put ashore in Virginia. Why the company chose John Smith as a councilor remains a mystery, and what happened to him on the way to Virginia is even more mysterious. His *Generall Historie* does not tell the whole story.

Of the seven council members who embarked for Virginia in December 1606, all but John Smith had special qualifications or connections. Four were seasoned mariners. Christopher Newport, forty-six, a wealthy privateer who invested in the Virginia Company, was in command of the *Susan Constant.* He had been sailing the Atlantic since he was nineteen. Bartholomew Gosnold, thirty-four, had explored the New England coast in 1602 (and named an island "Martha's Vineyard" after his mother-in-law). Now he was captain of the *Godspeed.* John Martin, in his early forties, had sailed with Gosnold to New England and commanded a ship in Francis Drake's expedition of 1585. Martin was also the son of Sir Richard Martin, a London goldsmith and master of the mint. John Martin's only son, also named John, was sailing with him.[2] John Ratcliffe (whose age is unrecorded) was the captain of the *Discovery.* Edward Wingfield, fifty-six, was from a prominent family and a patent holder in the Virginia Company. George Kendall, in his thirties, was kin to Sir Edwin Sandys, a member of Parliament and of the Virginia Company Council. (Kendall, who may have been a closet Catholic, was also rumored to be a spy for Spain. He was supposed to feed news about Virginia to Robert Cecil, the Earl of Salisbury, one of the Spanish ambassador's paid informants.) And last, there was John Smith. His biographer, Philip L. Barbour, wrote, "Only Smith's presence remains to be explained. Somebody must have recommended him, and that somebody must have had a basis to go on, for Smith was a nobody."[3]

John Smith, who would mark his twenty-seventh birthday on January 9, 1607, may have been the youngest of the group. The sandy-haired, sturdily built son of a Lincolnshire farmer, Smith had chosen to become a soldier of fortune in 1596 or 1597. Since then he had seen military service with English mercenaries in the Netherlands, fought in France, sailed on a pirate ship in the Mediterranean, served with the Austrian forces against the Turks in Transylvania, and returned from his adventures with the title of captain in the Hungarian army. He had also acquired a coat of arms bearing the heads of three Turks whom he claimed to have beheaded in one-on-one combat. The motto on the crest was *Vincere est Vivere* (To conquer is to live).

Now Capt. John Smith was one of 105 men and boys on the way to plant a colony in America. To avoid arguments about who was in charge on the way, the Virginia Company thought it wise to keep the identities of the seven council members a secret until they arrived. While they were at sea, Captain Newport was in command. The three ships set sail from Blackwall on the north side of the Thames on December 19, 1606, but when they reached the coast, "unprosperous winds" kept them pitching and rolling in the waves within sight of land for six long weeks. Many of the passengers were miserably seasick. The Reverend Robert Hunt, not a seasoned sailor, spent much of his time "making wild vomits into the black night."⁴ He grew so weak that many feared he might not recover. But he hung on, and he would later take John Smith's side in rough waters of another sort. Crowded aboard the three small ships (the *Susan Constant* was 111 feet long, the *Godspeed* about 68 feet, and the tiny pinnace *Discovery* only 49 feet in length), the passengers had plenty of time to get to know each other before the long Atlantic crossing began. Some of them may have come to know each other too well.

By the time they reached the Canary Islands on February 17, 1607, to rest and replenish their supplies, Smith was in trouble. Perhaps he had boasted too much of his own travels and adventures. He had been in the Canaries before, but so had Christopher Newport, and Smith, the brash farmer's son with a coat of arms, may have offended some of the gentlemen by flaunting his knowledge. For reasons to this day unknown, he was "restrained as a prisoner" when they left the islands on February 21. According to one report, some of the leaders feared that Smith "intended to usurp the government, murder the Council, and make himself king, that his confederates were dispersed in all the three ships."⁵ Whatever he said or did alarmed some people so much that there was talk of his execution. During their next rest stop at the West Indies island of Nevis from March 27 to April 3, "a pair of gallows" was made for him. Then Captain Newport decided that there was not enough evidence for an execution and talked Smith's enemies out of hanging him.⁶ But John Smith was kept a prisoner for the remaining three weeks of the voyage. Newport did not like him much, either, and these two would clash later on.

The sealed box with the seven council members' names (including Smith's) was opened April 26, the first night on Virginia soil. The six men (Smith not included) elected Edward Wingfield, the eldest and one of the richest of them, as their president. He refused to seat Smith. After "the gentlemen and all the company" talked to Wingfield for a few days, Smith was finally sworn in on June 10.⁷ The company's minister, the Reverend

Robert Hunt, may also have had a hand in Smith's return to grace. But the bad blood between John Smith and the men who hated him did not dissolve. Christopher Newport and John Ratcliffe, two of the ship captains, had no use for him, nor did Cambridge-educated colonist Gabriel Archer. At thirty-two Archer was also a seasoned mariner who had explored New England with Bartholomew Gosnold and John Martin in 1602. His bitter hatred for John Smith—whatever the reason—led him to make at least two attempts to end Smith's life.

Who were Smith's other enemies? No one knows. Smith had narrowly escaped one hanging in the West Indies, and he came within hours of another one a few months later. Every moment he spent in Virginia, John Smith had to watch his back, not just because of the Indians but also because of some of the English.

From the start, Virginia's hardships made harsh words inevitable: there was backbreaking, hand-blistering labor to do as soon as they had picked a place—marshy and unhealthy, as it turned out—to settle. Sailing more than thirty miles up the wide river that they named the James, after King James I, they chose a small, wooded peninsula about two miles long and a mile to a mile and a half wide. It was actually an island, separated from the mainland by a shallow creek, but the James River was six fathoms (thirty-six feet) deep, deep enough to moor their ships a stone's throw from the shore. By June 15, seven weeks after they arrived, 104 men and boys (one man had died on the voyage) had finished an enormous task: they had built a fort at the site they called Jamestown. Working and sweating in the hot Virginia sun, they dug more than sixteen hundred feet of trenches nearly three feet deep to form a huge triangle by the river's edge. They chopped down hundreds of pine and oak and elm trees. They dragged heavy logs of up to one foot in diameter, one by one, to set vertically in the trenches to make a palisade with walls eleven to fifteen feet high. When it was finished, the fort by the river covered about an acre and a half, or roughly the area of two football fields. It was 140 yards long on the side facing the river and 100 yards on each of the other two sides. With guns mounted at each angle and only one entrance, a massive log gate on the side facing the river, this palisaded fort would be a comforting defense against invaders—either Indian or Spanish.[8]

Three hundred years later, in 1909, a statue of John Smith would be erected on ground once occupied by the original fort. For many years the fort's site was believed to be lost, given up to the James River's tides. The truth was not discovered until 1994, when the Jamestown Rediscovery Project began. That summer a team of archaeologists made an earthshaking find: they uncovered "marks of decayed circular or split timbers once standing side by side and held upright by solid packed clay in a narrow, straight-sided flat-bottomed trench. . . . Carefully excavated, these marks left an exact mold of the timber, five inches to one foot in diameter."[9] They had found the first traces of Jamestown Fort's log palisade, erected four hundred years ago.

Inside their fort's stout walls the first colonists built a storehouse, a church, and two barrackslike structures, all made of wooden frames nailed to four posts planted in the ground, with earthen walls and thatched roofs. Buildings like this were known as "wattle and daub," or sometimes the more descriptive "mud and stud." They were simple to build, though ungainly to look at. Outside the fort were Indians, and inside, disease and death. John Smith would write later, "Within tenne daies scarse ten amongst us coulde either goe, or well stand, such extreame weaknes and sicknes oppressed us." Worse yet, there was not enough to eat. As an eminent twentieth-century historian wrote, "Gone were the meat and ale to which husky Elizabethan appetites were accustomed; daily rations now consisted of half a pint of wheat as little of barley, both wormy from months at sea."[10] Such a diet would be approximately six hundred calories.

Death took a terrible toll. From August 6 to September 5, twenty-one men died, sometimes two and three a day. As George Percy remembered, "Our men were destroyed with cruell diseases as Swellings, Flixes, Burning Fevers . . . but for the most part they died of meere famine."[11] One of them was councilor John Martin's son, John. Another was councilor Bartholomew Gosnold, the captain of the *Godspeed,* who left a wife and three small children at home in Bury St. Edmonds. As befitted an officer and a gentleman, he was buried with full military honors. Edward Wingfield, the colony's first president, allegedly hoarded food and refused to share the company's liquor supply (aqua vitae and sack). He lasted only four months in office. There were bitter quarrels, and Smith wrote mysteriously that he himself was "disgrac'd through others' malice." On September 10, 1607, Wingfield, who had plotted to sail for England in the pinnace, was deposed, and John Ratcliffe, who would later become one of Smith's enemies, was elected president. He turned out to be no better than Wingfield at controlling the fractious councilors and colonists. Councilor George Kendall, imprisoned by Wingfield, was tried and executed for "a mutiny." (Suspicions that Kendall was a spy for Spain may have had something to do with it.) One of the boys ran away to the Indians. A young man in his late teens or early twenties died of a gunshot wound to his leg. Who shot him, and why? No one knows. His name was not recorded, and neither was the date of his death, but his grave has recently been discovered. So far the skeletal remains in it are known only as "JR [Jamestown Recovery] 102C."[12]

John Ratcliffe, the councilor who became president, is a figure of mystery. His English background is unknown. He invested fifty pounds in the Virginia Company, and when he was in Virginia he called himself Ratcliffe. But sometimes he used the name Sicklemore.[13] George Kendall, condemned to be executed and hoping to save himself, declared that Ratcliffe's real name was Sicklemore, not Ratcliffe, and thus as President Ratcliffe he could not pronounce the sentence of execution.[14] But Ratcliffe did, and Kendall died. A few months later John Smith described Ratcliffe as "now called Sicklemore, a poor counterfeited imposture."[15] That may have been because Ratcliffe and others tried to hang Smith in January 1608.

Those troubles began when Smith went exploring up the Chickahominy River in December 1607. He hoped to trade beads and trinkets to the Indians for food, but instead the Indians killed three of his men. One of them, a carpenter named Thomas Emry, was apparently taken by surprise and never heard of again. His companion John Robinson died with "20 or 30 arrows in him."[16] The third man, a laborer named George Cassen who disobeyed Smith's orders and went ashore, suffered a hideous death by torture at the hands of Indians who were looking for Smith: they stripped Cassen naked, tied him to a tree, and with mussel shells or reeds they cut off his fingers one after the other, scraped the skin from his head and face, and finally disemboweled him. Then they burned him "with the tree and all."[17]

Meanwhile, Indians had captured Smith. He managed to hold his own among them, including the king of the Pamunkey Indians, a tall Indian named Opechancanough. His brother was Wahunsonacock, also called Powhatan, the chief of all the Chesapeake tribes. Taken for an audience before Powhatan, Smith narrowly escaped being bludgeoned to death.

This was the now-famous rescue, when Powhatan's daughter Pocahontas saved Smith's life. The Indians brought him before Powhatan, who sat "before a fire upon a seat like a bedsted . . . . On either hand did sit

C's own voice
Jeffrey L. Hartman
New element
History
Vol 23. No 1 Virginia
Otherwise Winter 1992
69-81

a young wench of 16 or 18 yeares, and along on each side the house, two rowes of men, and behind them as many women, with all their heads and shoulders painted red; many of their heads bedecked with the white down of Birds; but every one with something: and a great chayne of white beads about their necks.[18]

The Indians gave Smith food, a feast "in their best barbarous manner," and then, after a "long consultation . . . two great stones were brought before Powhatan: then as many as could layd hands on him, dragged him to them, and thereon laid his head, and being ready with their clubs, to beate out his braines, Pocahontas the Kings dearest daughter, when no intreaty could prevaile, got his head in her armes, and laid her owne upon his to save him from death; whereat the Emperor was contented he should live."[19]

Since the only account of this incident is this one in Smith's *Generall Historie,* it has raised many doubts. Modern scholars believe that it did take place, but was very likely an initiation ceremony that Smith misunderstood. But he did not misunderstand Pocahontas's feelings for him, and this was not the last time she would save his life.

We meet Pocahontas as John Smith later described her: "a child of tenne yeares old, which not only for feature, countenance, and proportion, much exceedeth any of the rest of his [Powhatan's] people, but for wit, and spirit, the only Nonpariel of his Country." William Strachey described Pocahontas as "a well featured but wanton young girle . . . som etymes resorting to our Fort, of the age then of 11, or 12. yeares." The word *wanton* in its Elizabethan context meant "undisciplined," "naughty," or "unruly." These Englishmen did not know that "Pocahontas" was her nickname. It meant "Little Mischief." Her real name was Matoaka. Strachey noted that Pocahontas would "gett the boyes forth with her into the markett place and make them wheele, falling on their handes turning their heeles upwardes, whome she would follow, and wheele so her self naked as she was all the Fort over." With Powhatan's approval, she also brought gifts of food and helped John Smith learn the Algonquian language. Her father may also have used her to spy on the English. But John Smith was also learning all he could about the Indians.[20]

In the two and a half years John Smith, the dauntless explorer, spent in Virginia, he traveled by boat on three thousand miles of waterways and met the Indians on their own ground. The land the English named Virginia, the Indians called *Tsenacommacah,* which means "densely inhabited land."[21] Smith worked at learning the Algonquian language and also wrote one of the earliest (and still one of the best) descriptions of Virginia's Native people:

> Tall and straight, of a comely proportion, and of a colour browne when they are of any age, but they are borne white. Their hayre is generally blacke, but few have any beards. The men weare halfe their heads shaven, the other halfe long; for Barbers they use their women, who with two shells will grate away the hayre. . . .
>
> [Smith found them to be] Craftie, timorous, quicke of apprehension, and very ingenious. Some of disposition fearfull, some bold, most cautious, all Savage. Generally covetous of Copper, Beads, and such like trash. They are soone moved to anger, and so malicious, that they seldome forget an injury. . . .
>
> For their apparell, they are sometimes covered with the skinnes of wilde beasts. . . . The better sort use large mantels [cloaks] of Deare skins. . . . Some embroidered with white beads, some with Copper, other painted after their manner. But the common sort have scarce to cover their nakednesse, but with grasse, the leaves of trees, or such like. . . . But the women are always covered about their middles with a skin, and very shamefast to be seene bare. They adorne themselves most with copper beads and paintings. Their women, some have their legs, hands, breasts and face cunningly imbrodered with divers workes, as beasts, serpents, artificially wrought into their fleshe with blacke spots. In each eare commonly they have 3 great holes, whereat they hang chaines, bracelets or copper. Some of their men weare in those holes, a small green and yellow coloured snake. . . . Others wear a dead Rat tyed by the tail. Some on their heads wear the wing of a bird, or some large feather with a rattle. . . . Their heads and shoulders are painted red. . . . Many other formes of paintings they use, but he is the most gallant that is the most monstrous to behold.[22]

When at last Smith returned to Jamestown on January 2, 1608, after his adventures upriver, he found disaster looming. Gabriel Archer, who hated him, had been elected to the council in his absence. As soon as Archer heard what had happened on Smith's expedition, he was ready to try Smith for the loss of his two men—John Robinson and Thomas Emry (nothing was said about poor George Cassen). Ex-president Wingfield wrote that Archer "indicted him [Smith] upon a chapter in Leviticus for the death of his two men." According to Wingfield, Smith would have had his trial "the same day of his return and . . . his hanging the same day or the next day"—but Smith was saved by a stroke of luck. On the very day he had returned, while Archer and the other councilors were preparing to try (and, some hoped, execute) him, Capt. Christopher Newport arrived. His ship's presence at the river's edge with a load of provisions and "near a hundred men" was so exciting that the councilors apparently forgot about trying John Smith. Captain Newport was horrified to learn that so many men had died: only 38 of the original colonists were there to greet him. He himself brought bad news: the *Phoenix,* another supply ship, had sailed with him but had disappeared and was presumed lost. Five days later, on January 7, 1608, a fire, perhaps accidentally ignited by one of the newcomers' tobacco pipes, burned all the houses in the fort. It was another in a string of misfortunes for the fledgling colony. Newport, who had arrived in Virginia in early January, stayed until April. He led an unsuccessful expedition to look for the lost Roanoke colonists (the 117 people sent by Sir Walter Raleigh in 1587 who had vanished by 1590 and whose fate is uncertain to this very day). Their story had fascinated all who heard it, and for years the English entertained the notion that the Roanoke colonists were alive and well somewhere across the sea. When the first Jamestown settlers asked the Indians about the Roanoke group, the Indians answered with tales of Indian "houses built with stone walls, and one story above another, so taught them by those English who escaped the slaughter at Roanoke." The Indians said that at Ritanoe, an Indian settlement some fifty miles from Jamestown, a chief name Eyanoco had "preserved seven of the English alive—four men, two boys and one young maid." He kept them to "beat his copper" (from a mine nearby) into utensils and ornaments.[23] But Newport's search and later searches found nothing. The English later learned from Powhatan that he had exterminated these Chesapeake Indians before Jamestown was settled. If so, the Roanoke survivors, if there were any, perished with them.[24]

Christopher Newport was more successful in his 1608 visit to Powhatan. Smith and a guard of about 30 men escorted a somewhat apprehensive Newport (who, according to Smith, harbored "many doubts, and suspitions of treacheries") to Werowocomoco. There, as Smith remembered, the shrewd Powhatan "strained himself to the uttermost of his greatnes" to entertain them, and "the most plenty of victuall hee could provide to feast us." As a present, Newport gave Powhatan one of the English boys at Jamestown: a thirteen-year-old named Thomas Savage, whom he called his "son." He was to live with Powhatan and learn his language. In exchange, Powhatan gave Newport his "trusty servant," a young Indian he called Namontack.²⁵ When Newport left Virginia on April 10, 1608, Namontack went with him to England.

Ten days later a small miracle happened: Capt. Francis Nelson and the *Phoenix* dropped anchor at Jamestown. Driven off course and separated from Christopher Newport on their voyage to Virginia months earlier, Nelson had made for the West Indies instead. He brought welcome provisions. Said the grateful colonists, "Wee would not have wished so much than he did for us."²⁶

When Captain Nelson left Virginia in early June, he did something else for Virginia: he carried with him the document that would be published in London as *A True Relation of such occurrences and accidents of note as hath happened in Virginia,* written by Capt. John Smith.

On September 10, 1608, Ratcliffe's term as president of the Virginia council was up. Who would be next? Of the original seven councilors, Newport was not now a Jamestown resident, Wingfield had already served and been deposed, Gosnold and Kendall were dead, and Martin, still mourning his son's death, was ailing. Gabriel Archer, Smith's avowed enemy, and Matthew Scrivener, a newcomer who became Smith's friend, were the councilors chosen to replace Gosnold and Kendall. When the vote was taken, Capt. John Smith was elected president of the Virginia council. Not everyone was pleased.

When Christopher Newport returned to Jamestown that same September, John Smith was not pleased. Newport brought seventy more colonists but, as before, not enough provisions. Newport also brought orders from the profit-hungry, image-conscious Virginia Company: hunt for gold, try again to find the Roanoke colonists, and stage a coronation for the Indian king Powhatan, to make him a vassal of King James I. All this, when food was in short supply and the colony was depending on corn from the Indians. Smith was furious. He criticized the Virginia Company for not sending more provisions and more men who knew how to wield an ax and saw a plank. In response, Captain Newport and ex-president Ratcliffe hatched a scheme to get rid of Smith. They claimed he had left on a food-trading expedition to Indian lands without asking their approval. On these trumped-up charges they wanted to depose him as president—and banish him from the fort. But Smith had friends as well as enemies at Jamestown, and the attempted coup failed. As one observer wrote of Newport and Ratcliffe, "Their horns were too short."[27] But they continued to watch John Smith, hoping for another chance.

Newport left for England sometime before the end of December 1608, bearing with him a letter from an angry, exasperated John Smith to the Virginia Company. Smith's letter shows Smith at his best: practical, witty, eloquent, and determined to make Virginia a success. The original letter has not survived, but Smith included a copy of it in his *Generall Historie* in 1624. Did he create it for his book? Did he embellish the original? Scholars disagree.[28] Smith's disgust with the Virginia Company's management is evident as he addresses company officials in an angry, one-paragraph tirade at the beginning of the document:

> I Received your Letter, [a Virginia Company document Newport had brought, now lost] wherein you write, that our minds are so set upon faction, and idle conceits in dividing the Country without your consents, and that we feed You but with ifs and ands, hopes, and some few proofes; as if we would keepe the mystery of the business to our selves: and that we must expresly follow your instructions sent by Captain Newport: the charge of whose voyage amounts to neare two thousand pounds, the which if we cannot defray by the Ships returne, we are like to remain as banished men. To these particulars I humbly entreat your Pardons if I offend you with my rude Answer.
>
> For our factions, unless you would have me run away and leave the Country, I cannot prevent them: because I do make many stay that would els fly any whether. For the idle Letter sent to my Lord of Salisbury, by the President [Ratcliffe] and his confederates, for dividing the Country, etc. What it was I know not, for you saw no hand of mine to it; nor ever dream't I of any such matter. That we feed you with hopes, etc. Though I be no scholer, I am past a schoole-boy; and I desire but to know, what either you, and these here doe know, but that I have learned to tell you by the continuall hazard of my life. I have not concealed from you anything I know; but I feare some cause you to beleeve much more than is true.[29]

Smith reports that Newport and other colonists, following the company's instructions, held a coronation ceremony with a crown and red cloak for Powhatan. The Indian Namontack, whom Powhatan had given to Newport on his last visit, had come back to Virginia with Newport, and he helped to stage the coronation ceremony. (Presumably young Thomas Savage, whom Newport had given to Powhatan, was present as well, though none of the accounts mentions him.) When the suspicious Powhatan was reluctant to don the scarlet cloak and "other apparel" that Newport had brought him, Powhatan was "persuaded by Namontack they would doe him noe hurt." At the crowning, the proud chief refused to kneel, but "at last by leaning hard on his shoulders, hee a little stooped," and the crown was set on his head. Namontack probably helped.[30] In return for his English presents, Powhatan then bestowed upon Captain Newport his "old shoes and his mantle." The mantle, or cloak, may be the elaborately beaded deerskin garment now known as "Powhatan's Mantle" in the Ashmolean Museum at Oxford.[31] Becoming fluent in English, Namontack would go back to London with Newport again. Though Namontack did not know it, the coronation was the last time that he would see Powhatan and the land of *Tsenacommacah*.

Smith also reports in his letter that Newport, as instructed, took 120 men upriver to look for gold and to seek out any survivors from the lost Roanoke colony of 1587. Both searches proved fruitless. Newport had brought a five-piece barge to be carried over the falls upriver and reassembled, but it did not go as planned. Smith writes scornfully, "And for the quartred Boat to be borne by the Souldiers over the Falles, Newport had 120 of the best men he could chuse. If he had burnt her to ashes, one might have carried her in a bag; but as she is, five hundred cannot, to a navigable place above the Falles." Smith chides the company for expecting to turn a profit from its colony so soon: "You must not expect from us any such matter, which are but a many of ignorant miserable soules, that are scarce able to get wherewith to live, and defend ourselves against the inconstant Salvages."

Food was always a problem. The men at Jamestown had inexplicably let spring and summer pass without planting enough corn to feed themselves, and the Indians were an unreliable source. Newport failed in his trading for corn with the Indians, and most of his men came back "sicke and neare famished." Smith reminds those in London that he and his countrymen in

Virginia were literally living from hand to mouth: "From your ship we had not provision in victuals worth twenty pound and we are more than two hundred to live upon this, the one half sick, the other little better. . . . Our diet is a little meal and water, and not sufficient of that."

Yet these 200 men lived on the banks of a river teeming with eight-foot-long sturgeon and many other fish; geese, ducks, and turkeys abounded; and deer, squirrels, rabbits, and other game roamed the woods. What was wrong with the English in Virginia? Sickness does not explain it, nor does Smith's next comment, eloquent as it is: "Though there be fish in the Sea, fowls in the air, and Beasts in the woods, their bounds are so large, they so wilde, and we so weake and ignorant, we cannot much trouble them."

Smith reports that he has done the best he can to be useful to the company: he is sending back a map "of the Bay and Rivers, with an annexed Relation of the Countries and Nations that inhabit them. . . . Also two barrels of stones, and such as I take to be good Iron ore." He is also sending back Gabriel Archer and John Ratcliffe. About Ratcliffe, he writes, "I have sent you him home, least the company should cut his throat. What he is now everyone can tell you: if he and Archer returne againe, they are sufficient to keepe us always in factions." Smith had not long to wait. Both Ratcliffe and Archer would be back in less than a year, as captains of ships that were in the *Sea Venture* fleet. When they arrived, Smith would again have reason to fear for his life.

The long letter to the Virginia Company ended with another warning not to expect profits too soon: "For in overtoyling our weake and unskillful bodies, to satisfy this desire of present profit, we can scarce ever recover our selves from one Supply to another." This "Supply" was already running short. During their three-month stay, from September through November, Newport's sailors ate and drank up most of their own provisions. Then they traded with the Indians, giving away most of the provisions meant for the colonists. When Newport was ready to sail for England, the hungry settlers, who had "but a pinte of Corne a day for a man . . . were constrained to give him three hogsheads of that to victual him homeward."

Smith wrote at the end of his letter, "These are the causes that have kept us in Virginia, from laying such a foundation, that ere this might have given much better content and satisfaction; but as yet you must not looke for any profitable returnes." Unfortunately, the Virginia Company did not take Smith's advice.

There were enough accounts for us to form the opinion that the new world was not much different from the old.

Newport sailed for England in early December 1608, leaving behind about seventy new colonists, including "eight Dutchmen [Germans] and Poles." Newport also brought the first two English women to Jamestown: a woman known only as "Mistress Forrest," who was no doubt the wife of one Thomas Forrest, and her fourteen-year-old servant girl, Anne Burras. They were the only Englishwomen among nearly two hundred men and boys.

With the departure of Newport's ship, he and two of Smith's chief enemies, Ratcliffe and Archer, were gone, but Smith's problems were not. Winter was coming, and people at Jamestown were desperately hungry. Sometime in December they managed to celebrate the nuptials of Anne Burras and a twenty-eight-year-old laborer named John Laydon. Smith wrote that this was "the first marriage we had in Virginia."[32] (Anne and John Laydon eventually had four daughters and prospered as landowners in Virginia.)

That same December, Powhatan, who well knew the condition of the colonists inside the little fort at Jamestown, invited Smith to visit him, promising to load Smith's ship with corn in return for some presents. The "presents" the old king wanted were English goods: a house built in the English wattle-and-daub style, a grindstone, a cock and a hen, some copper and beads—and English weapons: guns and swords.

Smith was not about to supply arms to his enemy, but he sent Powhatan three of the newly arrived "Dutchmen" and two English workers to start on the house. But as soon as they began working, the Dutchmen also began to hatch a plot to overthrow Smith as president. They quickly learned that Powhatan had no real love for the English, but what he loved most were English tools and weapons. With their countrymen at Jamestown, the Dutchmen conspired to filch axes, knives, and even guns and ammunition from the precious supplies inside the fort. These they would steal gradually and give to Powhatan. In return, when the time was ripe, he would give them his warriors to drive out Smith and the other English. Until then, the Dutchmen would watch and wait. Summer would be time enough.

Smith arranged for the building of Powhatan's house, but a promise to visit the newly crowned vassal of King James was not easy to fulfill: when Smith asked for volunteers to accompany him, many of the men at the fort grumbled and refused. It was a sailing trip of nearly a hundred miles in all, thirty-odd miles just to get down the James River to Point Comfort, then out into Chesapeake Bay and around the wide peninsula between the James and the Pamunkey rivers, then up the Pamunkey to Powhatan's royal seat at the Indian town of Werowocomoco. That meant twelve or fourteen days at best, in icy water and knife-sharp December winds—not to mention traveling among Indians who might or might not be glad to see them.

On December 29 Smith finally sailed downriver with the *Discovery* and a smaller pinnace, four days' worth of provisions, and forty-six volunteers.[33] Among them were Lt. George Percy, age twenty-eight, the eighth son of the Earl of Northumberland, who had been at Jamestown since 1607, and a newcomer, Francis West, age twenty-two, the younger brother of Lord De La Warr. For the time being, these two young noblemen were eager supporters, perhaps even admirers, of Capt. John Smith. In less than a year, they would be just as eager to see him brought down.

On the first night, after sailing downriver about twenty miles, the expedition stopped at the town of the friendly king of Warraskoyack, on the south side of the James. He fed them, housed them, and gave them provisions for their journey. In return they presented him with one of the English boys from the fort. Samuel Collier, who had once turned cartwheels with Pocahontas, was to learn this Indian king's language and teach him English in return. As they left, the king of Warraskoyack told them that Powhatan was waiting to cut their throats.

They sailed on. The wind was rising, and it had begun to snow. Taking refuge in Kecoughtan, another friendly Indian village near Point Comfort, they stayed for several days until the storm passed. As Smith remembered, "We were never more merry, nor fed on more plentie of good Oysters, Fish, Flesh, and Wilde-fowl, and good bread;, nor never had better fires in England than in the dry smoaky houses of Kecoughtan."

Why Smith's own people on the banks of the James could not fish, hunt, and feast in a like manner is a puzzle to this day. Instead, while Smith was gone, some of them took a skiff over to Hog Island, three miles across the river, and eleven of them drowned. They may have gone to get some of the hogs Smith had placed there earlier that year. Nearby Indians were the first to find the Englishmen's bodies. One of the colonists, Richard Wyffin, vowed to go and find Smith to tell him of this new disaster. The president needed to know he had lost eleven able-bodied men.

Wyffin went by land, fording streams and making his way through the snowy woods, and he reached Powhatan's house at Werowocomoco several days before Smith's pinnace and barges. Powhatan, just as the king of Warraskoyack had said, was planning to kill Smith and his men. But Pocahontas had heard her father's talk of a plan to murder the English, so as soon as she spied Richard Wyffin, somehow she managed to hide him. She warned him and sent him on his way. When Powhatan found out that Wyffin had been there and sent his men in pursuit, Pocahontas gave them the wrong directions. When at last Wyffin found Smith and told him the sad news of the drownings at Jamestown, Smith swore him to secrecy so as not to distress the rest of the men. Richard Wyffin must also have confirmed what the king of Warraskoyack had said: Powhatan was planning to kill them. They would be on their guard.

They kept doggedly on, building fires and sleeping "under the trees by a good fire" at night. They found refuge from sleet, snow, and "contrary winds" for three or four days with the Indians at Kiskiack, a village on the south side of the Pamunkey River. On January 12, 1609, the pinnace *Discovery* and the barge finally reached Werowocomoco, where the shallow two-mile-wide Pamunkey was frozen nearly a half mile from the shore. Leaving all but twelve of his men on the *Discovery,* Smith took the barge closer to the land by breaking the ice, and when the barge became trapped at ebb tide, he and his men waded ashore through the "muddy frozen ooze."

Freezing and desperate, Smith and his men sent word to Powhatan that they had arrived and asked for provisions. The crafty ruler sent them "plentie of bread, Turkies, and Venison"—and pretended surprise that they had come. He had not asked them, he said. The next day when they reached his house, he asked when they would be gone. But since they were there, he grudgingly offered to give them forty baskets of corn in return for forty swords. Smith's reply was a firm refusal: "As for swordes and gunness, I told you long agoe I had none to spare." Then a veiled threat: "And you must know those I have can keepe me from want."

The next day Powhatan made a speech to Smith and his men. Smith, who was by then the most proficient of all the colonists in the Algonquian language, was probably the one who later put Powhatan's speech on paper. It was first published in London in 1612 in a report on Virginia that Smith helped compile. The devious Powhatan and the shrewd young captain were well-matched adversaries. Each was not above lying to the other. Said Powhatan:

> What can you get by warre, when we can hide our provision and fly to the woods? . . . Thinke you I am so simple, not to know it is better to eate good meate, lye well, and sleepe quietly with my women and children, laugh and be merry with you, have copper, hatchets or what I want being your friend; than be forced to fly from all, to lie cold in the woods, feede upon Acornes, rootes, and such trash, and be so hunted by you, that I can neither rest, eate, nor sleepe, but my tyred men must watch, and if a twig but breake, everyone cryeth there commeth Captaine Smith: then I must flie I know not whether.[34]

Smith answered coolly in a long speech, the heart of which was, "Had we intended you any hurt, long ere this we could have effected it." Powhatan had asked Smith and his men to leave their weapons aboard their boats, but Smith had a counterargument: "Your people comming to James Towne are entertained with their Bowes and Arrowes without any exceptions; we esteeming it with you as it is with us, to weare our armes as our apparell."[35]

At that point, both leaders took stock of the situation and stalled for time. Smith and his men refused to surrender their weapons. Powhatan grudgingly agreed to trade corn for glass beads, knives, and copper. Smith asked for Powhatan's men to help free his boats from the ice in order to load the promised corn. Then Smith sent word for six more of his men to leave the boats and come ashore. Suddenly, Powhatan, "having knowledge his men were ready whilest the ice was a breaking, with his luggage, women and children, fled." But he left "two or three of the women talking with the Captaine, whilest he seceretly ran away, and his men that secretly beset the house."

Smith was on his guard. He had not forgotten the king of Warraskoyack's warning. When Powhatan's men surrounded the house, Smith fired his pistol among them and brandished his sword. These Indians, like Powhatan and his retinue, deserted the house.

Powhatan then sent word to Smith that he had departed, "fearing your gunnes." His messengers brought Smith a "great bracelet and a chaine of pearle" as a token of friendship. They also brought the requested baskets of corn.

Smith and his men, now numbering eighteen, faced the men Powhatan sent. Armed with bows and arrows and "grim as Divels," the Indians offered to guard the Englishmen's weapons while Smith and his men loaded the corn onto their boats. But Smith, equally grim, ordered his men to light the matches to fire their muskets. That action and "a few words caused them [the Indians] to leave their bowes and arrowes to our guard, and beare downe our corne on their own backes." Smith's boldness had won again.

But now the loaded barges had to wait for high tide to float them free from the icy mud. That would not happen until midnight. Smith and his men returned to Powhatan's house as though they "never had suspected or intended any thing." In like manner Powhatan's men passed the time until nightfall "with all the merry sports they could devise."

Darkness fell. Then the Indians all left. In this ominous absence another visitor came. It was Pocahontas. Smith (who often wrote of himself in the third person) later described their meeting with great tenderness:

> For Pocahontas his [Powhatan's] dearest jewel and daughter, in that darke night came through the irksome woods, and told our Captaine great cheare [food and drink] should be sent us by and by: but Powhatan and all the power he could make, wouild after come kill us all, if they that brought it could not kill us with our owne weapons when we were at supper. Therefore if we would live shee wished us presently to bee gone. Such things as she delighted in he [Smith] would have given her: but with the teares running down her cheekes she said she durst not be seene to have any: for if Powhatan should know it, she were but dead, and so she ranne away by her selfe as she came.[36]

Eight years would pass before John Smith and Pocahontas saw each other again.

After Pocahontas had left, in less than an hour "came eight or ten lusty fellowes, with great platters of venison and other victuall," just as Pocahontas had said. Smith and his men greeted them with muskets at the ready and the hempen cords of their matches smoldering. The Indians begged them to extinguish the matches, "whose smoake made them sicke" (this from a people who kept a constantly burning fire in their smoky houses). The request was not granted. The muskets remained at the ready.

The supper was served, but "the Captaine [Smith] made them taste every dish." When the meal was ended, Smith sent some of the Indians back to Powhatan to tell the old king to "make haste for hee was prepared for his comming." Powhatan then sent "more messengers, to see what newes," and "not long after them, others." The murder of the hated Englishmen had not taken place.

Pistols, swords, and muskets at the ready, Smith and his men passed the time in the house with Powhatan's men until midnight. They could not sail away until high tide lifted their boats from the mud. As Smith remembered, both sides—English and Indian—kept up a pretense of cordiality: "Thus wee spent the night as vigilantly as they, till it was high-water, yet seemed to the salvages as friendly as they to us."[37] When high tide came, the *Discovery* and the pinnace set sail with their baskets of corn.

Captain John Smith had won this time, but his triumph over Powhatan was short-lived. Smith had humiliated him before his men, and Powhatan would not forget that. Besides, he still had the friendship of the traitorous Dutchmen and the promise of more weapons.

Knowing too well that the baskets of corn were not enough to last until spring, Smith paid a visit farther upriver to Powhatan's brother, Opechancanough. But the king of the Pamunkey had obviously heard that the captain of the English was coming. When Smith and fifteen of his men entered Opechancanough's great bark house, seven hundred armed warriors appeared outside as if by magic. Bristling with bows and arrows, they surrounded the house.

Smith, undaunted, surveyed the forces assembled against him and spoke to his men: "We are sixteene, and they but seaven hundred at the most; and assure your selves, God will so assist us, that if you dare stand but to discharge your pieces [fire your muskets], the very smoake will be sufficient to affright them. Yet howsoever, let us fight like men, and not die like sheepe. . . . God hath oft delivered mee and so I trust will now." Then Smith had a sudden inspiration: he would challenge Opechancanough to fight him one-on-one, and winner take all. He told his men, "If you like this motion, promise me you will be valiant."[38]

All agreed, though there must have been doubts. Opechancanough was a big man, a head taller than their short, stocky captain. Then Smith spoke to Opechancanough:

> I see, Opechancanough your plot to murder me, but I feare it not. As yet your men and mine have done no harme, but by our direction. Take therefore your armes, you see mine, my body shall bee as naked as yours: The Isle in your river is a fit place, if you be contented: and the conquerour (of us two) shall be Lord and Master over all our men. If you have not enough, take time to fetch more, and bring what number you will; so everyone bring a basket of corne, against all which I will stake the value in copper, you see I have but fifteene, and our game shall be, the Conquerour take all.[39]

The shrewd old king pretended agreement. Then he motioned for Smith to step outside ahead of him. The seven hundred warriors were still waiting, silent and still as the woods around them. Smith refused to step outside.

With a quick word to his men to be on guard in the house, Smith suddenly reached up and caught Opechancanough by his topknot. Pulling the king's hair tightly, he put a pistol against his bare chest and forced him outside. Opechancanough's men were astonished. Seeing their king trembling with fright in the Englishman's grasp and "little dreaming that any durst in that manner [would] have used their King," the seven hundred warriors threw down their bows and arrows.

Smith then spoke to them: "If you shoot but one Arrow to shed one drop of bloud of any of my men . . . I will not cease revenge (if once I begin) so long as I can heare where to finde one of your Nation." That said, Captain Smith had not forgotten the reason for his visit: "You promised to fraught my ship ere I departed, and so you shall, or I meane to load her with your dead carcasses." Suddenly, Smith turned conciliatory: "Yet if as friends you will come and trade, I once more promise not to trouble you, except you give me the first occasion, And your King shall be free and be my friend, for I am not come to hurt him or any of you."

In the end, Indians "from all parts of the Country with ten or twelve miles in the extreame frost and snow, they brought us provision on their naked backs." Smith and his men had traded 25 pounds of copper and 50 pounds of "Iron and Beads" for enough food, they reckoned, to "keepe 46 men six weekes." They returned to Jamestown with 479 bushels of corn and nearly 200 pounds of deer suet. Jamestown would not starve this winter. The "Starving Time" would come later.

For the rest of his presidency John Smith managed to keep an uneasy peace with the Indians along the rivers and to keep order among the unruly colonists at Jamestown. Even though there was food in the storehouse, Smith issued his now-famous dictum: "He that will not work shall not eate."[40]

There were too many gentlemen at Jamestown who had never done a day's manual labor in their lives. There were goldsmiths and glassblowers and tailors who disdained to chop down trees and till fields and catch fish. That left the farmworkers and the bricklayers and carpenters and blacksmiths to do the heavy work. Said the president, "The labours of thirtie or fortie honest and industrious men shall not be consumed to maintaine an hundred and fiftie idle loyterers." Under Smith's direction the colonists dug a well "of excellent sweet water" in the middle of the fort, built twenty new houses, repaired the church, constructed weirs for fishing, and cleared and planted "thirtie or forty acres of ground." The well of "sweet water" has recently been unearthed, along with other remains of the fort, by archaeologists in the Jamestown Recovery Project.[41]

Smith's enemies were still at work. The Dutchmen he had sent to build a house for Powhatan at Werowocomoco were ready to kill John Smith and take over Jamestown—with Powhatan and his men, using guns and swords stolen from the English. There were disaffected confederates among the colonists at Jamestown who had been helping to smuggle hatchets, knives, guns, and swords to arm the Dutchmen and Powhatan's Indians. Soon the Indians had learned how to shoot more than bows and arrows.

Before summer came, Smith had discovered a plot by the Dutchmen to have forty of Powhatan's men ambush him in the woods near Jamestown. But Smith had the ringleader captured and managed to foil the plot (the record does not explain how).

Then the king of Paspahegh, an Indian town about six miles south of Jamestown, meeting Smith alone, tried to shoot him and dragged him into the river to try to drown him. In retaliation Smith's men "burnt the Kings house."[42]

Then Smith took his own revenge among the Indians, "whereby six or seaven were slaine, as many made prisoners. He burnt their houses, took their Boats, with all their fishing wires [weirs], and planted some of them at James towne for his own use."[43] The Indians were intimidated—at least, for the time being.

They were also impressed by John Smith's mysterious powers. He revived one of the Indian prisoners who was found unconscious in the Jamestown jail. The weather was cold, and Smith had allowed him to build a charcoal fire. But it was an enclosed, ill-ventilated space, and the prisoner was evidently overcome by the carbon monoxide fumes. Smith and his men revived him with "Aqua vitae and Vinegar," and soon word spread among the Indians that "Captain Smith could make alive a man that was dead." Archaeological evidence at Jamestown has discovered what may be the site of that prisoner's jail cell—and the charcoal fire he built.[44]

Smith's actions, combined with the accidental killing of some of Powhatan's Indians by an exploding bag of gunpowder, "amazed and affrighted both Powhatan, and all his people, that from all parts . . . they desired peace."[45] They would not be peaceful for long.

In early summer, 1609, the weather in Virginia was turning hot. Mayflies, the small, pesky insects whose bites made red, itchy welts, swarmed everywhere. But the forty precious acres of corn would be ripe in September, the hogs on Hog Island had produced litters of "60, and odd Piggs," and there were "neer 500 chickings brought up themselves without having any meat given them." And best of all, the storehouse had plenty of bushels of corn to last until harvest time in the fall. The Indians, for the time being, were quiescent. Jamestown's two hundred colonists were hopeful. Anne and John Laydon were expecting their first child. Since John Smith took over as president (the other councilors having died or gone back to England), Virginia had been a one-man government. In all this time, except for the eleven men who drowned the previous winter, only "7 or 8" had died. Under Smith's direction the colonists built a blockhouse on the narrow neck of Jamestown Island, with a garrison to allow no one to pass, "Salvage nor Christian, without the presidents order." There was now a blockhouse at Hog Island, and a half-built fort on a "high commanding hill, very hard to be assaulted, and easie to be defended."[46] Come what may—hunger or Spanish or Indians—the English at Jamestown, well fed and snug in their log fort, would be ready. There was reason to hope that at last, their troubles were over. They were mistaken.

One hot midsummer day, Jamestown's good fortune came to an end. The person who first discovered it is not known. No doubt that person, unbelieving, called for others to see: the precious bushels of corn in the storehouse had rotted. Bushel after bushel were filled with blackened and stinking ears of corn. Worse yet, on breaking open the rest of the bushels they found that what dampness and heat had not destroyed, rats had devoured. "So many thousands rats (increased first from the ships)" had done damage beyond belief. "This did drive us all to our wits end," as Smith wrote, "for there was nothing in the country but what nature afforded."[47] And there was no point in going to the Indians for help. The Indians Smith had strong-armed so successfully to trade corn the previous winter had none to spare. All of Virginia was in the throes of a severe drought. The Indians' first crops of corn, planted in May, would not be ripe until August, and even now, as June began, the young plants were spindly, with leaves that curled inward to conserve what little moisture they were getting. The Indians would be hungry, too. They generally ran short of their store of dried corn by winter's end. Spring and early summer were their leanest times, when they lived mostly on fish, small game, and wild berries.

Smith decided that his Jamestown people would imitate the Natives. He dispatched Ens. William Laxon, a brawny young carpenter, with a company of sixty men to spread themselves up and down the riverbanks and "live upon oysters." The wide James River south of the fort had plenty of them. Roasted over a fire, they made a tasty meal. Farther downriver Smith sent Lt. George Percy with twenty men to fish at Point Comfort. Chesapeake Bay abounded in all kinds of fish: herring, shad, perch, flounder, and some the English did not even know the names of. Sending the groups with Laxon and Percy would relieve Jamestown of about a hundred mouths to feed. But that still left too many with too little to eat, so Smith sent Francis West and another company of thirty men upriver near the Falls (near modern Richmond, Virginia) to hunt rabbits and squirrels and forage for wild berries.

As the long summer days passed, the fruits of all this food gathering were disappointing. Laxon and his oyster hunters managed to sustain themselves, but they were not well fed and certainly not happy. Poor Percy had a gunpowder accident that left him badly burned and in no condition to supervise his fishermen. They quarreled so much that "in six weekes they would not agree once to cast out the net."[48] And up at the Falls, West and his men were eating little but red mulberries and boiled acorns—not a satisfying diet.

At Jamestown the malnourished and the malcontents made for more misery. Some people had heard that Powhatan had a basket of corn at his town, some fifty miles away. They demanded that Smith trade for it, and though he "bought neere halfe of it to satisfie their humors," they were not satisfied. Some of them wanted to abandon Virginia.

Smith discovered that William Dyer, who had been one of his trusted band of explorers in 1608, was the man behind this plot. Now Dyer was a defector, a determined troublemaker, "a most crafty fellow . . . whom he [Smith] worthily punished."[49] The nature of Dyer's punishment was not recorded, but William Dyer would not forget what Smith had done to him. Dyer began to nurse a grudge.

Besides the malcontents at Jamestown, there were the sick—their number is not known. But Smith mentioned them in a speech to the colonists, declaring that "the sick shall not starve, but equally share of all our labours; and he that gathereth not every day as much as I do, the next day shall be set beyond the river, and be banished from the Fort as a drone, till he amend his conditions or starve." "He that will not work shall not eate" had suddenly escalated. Surviving reports do not say if any men were banished, but "many" of the Jamestown colonists were "billetted among the Salvages, whereby we knew all their passages, fields and habitations, how to gather and use there fruits as well as themselves; for they did know wee had such a commanding power at James towne they durst not wrong us of a pin."[50]

Just how close were the English and Indians? In recent excavations of a cellar in the fort at Jamestown, an Indian cooking pot was discovered, "still containing traces of turtle bone. A butchered hip-bone of a pig and a butchered turtle shell lay nearby." Archaeologist William Kelso speculates, "So was the cook a Virginia Indian—perhaps a woman?"[51] The remains here point to a very early period in Jamestown's history, but the exact date is impossible to know, as is the story behind these remains. Why was an Indian woman cooking turtle meat and ham inside the fort? Was she perhaps the wife of one of the Englishmen? For nearly two years Jamestown (except for the two Englishwomen) was an all-male camp, ranging in age from ten or twelve to forty or fifty. Small wonder if some of the men took up with Native women. But that was not the sort of news the Virginia Company wanted to publicize.

Meanwhile, some of the men at Jamestown tried to escape their hunger by escaping Virginia. The details are not recorded, but Smith issued them a stern warning: "If I finde any more runners for Newfoundland with the Pinnace, let him assuredly look to arrive at the Gallows."[52] This threat was enough to keep the colony's one oceangoing vessel, the *Discovery,* in Virginia. The colonists at Jamestown would be glad of that later.

If these troubles were not enough, the Dutchmen living with Powhatan decided to take advantage of Jamestown's weakened condition. With most of the able-bodied men now scattered up and down the James River, Powhatan's foreign-born confederates reckoned it would be easy to destroy the English colony. With Powhatan's help they proposed to burn the fort, seize the *Discovery,* and make the colonists Powhatan's prisoners. Rumors circulated, and many of Jamestown's "Discontents" agreed to "their Devilish practise." Two of the others leaked the plot to Smith, who swore them to secrecy and schemed with them to "bring the irreclaimable Dutch men and the inconstant Salvages" to an ambush. When some of the "impatient multitude" at Jamestown heard about the Dutch plot, they were furious and "offered to cut their [the Dutchmen's] throats before the face of Powhatan." George Percy and a colonist named John Cudrington, "two Gentlemen of as bold resolute spirits as could possibly be found," volunteered to kill the foreigners. (Percy had obviously recovered from his gunpowder accident.) But Smith "had occasion of other imployment for them." He sent two other men, to whom the Dutchmen and Powhatan issued deceitful disclaimers.[53]

In the midst of this delicate diplomacy a ship sailed upriver to Jamestown. Capt. Samuel Argall, an "ingenious, active, forward young gentleman" in the employ of the Virginia Company (he was a cousin of Sir Thomas Smith by marriage), arrived on the *Treasurer* on July 13, 1609, after a record-breaking voyage across the Atlantic. He had sailed the more direct course westward, avoiding the longer southern route by way of the Canary Islands and the West Indies. Argall made the crossing in nine weeks—including two weeks when his ship was becalmed. Best of all, that ship was "well furnished, with wine and much other good provision." Though Argall's supply was not brought for the colonists (the Virginia Company had sent him on the new route across the Atlantic, and he had then planned to fish and trade), the hungry Jamestown settlers feasted. Argall also brought letters (now lost) from the Virginia Company criticizing Smith's harsh treatment of the Indians and his failure to send back profitable cargoes. From Argall, Smith and the others learned of a "great supply and preparation for the Lord de La Warre."[54] This was the Sea Venture fleet Argall had left England on May 5, 1609, and James I had signed the Virginia Company's new charter on May 23. London had been abuzz with talk of the *Sea Venture* expedition long before that, but neither Argall nor Smith knew that the nine-vessel fleet had left England on June 2 and was then somewhere in the mid-Atlantic. And no one knew of the *Sea Venture* wreck and the scattering of the rest of the fleet.

Less than three weeks later, in early August, four ships hove into Chesapeake Bay. Smith's lookouts at Point Comfort quickly sent word of the unknown vessels to Jamestown. Smith "supposed them Spaniards" and prepared for an invasion. Indians who lived near Jamestown stood by to help. They hated the Spanish even more than the English. But when the four battered ships made their way nearer Point Comfort, all ashore were surprised to discover that they were not Spanish at all. They were what was left of the great Sea Venture fleet.

By August 11, 1609, the *Blessing, Lion, Falcon,* and *Unity* were moored to trees on the riverbank at Jamestown. Neither the ships nor their passengers were in good shape. Gabriel Archer (Smith's old enemy) had returned as captain of the *Blessing.* A few days after he arrived he wrote a letter to a friend in London who happened to be one of the Virginia Company investors. Archer wrote frankly of the conditions of the newcomers: "The *Unity* was sore distressed when she came up with us, for of seventy land men, she had not ten sound, and all her Sea men were downe, but onely the Master and his Boy, with one poor sailor. . . . In the *Unity* were borne two children at Sea, but both died, being both boyes." A few days later the *Diamond* arrived, with its mainmast gone, and "many of her men very sick and weake. . . . And some three or four dayes after her, came in the *Swallow,* with her maine Mast overboord also, and had a shrewd leake."[55]

Archer also wrote of the colony's perpetual food shortage. He blamed "Captain Newport and others" for leading the Virginia Company in London to believe that there was "such plenty of victuall in this Country, by which meanes they [the Virginia Company] have been slack in this supply." "Upon this," Archer told his friend, "you that be adventurers [investors] must pardon us, if you find not return of Commodity so ample as you may expect, because the law of nature bids us seek sustenance first, and then to labour to content you afterwards. But upon this point I shall be more large in my next Letter."[56] Unfortunately, Archer's "next letter" has been lost. But his criticism of the Virginia Company's failure to send enough provisions was not new. John Smith had complained of the same failing in his letter to the company almost a year earlier.

Now there were even more mouths to feed in Virginia: the incoming ships' crews and passengers numbered about three hundred in all, including an unknown number of women and children. The Virginia Company claimed that it had sent "five hundred men with some number of families—of wife, children, and servants—to take fast hold and root in that land."[57] One hundred fifty of them had been on the *Sea Venture*. The rest had been at sea since June. It was now early August.

None of them had seen the *Sea Venture*. Many of them were sick. All of them were hungry. Smith was not glad to see them. Worse yet, some of the newcomers were his sworn enemies.

Here was his old nemesis, John Ratcliffe, whom he had sent home a year ago. Here was Gabriel Archer, whom he had sent along with Ratcliffe. Now they were back. Ratcliffe, who had captained the *Discovery* in 1607, was now captain of the *Diamond*. Another of Smith's old adversaries was John Martin, who had sailed back to England in 1608 and had now returned as captain of the *Falcon*. Smith was in command at Jamestown, but the trouble was that the lost *Sea Venture* had carried not only Sir Thomas Gates, the new deputy governor of Virginia, but also the new charter and instructions for the Jamestown colonists. Without a governor, who was in charge? Smith's term as president would expire on September 10.

Meanwhile, besides the two hundred colonists already in Virginia, there were now some three hundred more who needed food and shelter. But mostly food. As the days passed, people were getting hungrier and hungrier. Besides the governor and the charter, the *Sea Venture* had carried the bulk of provisions intended for Virginia and all the bills of lading to distribute them. How should they parcel out the few supplies they had left? There were the captains of the *Blessing, Falcon, Lion, Falcon, Unity, Diamond,* and *Swallow* who thought they should decide. There were people of distinguished families, like George Percy and Francis West, whose

It would take all of P's magic to tame this bunch!

status, they thought, entitled them to share in decisions. There were the ships' officers and crews, eager to provision their ships and be gone. There were the sick and weak and the newly arrived women and children to be considered. And there was John Smith, the lame-duck president.

Capt. Gabriel Archer (who bore no love for Smith) wrote, "Now did we all lament much the absence of our Governour, for contentions began to grow, and factions, and partakings, &c. Insomuch as the President [Smith], to strengthen his authority, accorded with the Mariners, and gave not any due respect to many worthy Gentlemen, that came in our Ships."[58] These "worthy gentlemen" decided to choose young Francis West, the brother of Lord De La Warr, Virginia's governor-to-be, as the interim president after Smith's term expired. West refused, and the bickering and backbiting went on.

As one of the pro-Smith colonists reported, "Happie had we beene had they never arrived, and we forever abandoned and as we were left to our fortunes: for on earth for the number there was never more confusion, or misery, than their factions occasioned. . . . It would be too tedious, too strange, and almost incredible; should I particularly relate the infinite dangers, plots, and practices, he [Smith] daily escaped amongst this factious crew." Smith tried to persuade Capt. John Martin, who had been in Virginia before, to take the presidency, but Martin, "knowing his owne insufficiency and the companies untowardnesse and little regard of him, within three houres . . . resigned it againe to Captaine Smith."[59]

Smith decided to act. If Martin would not take the presidency, instead he could lead a group of men to forage for food and live among the friendly Indians at Nansemond, some thirty miles downriver, across from Point Comfort. Soon John Martin and 120 disgruntled men went south, and the same number went northward to the Falls under the command of Francis West.

Neither group succeeded. Martin was so fearful of the Indians at Nansemond that he took over their king's house and made "this poor naked King" his prisoner. The king's people attacked Martin, killed many of his men, and left—taking with them "a thousand bushels of Corne." Martin, still terrified, sent to Jamestown for 30 more men. But when the men reached Nansemond, he did not use them and finally returned to Jamestown, leaving the remnants of his men to fend for themselves. Some were wounded. One of them, a man named George

Forrest, "had seventeene Arrowes sticking in him and one shot through him, yet lived six or seaven dayes, as if he had small hurt, then for want of surgery died."[60]

Meanwhile, there was more trouble upriver. At the Falls, Francis West had chosen to make his camp at a low-lying place where the river regularly flooded. Smith made a shrewd offer to Powhatan for an Indian village nearby, for West and his men to occupy. In return, the English would help Powhatan against his enemies, the Monacans. Powhatan Village was a well-located site with more than two hundred acres of land ready to be planted, but West and his unruly men would have none of it. Instead, West returned to Jamestown, while his men at the Falls robbed the neighboring Indians' gardens, stole their corn, and took some of them as prisoners. The Indians came complaining to Smith that the men he had sent them to defend against the Monacans were "worse enemies than the Monacans themselves." Smith spent nine days upriver trying to persuade West's men to come to terms with the Indians, but failed. He sailed away in disgust. As soon as Smith departed, the Indians, still angry, attacked West's men, "slew many," and retired to the woods "with the swords and cloakes of those they had slaine." After that attack, the frightened survivors were more than willing to listen to Smith, whose ship had accidentally run aground "halfe a league" (about three miles) downriver. Perhaps hearing from the Indians of their surprise attack on West's camp, he took a boat and returned once more to West's men. There he "put by the heeles [put in irons, confined] six or seaven of the chiefe offenders." He then settled the rest at Powhatan Village, "readie built and prettily fortified with poles and barks of trees, sufficient to have defended them from all the Salvages in Virginia."[61] Smith mollified the Indians once more, returning to them the corn West's men had stolen.

"At that instant" West himself arrived to take command, and "new turboyles [troubles] did arise" between Smith and West and West's unruly men. Smith, presumably with the half-dozen troublemakers he had taken into custody, made ready once again for the long journey back to Jamestown. But as Smith departed, West and his men immediately abandoned Powhatan Village and moved back to sleep in the open air at their original camp. Smith, no doubt disgusted and exasperated, set sail. What happened next is not clear. There are two versions of a mysterious accident aboard Smith's boat, one written by Smith, and the other by George

Percy, who had no love for Smith. According to Smith's account, he had sailed "with his best expedition," but there is no record of who was aboard the boat with him. While Smith was "sleeping in his boat, (for the ship was returned two daies before) accidentallie, one fired his powder-bag, which tore the flesh from his body and thighs, nine or ten inches square in a most pitifull manner; but to quench the tormenting fire, frying him in his cloaths he leaped over bord into the deepe river, where ere they could recover him he was neere drowned. In this state, without either Chirurgeon, or chirurgery, he was to goe neere 100 miles."[62]

George Percy's version of this incident is somewhat different. When he wrote his "Trewe Relacyon" years later, he described the "greate devisyon" between West and his men and Smith at the Falls, where "Capteyne Smithe perceavinge bothe his authorety and person neglected, incensed and animated the Salvages ageinste Capteyne West and his company, Reporteinge unto them [the Indians] thate our men had noe more powder left them then wold serve for one volley of shott. And so Capteyne Smithe Retourninge to James Towne ageine [was] fownd to have too mutche powder aboutt him, the which beinge in his pockett where the sparke of a matche lighted, very shrewdly [sharply] burned him."[63] A pocket was a small bag tied around the waist, by men or women, to carry miscellaneous objects. A match was a slow-burning wick made of hemp, used to ignite a charge of gunpowder to shoot a musket. What Smith probably had was a leather gunpowder bag attached to a belt around his waist. In his sleep, the bag could have slipped from his side to the front of his body. As he slept, one of his men standing watch on deck, with a match kept burning at the ready, could have accidentally ignited the bag. A spark from the match, caught by a gust of wind, perhaps, could have been the cause of the accident. Percy, however, does not use the word *accident*. Smith was a seasoned soldier, and it is unlikely that he had "too much powder" in his bag. But in Percy's view, gunpowder was an issue: if, as Percy said, Smith had told the Indians that West's men had very little powder left (and therefore were not to be feared), it is possible that the ignition of Smith's gunpowder bag was no accident, but a deliberate act of retaliation by one who wanted Smith dead. West's men, after all, would have blamed Smith for the deaths of their comrades slain by Indians friendly to Smith. And there would be another attempt on Smith's life when he returned to Jamestown.

Like so many things about early Jamestown history, the source of John Smith's accident remains a mystery. But the accident changed his life forever. Miraculously, he survived the severe injury and did not die of infection. But it is possible that, as a twenty-first-century scholar bluntly put it, the accident "destroyed Smith's genitals."[64] There is, however, no evidence of that. But the description of the injury's location was very specific, and the gunpowder explosion in that area damaged "flesh" as well as skin. Medical evidence suggests that such a wound and its scars could have caused infertility, serious problems with sexual relations, or both.[65]

John Smith returned to England, and never returned to Virginia, and he did not go to sea again until 1612. He never married. He put his formidable energies into writing about Virginia and New England. Years later, he wrote, "By that acquaintance I have with them [the colonies] I may call them my children, for they have been my wife, my hawks, my hounds, my cards, my dice, and total my best content."[66]

If the gunpowder accident had been a deliberate attempt on Smith's life, it had fizzled. Smith's enemies would have to devise another scheme to get rid of him. They would not be long in doing so.

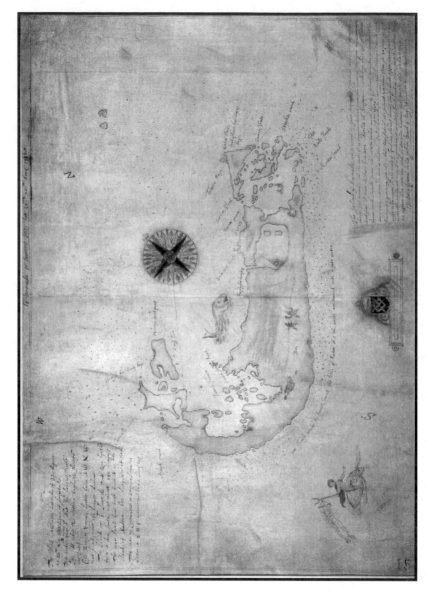

Sir George Somers's map of Bermuda, 1609. *Courtesy Bermuda Archives: MP/08/001/01.*

3

TROUBLES IN PARADISE

Henry Ravens was expendable. No one dared to voice this, not even in a whisper, but every one of the Bermuda castaways knew it. If they were ever to get off these remote islands, someone had to go for help. Virginia was the closest place, but between Bermuda and Virginia lay seven hundred miles of foaming, swelling waves that could swallow a tiny boat in one gulp. They could not risk losing Admiral Somers or Lieutenant-General Gates or Vice-Admiral Newport on such a voyage. Christopher Newport had sailed to Virginia before, but this boat's captain was going to be Henry Ravens. As the master's mate of the *Sea Venture,* he knew how to steer a vessel. And as William Strachey remembered, Ravens "was supposed a sufficient pilot." Well he should be, with his years of experience. He had sailed the West Indies as ship's master with Christopher Newport in 1594.[1] When they asked Ravens to go, he was "easily won"—but he knew the odds.

Meanwhile, Raven's boat had to be readied, and 150 people had to survive on Bermuda, one of the most remote islands in the Atlantic. Most of their shipboard provisions of "bread, beer, and victual being quite spoiled, in lying long drowned in salt water," they had to look for sustenance on land.[2] When they came ashore, they had not eaten for three days. Soon it would be night, and they were, after all, on the fearsome Isle of Devils. Who could say what lay in the dark woods nearby and in the hidden coves by the sea? The braver ones set out "to search the islands for food and water; others to get ashore what they could from the ship." The indomitable Adm. Sir George Somers, unfazed by his seventy-two hours without sleep on the deck of the *Sea Venture,* went fishing. Soon he "found such a fishing, that in half an hour with a hook and line, he took so many as sufficed the whole company."[3]

That first night, July 28, 1609, the soft white sands of "Gates's Bay" must have glowed with dozens of fires. On them newly caught fish, fat and succulent, roasted in the ashes. This was the castaways' first fresh food since the *Sea Venture* had left England eight weeks earlier. But what did they have to drink? Their beer was all spoiled, and their personal stores of wine and aqua vitae had been jettisoned during the storm. They were desperate for fresh water, but Bermuda is a volcanic island group with no natural springs and no rivers. William Strachey recalled that "when wee came first we digged and found certain gushings and soft bubblings . . . onely fed with rain water."[4] It may have been the search for water that led to the murder.

The ever-observant Strachey left a frustratingly brief record of the killing: a sailor named Robert Waters "on his first landing on the Iland . . . killed another fellow Saylor of his" with a shovel. Strachey gives no details except that Waters struck the victim, Edward Samuel, "under the lift of the Eare." Was this a quarrel between two exhausted, thirsty men digging for fresh water? It may have been a blow struck in anger, not meant to kill, but it was the end of Edward Samuel. Waters was "apprehended" (by whom, Strachey does not say). Since it was nearly dark, Waters was "appointed to be hanged the next day." That would have been by Lieutenant-General Gates's orders, which would have been carried out by his military officers (Capts. George Yeardley and William Pierce, perhaps), but the convicted murderer was one of Admiral Somers's sailors. To await his hanging, Robert Waters was "bound fast to a Tree all night, with many Ropes, and a Guard of five or six to attend him." As soon as the exhausted sentinels dozed off (after all, the *Sea Venture*'s company had been sleep deprived for three days and nights), some of Waters's fellow sailors crept stealthily up to the tree and cut his bonds. Ignoring the "unmanliness of the murder" and the "horror of the sinne," the sailors "conveyed him into the Woods, where they fed him nightly, and closely [secretly]." But after a time (Strachey's account does not say how long), the sailor Robert Waters was forgiven. "By the mediation of Admiral Somers, upon many conditions," Lieutenant-General Gates granted Waters a reprieve.[5]

Waters went free, but his narrow escape from hanging, and Somers's role in it, may have rekindled the dangerous rift between Sir George Somers and Sir Thomas Gates. The source of their bitterness toward each other lies long buried with the two knights, but there are eyewitnesses to

[handwritten: Two hostile camps / no different from European — in fact]

their anger: "Such a great difference fell amongst their commanders, that they lived asunder in this distress, rather as mere strangers than distressed friends." A narrative probably written in 1622 by a Bermuda governor offers an explanation: "The sea and the land commandours, being alienated one from another (a qualetye over common to the English) and falne into jealousies, there was produced, not only a separation of the company (even in this extremitie, even in this streight place), but an affection of disgraceinge one another, and crossinge their designes."[6] For much of their stay in Bermuda, Gates and Somers, with the factions loyal to each, lived apart. The castaways were split into two hostile camps.

John Smith wrote of this division in his *Generall Historie of Virginia, New-England, and the Summer Isles.* But how did Smith, who published his book in 1624 and who was never in Bermuda, know what happened to the castaways during their ten months there? In this case Smith, who did not always give credit where credit was due in his writings, was quite clear where his Bermuda material came from. He acknowledged his debt to men who were among the castaways: "Master Jordan, Master John Euens, Master Henry Shelly, and divers others." Silvanus Jourdain (or Jordan or Jourdan) wrote a pamphlet, *A discovery of the Barmudas, otherwise called the Ile of Divels,* published in London in 1610. A second edition appeared in 1613. In the preface to the 1613 edition Jourdain wrote, "Good Reader, this is the first book published to the world touching [the] *Sommer Ilands.*"[7] Poor Strachey. Jourdain got there first. William Strachey's much more vivid, detailed narrative did not see print until 1625—a year after John Smith's *Generall Historie* was published. The other sources Smith named—John Euens (Evans?) and Henry Shelly—had either talked to Smith in London or written their own accounts, which have not survived. John Euens's identity is not known, but Henry Shelly was one of Somers's sailors. He went fishing and discovered Mullet Bay on the island of St. George's. Shelly Bay, a large, shallow bay on Bermuda's north shore, was also his discovery. These men and the "divers others" who were cast away on Bermuda shared their memories later with John Smith. Smith probably also read Strachey's manuscript, which was sent to London in 1610. These various accounts, taken together, are the only surviving record of what happened to 150 men, women, and children who were shipwrecked for ten months on an uninhabited island more than six hundred miles from the nearest land.

[handwritten margin notes: 1610, 1613, 1625, 1610]

[handwritten at bottom: Jourdain / Strachey / Smith]

They had already been through hell and back, and they knew each other well. History knows the names of only about 50. There were young married couples like Edward Eason and his wife (known only as "Mistress Eason") and John Rolfe and his wife (known only as "Mistress Rolfe"). Both couples would become parents while they were in Bermuda. William Strachey mentions children among the castaways, but does not name any. At least one of the named passengers, Stephen Hopkins, may have had his family with him. His wife, Mary, and their three young children—Elizabeth, age five; Constance, three; and their little brother, Giles, who was not yet two—may have been in Bermuda. Among the other married passengers was Mistress Horton, whose husband, if he traveled with her, does not appear in the records. Her servant girl, Elizabeth Persons, would marry the *Sea Venture*'s cook, Thomas Powell, perhaps as the happy end to a shipboard romance. Their wedding took place when they had been in Bermuda for four months. Another servant girl, Elizabeth Jones, did not get married, but considering the goodly number of young and able-bodied men around, it was probably not for lack of opportunity. There were young soldiers like Capts. George Yeardley and William Pierce, whose loved ones, Temperance Yeardley aboard the *Falcon* and Joan and little Jane Pierce aboard the *Blessing*, might be lost at sea with the rest of the *Sea Venture* fleet. No one knew. There were the men like Strachey and Gates and Somers and Newport, and many others, whose wives and children were at home in England. Would they ever be together again? No one knew. And there were the sailors, twenty or more of them, young and agile or grizzled and slow, single or married, all of them fiercely loyal to Admiral Somers. They, too, had loved ones who waited for them somewhere.

For spiritual consolation the castaways looked to the young Reverend Richard Buck. He, too, missed his wife and daughter in England. He would soon be preaching Sunday mornings and Sunday evenings under a palmetto-thatched roof and ringing a bell morning and evening for daily prayers. As division and discord began to grow among the company, they needed all the prayers they could get. One of Buck's first official duties would have been to conduct a burial service for poor Edward Samuel. It would not be the last burial on these islands.

Gates and Somers had been at odds since before the *Sea Venture* sailed. They had boarded it grudgingly, not even wanting to sail on the same ship. Now they were marooned together on a deserted island. Their clash over the killing of Edward Samuel, with Gates determined to hang the culprit and Somers equally determined to get him off, was a sign of troubles to come. The other cause of discord was the fault of Bermuda itself: some people quickly decided that they did not want to leave it. Instead of the Isle of Devils, they found it a paradise: uninhabited, lush green islands set in aquamarine seas, nestled inside a protective barrier of coral reefs, with balmy breezes and, above all else, an incredible, astounding abundance of food. Few of the castaways had ever had so much to eat with so little effort. Within a few days they were charmed by the "ease, and pleasure," of the place.[8] Some of them began to wonder why they had to go on to Virginia.

At first the whole company camped together in a small area they called "the quarter" near Gates's Bay. They settled on the southeast tip of St. George's Island, on a narrow point of land about the size of a football field, with the sea on three sides of them. Summer's warm nights meant that for the time being they could sleep in the open air. Simple framed cabins with palmetto-thatched roofs would be their shelters later on. Silvanus Jourdain remembered that at first they had "time and leasure to save some good part of our goods and provision, which the water had not spoyled, with all the tacking of the ship, and much of the iron about her."[9] Rowing the skiff or maneuvering the longboat through the surf and out to the wreck, nearly three-quarters of a mile from shore, was not easy. Neither was the return trip with a heavily laden boat.

Among the provisions they salvaged were several hundred wooden casks of meal, more than four tons in all, that the *Sea Venture* had been carrying to the hungry colonists in Virginia. The flagship had also been transporting live hogs for the same purpose. Strachey recalled "our own Swine preserved from the wreck and brought to shoare."[10] Squealing and grunting, these hapless creatures were freed from their seawater prison only to become part of the food supply ashore.

Though the castaways did not know it, Bermuda had its own supply of hogs. They found out as soon as some of their sows strayed into the woods. It was not long before "an huge wilde Boare followed downe to our quarter." Strachey remembered what happened next: "One of Sir George Somers's men went and lay among the Swine, when the Boare being come and groveled by the Sowes, hee put over his hand and rubbed the side gently of the Boare, which then lay still, by which meanes hee fastened a rope with a sliding knot to the hinder legge and so tooke him, and after him in this sort two or three more."[11]

As Somers had been the first to fish, he was now the first to hunt for wild hogs. Among the castaways was the ship's dog, whose task aboard the *Sea Venture* had been to catch rats, but now it was promoted to a boar-hunting dog. The first hunting party, led by Somers, took the astonishing number of thirty-two wild hogs. These, according to Jourdain, he "brought to the company in a boate, built by his own hands." If so, he must have made several trips. This may be the same boat that Strachey remembered as the "flat bottome Gundall [gondola] of Cedar" they used for fishing "farther into the Sea." Bermuda's wild hogs were so plentiful that sometimes a hunting party would bring in "thirtie, sometimes fiftie, Boares, Sowes and Pigs in a weeke alive." The eager ship's dog "would fasten on them and hold, whilest the Hunts-men made in."[12] They brought the hogs back, penned them up, and kept them fat with twice-daily feedings of berries from the cedar and palmetto trees.

Hogs were not the only ones who ate palmetto berries. The castaways took a liking to these berries, which Strachey described as "luscious" and "blacke and rounde, as bigge as a Damson [plum]." Jourdain remembered that these berries often took the place of bread at mealtime. He wrote that they then could save more of their supply of meal for Virginia—assuming they would get there eventually. Bermuda's tall, graceful palmetto trees produced not only berries, but also large green leaves that grew from a top, or head, that tasted good raw or cooked. Some people thought them "far better than any cabbage" when stewed. Roasted, the heads, some weighing as much as twenty pounds, tasted like "fried melons." On Bermuda's rocks they found prickly pears, which tasted to them like mulberries, raw or baked. No doubt these, along with the palmetto heads and berries, made a fine accompaniment to roast pork.[13]

William Strachey wrote a lyrical description of the palmetto tree, whose head he found "so white and thin as it will peel off into pleats as smooth and delicate as white satin into twenty folds (in which a man may write as in paper) where they spread and fall downward about the tree like an over-blown rose, or saffron flower not early gathered." The palmetto's leaves had their uses as well: "So broad are the leaves, as an Italian umbrella, a man may well defend his whole body under one of them, from the greatest storm that falls. For being stiff and smooth, as if so many flags were knit together, the rain easily slides off." No doubt the castaways soon discovered this in Bermuda's frequent summer rain showers. And these broad, tough palmetto leaves also served as roofs for their church and their houses. Houses were easy to build, and food was easy to come by. Hogs were hunted for sport, and fishing was so simple it could hardly be called recreation. "And fish is there so abundant," Jourdain wrote, "that if a man steppe into the water, they will come round about him: so that men were faine to get out for feare of byting. These fishes are very fat and sweete, and of that proportion and bignesse that three of them will conveniently load two men: Those we called rockfish." Rockfish are still a Bermuda favorite. "Besides," said Jourdain, "there are such store of mullets that with a seine might be taken at one draught one thousand at the least, and infinite store of Pilchards, with diverse kinds of great fishes, the names of them unknown to me."[14]

Strachey knew many and listed them: angel fish, bream, snappers, hog-fish, dogfish, pilchards, mullets, rockfish, stingrays, and sharks.[15] Under rocks they found crawfish as large as English lobsters, and they discovered they could attract them by building a fire at night. Besides crawfish there were crabs, oysters, and whelks. Henry Shelly found a bay just a short walk to the northwest of Gates's Bay, on the south side of St. George's Island, which was "so full of Mullets, as none of them before had ever seene or heard of the like."[16] Mullet Bay is still called by that name. It is a small, sheltered bay less than a fathom (6 feet) deep, and about 320 yards wide, with a tiny island, now called Bartram's Island, in its center. Mullet Bay was a perfect place for fishing. The castaways went back there the day after Shelly found it, armed with fish gigs. They "strucke so many the water in many places was red with blood, yet caught not one." Then they brought a net, cast it, and "caught as many as they could draw a shore." Strachey thought that "no island in the world may have greater store or better fish."[17]

And then there were the tortoises, so enormous that one would make a meal for fifty people. Strachey thought tortoise meat looked and tasted like veal.[18] It was delectable stewed, baked, or roasted. Jourdain wrote that the tortoise was "all very good meate, and yieldeth great store of oyle, which is as sweete as any butter." With their two small boats the tortoise fishermen could take as many as forty turtles in one day. Besides the savory meat, there were the eggs: one female tortoise could have as many as "a bushell of egges . . . sweeter than any Henne egge." There were other eggs in profusion besides turtle eggs: Bermuda had birds so tame they laid their eggs on the sand "daily, although men sit down among them." The numbers of eggs the castaways took are hard to believe. Jourdain recalled that Gates's men took a thousand eggs in a morning, and then Somers's men, "coming a little distance of time after them," stayed there "whilest they came and laid their eggs amongst them," and got again as many eggs, along with "many young birds very fat and sweet."[19] These birds were probably terns, which lay four eggs a day.

Most abundant of all Bermuda's birds were the cahows, which then numbered in the hundreds of thousands. Now the cahow is Bermuda's national bird and an endangered species. As Strachey described them, "A kind of webbe-footed Fowle there is, of the bigness of an English green Plover. . . . Their colour is inclining to Russet, with white bellies, as are likewise, the long Feathers of their wings Russet and White, these gather themselves together and breed in those Ilands which are high, and so farre alone into the Sea, that the Wilde Hogges cannot swimme over [to] them, and there in the ground they have their Burrowes, like Coneys [rabbits] in a Warren."[20]

John Smith later wrote of these birds: "The Cahow is a Bird of the night, for all day she lies hid in holes in the Rocks, where they and their young are also taken with as much ease as may be, but in the night if you but whoop and hollow, they will light upon you, that with your hands you may chuse the fat and leave the leane."[21] Said Strachey:

> I have beene at the taking of three hundred [cahows] in an houre. . . . Our men found a prettie way to take them, which was by standing on the Rockes or Sands by the sea side, and hollowing, laughing, and making the strangest out-cry that possibly they could: with the noyse whereof the Birds would come flocking to that place, and settle upon the very armes and head of him that so cryed, and still creepe neerer and nearer, answering the noyse themselves: by which our men would weigh them with their hand, and which weighed heaviest they tooke for the best and let the others alone, and so our men would take twentie dozen in two houres.

But, Strachey added, "They will bite cruelly with their crooked Bills."[22]

The English predators were the first humans who had ever lived in Bermuda. No wonder the birds were incredibly tame. Jourdain wrote that "a man walking in the woods with a stick and whistling to them, they will come and gaze on you so near that you may strike and kill many of them with arrowes fat and plump like a Bunting, bigger than ours, Robbins of diverse colours greene and yellow, ordinary and familiar in our Cabbins. . . . Bitterns, Teals, Snites, Crowes and Hawkes . . . Goshawkes and Tassells, Oxen-birds, Cormorants, Bald-Cootes, Moore-Hennes, Owles and Batts in great store."[23] For most of the castaways, Bermuda was a gustatory paradise. In England ordinary folks were lucky if they ate meat twice a week: a bit of mutton, or a sausage carefully put by, or fresh pork if they were fortunate enough to have a hog to kill. The rest of their diet was grain and vegetables: coarse bread, porridge, turnips, cabbage, and peas, perhaps with a little cheese if they had a cow. In Bermuda they feasted every day on crabs and oysters and turtles, rockfish and mullets and snappers and bream, and cahows and other fowl, with palmetto heads and berries and prickly pears on the side. Occasionally, they made bread from their precious store of meal. And they washed it all down with a drink they learned to make from cedar berries, stewed, strained, and the juice left to "stand some three or four daies."[24] No wonder many people began to wonder why they had to leave this place.

But some of them had work to do: as the hot August days passed, the *Sea Venture*'s four carpenters, directed by Robert Frobisher, the shipwright, worked feverishly at making the longboat ready for an ocean voyage. They converted it to "the fashion of a Pinnace, fitting her with a little Deck . . . so close that no water could goe in her."[25] Its deck was made of planks from the hatches of the *Sea Venture,* and it had both sails and oars. With luck, the little boat could make it to Virginia.

All through August, as Henry Ravens and his crew watched the construction of their longboat-turned-pinnace, the *Sea Venture* castaways built their palmetto-thatched cabins, explored, and hunted and fished. Somers, who had caught the first fish and brought in the first hogs, put two of his best men, Henry Shelly and Robert Walsingham, in charge of hunting and fishing for the whole company. Or perhaps he persuaded Gates to appoint them. Somers himself went fishing with his men. They had a flat-bottomed cedar boat, very likely the one he built. On one occasion the admiral cast his line and hook and twice had it pulled from his grasp. This was no doubt a large rockfish. The third time Somers held on so tightly he would have been pulled into the sea "had not his men got hold of him."[26] When they brought the fish in and opened it, they found Somers's three hooks in the fish's belly.

Meanwhile, on land, Lieutenant-General Gates did his share of the work in the time the two leaders were still living in the same place. Gates began a saltworks. He had a little house built a short distance from the bay and the quarter and put two or three of his men to work there, boiling brine to make salt. During their stay in the islands Gates and his workers dried, salted, and stored in barrels about five hundred rockfish. If and when they could leave Bermuda, they would have food for the voyage.

When he was not hunting and fishing, Somers kept busy by laying out a garden in the quarter and planting the seeds they had brought with them to sow in Virginia. Muskmelons, peas, onions, lettuce, radishes, and other seeds went into the ground, produced little green seedlings in about ten days, but they turned spindly and eventually died. Perhaps it was the August heat in Bermuda. The birds may have eaten some of the seeds. Strachey puzzled over the garden's failure, since he saw no insects in Bermuda except flies and a kind of beetle. It would take another decade or more for mosquitoes, flies, and ants to appear, as well as the later ubiquitous cockroach. Another marvel was that there were no toads, snakes, or venomous creatures in all of Bermuda. There were some spiders with long, slender legs that got into their linen chests and drinking cans, but these apparently were not poisonous. Somers also planted sugar cane (which they had carried to plant in Virginia), but the hogs broke in and ate them.[27]

Seeds of discontent were planted as well. Some people grumbled at having to attend church. Others did not care for the doctrines in Buck's sermons. By the early 1600s Puritans in England were beginning the religious upheaval that would put Pilgrims on the *Mayflower* in 1620 and found the colony of Massachusetts by 1630. Bermuda, too, turned out to have its share of religious dissidents. But they had to conform: besides two sermons every Sunday, on weekdays there were daily prayers, announced every morning and evening by the clanging of a bell. At prayer time the names of the whole company would be read out, and anyone not present, said Strachey, "was duly punished."[28] (Strachey neglected to say what this punishment was, or to whom and by whom it was administered.) These punishments, whatever they were, bore fruit that would mature later.

At the end of August the boat that was to sail for Virginia was finally ready to leave from Gates's Bay. Ravens was taking a crew of six, and Thomas Whittingham, the expedition's cape merchant (supply officer), was to sail with them. They carried letters from Lieutenant-General Gates explaining what had become of the *Sea Venture* and appointing an interim governor of Virginia, a colonist named Peter Winn, to serve until either he or Captain-General De La Warr could get there. (Gates had no way to know that Winn had died at Jamestown some months before and that John Smith was currently the only councilor left in Virginia.) Gates also sent Winn a letter to be forwarded to the Virginia Company in London. The rescue plan was for the Virginians to send their pinnace, the *Discovery*, back with Ravens and his converted longboat. These were all the vessels at hand, and they were too small to transport 150 people. They would have to make more than one trip to get all the castaways off Bermuda. Leaving was not going to be a simple matter. Who would go, and who would stay?

At first light on Monday, August 28, 1609, one month from their landing in Bermuda, Ravens, Whittingham, and their crew set sail for Virginia, sailing a course south-southwest from the islands. They left, but they would not get far.

As soon as he had wished the Ravens boat a safe voyage, Lieutenant-General Gates turned to another crucial part of his rescue plan: he was going to build a ship. Before that day was out, Robert Frobisher, the shipwright, began supervising the laying of the keel for a pinnace. To build it he and Gates had chosen a broad, shallow bay just a few feet deep and a short walk up the shoreline from Gates's Bay. They called it Frobisher's Building Bay. Today it is known as Buildings Bay. Preparations had been in the making for several days, because the carpenters and their men first had to cut and saw trees to build the wooden stocks that would hold the keel. For this vital part of the ship, they had managed to find a tall, straight tree whose trunk would make the keel. Cut and ready to lay, it was a stout cedar timber forty feet long. From it would rise two other large timbers, the curving stem at the bow end, and the sloping stern post at the other. That was the skeleton of every vessel built. This one would be broad in the beam, at nineteen feet, but even with that, Gates's ship would not be large enough to carry 150 people. All of them could see that.

When they waved farewell to Ravens's boat and witnessed the laying of the keel for Gates's pinnace, each of them began to wonder what lay ahead. When this little ship was ready to put to sea, who would be aboard it? But they had many weeks, perhaps many months, to think about their future. Shipbuilding was a long and laborious task, and the keel was only the beginning. Then would come the laying of the floor timbers crosswise of the keel and then the keelson, another timber the same size of the keel, laid on top of them. It would be at least February before all the beams and timbers and planks were in place. Then they would have to caulk. Every seam had to be tightly sealed so it would not leak. The *Sea Venture* survivors knew all too well how important caulking was.

Two nights after Ravens set sail for Virginia, before the castaways had time to think much about the work at Frobisher's Building Bay, they spied a tiny, mysterious light blinking far out to sea, across the dark waters to the northwest of Gates's Bay. Word spread quickly. Knots of frightened people gathered on the sandy shore, peering out into the blackness. Was it a sea monster? A devil returning home to the Isle of Devils? A Spanish ship coming to attack them? As the bobbing, flickering light drew closer, they could see that it was the lantern at the stern of a small boat. Closer still, and they could see that it was Henry Ravens's boat. His converted longboat-pinnace had been at sea for more than two days and nights. It was now Wednesday night, August 30. Since Monday Ravens had been piloting his boat among the coral reefs that ring Bermuda, trying to find a passage out. Their boat drew barely twenty inches, but even with such a shallow draft Ravens could not find water deep enough to clear the reefs and reach open water.

John Smith wrote of Bermuda's treacherous undersea barriers: "By reason of those Rocks the Country is naturally very strong, for there is but two places, and scarce two, unlesse to them who know them well, where shipping may safely come in. . . . It may well be concluded to be the most impregnable place in the world." Strachey wrote: "It is impossible without great and perfect knowledge, and search first made of them, to bring in a bable Boat so much as of ten Tun without apparent ruine. . . . There is one onely side that admits so much as hope of safetie by many a league, on which . . . it pleased God to bring us. Wee had not come one man of us else ashore, as the weather was."[29] By the grace of God, the castaways would say, the Sea Venture had come in by way of one of the two safe passages through the reefs. Strachey made note of the other one later. It lies southwest of St. George's Island, a passage only three fathoms (eighteen feet) deep and so narrow and straight that Strachey thought it could be easily fortified and defended. A few years later, it was. It is the entrance to what is now called Castle Harbor.[30] If no ship could get in, no ship could get out, either.

On their return, the discouraged Ravens, Whittingham, and the six sailors finally decided they must go out from Bermuda the way the *Sea Venture* had come in. They spent the night ashore and set out as soon as it was light the next morning. They went out by the passage they had named "Somers Creek," a channel that took them north-northeast through the reefs. But the way to Virginia lay south-southwest. They would have to sail the long way, around Bermuda first. Two days passed. Ravens's boat did not make the open Atlantic until Friday, September 1. Those ashore knew, because they kept scanning the sea from northeast to southwest, the course they knew Ravens must take. Eventually, they spied a tiny dot on the horizon, and they watched it until it disappeared.

Ravens had estimated he could make Virginia and return with that colony's pinnace, the *Discovery*, by the next new moon. That would be around September 16. Two weeks, more or less. It was a rough guess. When the *Sea Venture* had been hit by the hurricane, Christopher Newport had calculated it was maybe eight days from landfall in Virginia. So Ravens reckoned he could sail from Bermuda to Virginia, make a quick turn-around, and be back by mid-September.

In the meantime the castaways were to keep beacon fires burning on the nearest "promontory," probably on what is now the part of St. David's Island called St. David's Head, the site of a lighthouse in modern Bermuda. As the crow flies, it is about a mile and a quarter from Gates's Bay. But the lookout point could be reached only by water. Those who kept watch had to take the flat-bottomed boat or the skiff to get there. But building beacon fires and keeping watch were not on anyone's mind the day that fateful Friday that Ravens's boat reached the open sea. That was the day the conspiracy broke out.

Perhaps John Want, the ringleader, deliberately timed it to coincide with a day when everyone was busy watching Ravens's boat. Or perhaps it was the laying of the keel for Gates's pinnace four days earlier that moved John Want to do what he did. Both Ravens's departure and Gate's pinnace meant the same thing: eventually, the castaways would be leaving Bermuda. John Want was one of those who did not fancy going. Besides that, he had developed a strong dislike of the Reverend Richard Buck, and he resented having to attend church services. Want was rumored to be a "Brownist," a religious dissident who favored separation from the Church of England. Suddenly, Want saw a chance to break free: Why should he have to work on Gates's pinnace when he did not want to leave Bermuda? And why did he have to attend sermons and prayer services that irritated him?

Want had been thinking about all this before work on the pinnace began, but it was the labor at Frobisher's Building Bay that put him with five other disaffected men. As they sawed and planed and hammered, they muttered among themselves that they did not want to help build a vessel to take them away from Bermuda. John Want had found kindred spirits. Strachey carefully set down their names: Francis Pierpont, William Brian, William Martin, Richard Knowles, and Christopher Carter. Almost nothing is known about the first four, but Christopher Carter would have a long history of troublemaking in Bermuda. Now John Want and his fellow conspirators swore to each other that they would quit working on the pinnace and move to another island to live. Before the day was over they persuaded at least two more to join them, recruiting the company's blacksmith (whose name is not known) and one of the carpenters, named Nicholas Bennett. But someone heard them, and that someone told Lieutenant-General Gates.

William Strachey, so careful in some details, left a good many blanks here. Who gave away the plot? Strachey does not say. But Gates tailored the renegades' punishment to fit their crime: they had wanted to live on another island, so Gates sent them "to an Iland farre by it selfe" and put them ashore with orders to stay there. After a while (Strachey does not say how long—days? weeks?), the would-be rebels grew tired of fending for themselves. They missed the ease of living in the quarter and having Somers's men hunt and fish for them. They missed having women to cook for them. They sent "many humble petitions" to Lieutenant-General Gates, begging forgiveness, vowing to make amends, and promising to work for the good of the whole company.

There is a puzzle here. If the outlaws were on an island "farre by it selfe," how did they get word to Gates? It is possible, in fact, very likely, that some if not all of these men were sailors with a strong loyalty to Admiral Somers. In that case, Somers himself may have seen to it that their messages reached Gates. And it is also possible, as in the case of Robert Waters's pardon for the murder of Edward Samuel, that it was Somers who persuaded Gates to pardon the miscreants. Strachey wrote that in light of their repeated pleas and resolutions, the lieutenant-general "was easily content to reacknowledge them againe."[31]

On Sunday, October l, a month after the conspiracy had been discovered, Mr. Buck held a communion service. No doubt the penitent rebels, including the religious dissident John Want, attended with the rest of the company. Strachey noted, "The contents (for the most part) of all our Preacher's Sermons, were especially of Thankfulnesse and Unitie, &c."[32] Unity was restored, but not for long.

The outlaws were back, but Henry Ravens's boat was not. He had put to sea on September l, his first night out lighted by a full moon. That moon had waned. September 16, the date of the new moon, had come and gone. "Ah, a few days more," people said. "Any time now." The watch fires on the hill high above the sea burned brightly, but as each day passed, hopes for the sighting of Ravens's boat with a Virginia rescue mission grew fainter. Strachey, who took his turn as one of the lookouts, remembered "many a long wished look round the horizon from the northeast to the southwest, but in vain, discovering nothing all the while . . . but air and sea."[33]

Meanwhile, Gates and Somers kept busy—but not together. Gates, growing more worried as the days went by and rescue from Virginia looked more and more unlikely, worked frantically on his pinnace at Frobisher's Building Bay. He did not shirk hard labor, and Strachey wrote admiringly that the lieutenant-general worked with a will: he did not disdain to "fell, carry, and sawe Cedar . . . for what was so meane, whereto he would not him selfe set his hand, being therefore up earely and downe late."[34] Sunup to sundown, day after day, Gates and his work crews labored. It was back-breaking, bone-wearying work.

Meanwhile, Admiral Somers set himself to exploring. He sailed his little boat around Bermuda, exploring the islands, large and small. Strachey thought that Bermuda's main island was shaped like a croissant; Jourdain called it a half moon. St. George's Island, where the castaways landed, lies like a small inverted triangle northwest of the croissant. But from one end to the other, all of Bermuda is only about twenty miles long. Somers also drew a map, the first English map of Bermuda. (An earlier Bermuda castaway, the Spanish sea captain Diego de Ramirez, had drawn the first surviving map in 1603.) Somers's map is a very good one, considering his sea-level perspective and his rough drawing materials. His talent is evident in this map, as is his sense of humor. In the left-hand corner he sketched a tiny picture of himself standing on the back of a large tortoise, clutching a pennant, and pointing toward Bermuda. On the land he drew two men hunting with their guns and the ship's dog gamboling ahead of them. Somers and his men Shelly and Walsingham (each would have a bay named after him) continued to hunt and fish for the whole company. But that was soon to end.

As the weeks went by, summer's steamy heat gave way to autumn's cooling breezes. In the quarter, life went on as it had since July. Young Mistress Rolfe was growing rounder and heavier as her lying-in time drew near. February, she thought. Thomas Powell and Elizabeth Persons, the courting couple, like many couples who would come after them, strolled Bermuda's beaches and planned their future. The hogs in the pen grew fat on palmetto berries. People washed their clothes in sea-water and hung them in the bright sunshine to dry. They built fires and cooked. They ate and drank heartily and went to sleep with full bellies every night. Before they went to bed they looked at the stars, which were as brilliant in Bermuda's remote location as they were when seen from a ship at sea. At night they listened to the eerie cries that they now knew were only cahow birds coming out to feed at night. Hundreds of them hovered over the dark sea, diving for fish and calling out what sounded like "Cahow! Cahow!" The castaways also listened to another unearthly sound: the calls of whales at night. Jourdain wrote that the whales swam "so usually and ordinarilie to the shore, that wee heard them oftentimes in the night abed: and have seene many of them neare the shoare, in the day time."[35]

But there was no sighting of a ship from Virginia. There were many reasons, as the *Sea Venture* survivors well knew, that could have delayed Henry Ravens. But as the chilly winds of November blew, hope dwindled. No one liked to talk about it. There had been three new moons since Ravens had left.

November brought colder weather, though nothing like the cold they had known in England. November also brought a wedding. On Sunday, November 26, Thomas Powell, the *Sea Venture*'s cook, and Elizabeth Persons, Mistress Horton's serving maid, were joined in holy matrimony by the Reverend Richard Buck. Afterward, no doubt, they had a wedding celebration with feasting and singing and dancing.

But the next day, Monday, November 27, Adm. Sir George Somers held a grim consultation with Lt.-Gen. Sir Thomas Gates. It was painfully, sadly obvious that Ravens and his boat and crew had been lost at sea. Help was not on the way. No one in the whole world knew where they were. But what was to be done? The two leaders disagreed. It was clear that Gates's pinnace was too small to carry the whole company, though now, minus the eight men lost in Ravens's boat and the murdered Edward Samuel, they no longer numbered a hundred and fifty. But some of them would have to stay behind while the rest sailed away.

The admiral had a better idea: he himself would build another pinnace, and then there would be room for all. He would need two carpenters (Gates was using all four at Frobisher's Bay) and twenty men to help him—and he would build his vessel "on the main" (the main island). He and his men would no longer live in the quarter with Gates and the rest of the company. The two leaders would now have separate commands. The men who chose to go with Somers were no doubt his sailors, who had a special affection for the admiral. Among them may have been Robert Waters, whom Somers had persuaded Gates to pardon for the murder of Edward Samuel. The move meant that Admiral Somers and his crew would be working and living on the main island, at least three miles from Lieutenant-General Gates and the rest of the company on St. George's Island.

What had brought about this parting of the ways? None of the existing narratives has a clue: Jourdain does not mention it at all. Strachey describes the separation, but never exposes the root of the bitterness between Gates and Somers. Smith's version merely observes the two leaders' rift.

Exactly where Somers and his men took up residence is not known. But he had explored the entire coast and would have chosen a sheltered cove or bay with shallow water to build his pinnace. The map of Bermuda that Somers drew offers some clues. On the north shore of the main island are two small dots, one labeled "Wattors [Waters's] house," the other labeled "Bailey's house." Both houses were on a bay now called Bailey's Bay. It is a small one, sheltered from the open sea by a tiny island and protected from northwest gales by a curve of land.[36] Somers may well have chosen to start building his pinnace here. Another possible building spot could have been Shelly Bay, named for another of Somers's men, Henry Shelly.

This bay is larger than Bailey's Bay, and it is also sheltered and shallow. By the eighteenth century it was a major shipbuilding site in Bermuda. But Bailey's Bay is closer to St. George's, and the two houses near it on Somers's map are clues that Robert Waters and Bailey (whose given name is unknown) built houses where Somers and his building crew lived.

Somers, with his customary energy, set to work with a fervor to match Gates's. Jourdain recalled that "he labored from morning unto night as duly as any workman doth labor for wages." Somers's boat, a smaller (thirty-ton) version of Gates's eighty-ton pinnace, was built completely of cedar. Gates had already commandeered the salvageable oak timbers from the *Sea Venture*. He had also taken its cables, iron, and nails, as well as a barrel of pitch and a barrel of tar. Somers built his boat, so both Jourdain and Smith said, entirely with hand-hewn wooden nails, except for one iron bolt. That was used to fasten the keelson to the keel and the other timbers. Lime made from Bermuda limestone, mixed with some wax "cast up by the sea, from some ship wracke," served to caulk the seams of Somers's pinnace.[37] One of Somers's carpenters was Nicholas Bennett, who had been numbered among the renegades who tried to desert the company back in September. John Want and the six other rebels, for whom Somers may have begged Gates's forgiveness, were also very likely in Somers's camp. They may have been the cause of what happened later.

All that winter, work on both pinnaces took most of the able-bodied men and the lion's share of time. Cutting down cedar trees, hauling the logs, hewing them into timbers, fashioning wooden nails and pegs, and fitting all the pieces together like a great puzzle were hard labor. Besides, the weather was cold. An Englishman who lived in Bermuda years later wrote that "noe cold ther is beyonde an English Aprill, nor heate much greater than a hott July in France." But English Aprils can be cold. In Bermuda's winter months the mild sea breezes of autumn turned to biting north winds, numbing fingers and reddening noses. The sun did not shine as often, and sometimes hailstones, hard and icy, came with rainstorms. Strachey remembered that the winter was "heavy and melancholy."[38] Some people began to wonder if they would ever see home again. Others did not want to sail the ocean in vessels as small as these pinnaces. They kept thinking about what happened to Henry Ravens and the longboat. Murmurs of discontent began to grow.

But even in wintertime there were pleasures to be had in Bermuda. The weather was chilly, but there was plenty of wood for firewood. Wood was scarce in England, and a large wood fire was a luxury. Here the castaways could build fires that were warm and cozy to sit beside. Here they could eat their fill. Winter was good hog-killing time, and they had plenty of hogs. When the weather was not good for fishing and catching tortoises, they feasted on fresh roast pork. The terns did not lay their eggs on the beaches, but on the small islands the cahow burrows were full of eggs. Two or three men could take the skiff and gather enough to feed the whole company. For those so inclined, there was tobacco for smoking. There was some tobacco already growing near a bay on the northeast corner of St. George's Island, a short walk from the quarter. Seeds planted by some earlier castaways may have been the start of this small crop, or birds could have spread the seeds. Somers named the spot "Tobacco Bay," a name it still carries, and the line of limestone crags on its outer edge is called "Tobacco Rock."

On Christmas Eve the Reverend Richard Buck preached a sermon and held another communion service like the one in October, but this time not everyone attended. Strachey recalled that Gates was there and "the greatest part of our Company."[39] But not all. And not Somers.

On New Year's Day, a fine winter morning, Lieutenant-General Gates and his friend James Swift went for a walk with their guns, and each of them bagged a wild swan.

On January 2 the sky turned dark, ominous clouds gathered, the temperature dropped, and a howling gale from the north lashed the islands. Enormous wind-driven waves, their white foam caps slowly cresting and falling and cresting again with majestic, angry force, battered Bermuda's northern shores—and Frobisher's Building Bay, which opens to the north. A narrow strip of land forms the outer edge of the bay, like an arm embracing the sea. Here, resting on wooden stocks, was Gates's fragile pinnace with its framing still unfinished, its "knees . . . not set to, nor one joynt firme." As the churning seas filled the bay and crashed on the shoreline, they nearly washed the half-finished pinnace off its supports. Each wave made it rise and fall on its wooden stocks, loosening painstakingly fitted joints, dislodging hand-hewn nails. It was about to become a pitiful pile of timbers washed into the sea. With grim desperation and sheer brawn, the men of the pinnace's work crew managed to hold it in place as the icy waves swept over them. Strachey, who was himself among these determined men, wrote with characteristic understatement that "with much difficultie, diligence, and labour, we saved her."[40]

As soon as the winds died down, Gates gave orders for the men to start gathering "an hundred load of stone" from the hills to build a sort of pointed bulkhead around the pinnace to break the force of the waves. Winter was far from over, and there would be other northeast gales. While they were at it, the men also wedged stones around the pinnace's ribs from stem to stern to steady the vessel against the waves while it was still "green" on the stocks.

And what of Somers's pinnace, also a-building, in this storm? There is no mention of any trouble with wind or waves. But Somers (who, after all, had sailed the entire coast of Bermuda before he began building his own vessel) had chosen his spot with care. Bailey's Bay is on the main island's north shore, but it opens to the southwest, and a strip of land shelters it from winter gales.

Toward the end of January there was a storm of another kind. It was far more dangerous than a gale, and it came from an unexpected source. Stephen Hopkins was a thoughtful, studious young man in his early thirties, a husband and family man with two young daughters and a son. On Sundays he had been reading the Psalms and the lessons for the Reverend Richard Buck. Hopkins had impressed Buck and others with his knowledge of the scriptures and his grasp of theology. But Stephen Hopkins was a wolf in sheep's clothing. For some time he had been secretly pondering what the Bible had to say about authority, and what he said secretly made some people very nervous. He had decided that they did not have to obey Lieutenant-General Gates. The wreck of the *Sea Venture,* said Hopkins, was the end of Gates's authority. It was "no breach of honesty, conscience, nor Religion, to decline from the obedience of the Governour" nor to be "led by his authority . . . since the authority ceased when the wracke was committed, and with it, they were all then freed from the government of any man."[41] That meant they did not have to leave Bermuda.

Hopkins touted two reasons for staying in Bermuda. The first was the "abundance by Gods providence of all manner of good foode." They ought not to fly in the face of divine Providence. The second reason was independence: stay in Bermuda, said Hopkins, and "in reasonable time," they could build their own small boat and "get cleere from hence at their owne pleasures." Nicholas Bennett, the carpenter, would help them build a "small Barke." Everyone knew that Nicholas Bennett was one of the rebellious seven who had been banished for a time to another island last September. What was Stephen Hopkins up to?[42]

He was obviously aiming to rekindle earlier discontents that had been quieted, but not quenched. There were still many people—Strachey thought they were a majority—who had learned to enjoy a life of ease in Bermuda. Why should they go to Virginia? The majority of the castaways were the ordinary folk: the sailors, the farmers, the blacksmiths, the stonemasons, the barrel makers, the carpenters, and the like. They were the ones who knew they would break their backs toiling for the Virginia Company once they reached Jamestown. They knew from the reports and rumors about Jamestown so far that there "*nothing but wretchednesse and labour must be expected.*"[43] Who in his right mind would want to go to Virginia when he could stay in Bermuda? Many people felt that Stephen Hopkins was right.

William Strachey is the only one who wrote about the attempted revolts that took place during the castaways' time in Bermuda, and he makes a distinction between the majority and what he calls the "better sort," or the ones with upper-class backgrounds and good families. These were men like himself, and John Rolfe, and Ralph Hamor, and Robert Rich, and the military men like George Yeardley and William Pierce who were loyal to Gates. With them as well was Christopher Newport, the veteran of so many Virginia voyages, who was determined to get back to Jamestown at all costs. But the "better sort" were the minority.

A discontented majority is a dangerous thing, and Lieutenant-General Gates knew it. When two of the men in the quarter, Humphrey Reade and Samuel Sharpe, came to him and told him what Hopkins was saying, he knew he had to act—and quickly. He arrested Stephen Hopkins and put him in chains.

Did Gates consult with Somers on this matter? There is no evidence that he did. The two men had been living apart with their respective followers—Gates with the people in the quarter and Somers with his sailors on the mainland—since November. To consult Somers would have meant sailing four miles around St. George's coast and over to the mainland.

What words passed between Lieutenant-General Gates and his prisoner? Strachey, who was a diligent recorder, did not say, if in fact he knew.

How long did Hopkins languish in chains? Did Gates give him ample time to ponder his fate? The record is silent. The punishment for mutiny is death.

After some time had passed—a few hours, a night, a day?—Gates ordered the bell rung. Not for church, not for prayer this time, but for a hearing. Humphrey Reade and Stephen Sharpe would confront Hopkins. As the deep tones of the bell called them, the residents of the quarter gathered obediently. Shivering in the chill January air, they huddled together, murmuring, anxious. Gates had Stephen Hopkins "brought forth." The crowd kept silent, mute with shock and disbelief. This was a husband and father, the man who read the scriptures on Sundays, the one who helped Reverend Buck with the services. Now Stephen Hopkins was wearing manacles. The heavy iron rings around his wrists were connected by a short chain. With his slightest movement, the chain clanked. It made a mournful sound.

Then Lieutenant-General Gates began to speak, slowly and solemnly, about a dangerous mutiny in their midst. Then he asked Reade and Sharpe to lay before Hopkins what they had heard him say. When their grim testimony was finished, there was time for Hopkins to answer the charges against him. Strachey did not set down any exact words from accusers or accused, but he did note that the accused man's speech was "full of sorrow and teares." It was also an impassioned denial.

The lieutenant-general was unmoved. He spoke of the seriousness of the crime. Hopkins was "both the Captaine, and the follower of this Mutinie." He would be tried by court-martial and, if found guilty, condemned to death.

The prisoner broke down. He wept in loud, gulping sobs. He begged forgiveness. He pleaded for mercy for his family's sake: his wife, Mary; his two young daughters, Elizabeth, five, and Constance, three; and their little brother, Giles, who would be two years old the next week. According to Strachey, Stephen Hopkins was so penitent and "made so much moane" pleading on behalf of his wife and children that "all the better sort of the Company" later went to Gates with "humble intreaties, and earnest supplications" to cancel Hopkins's trial. This determined group, including Strachey and Newport, used all their eloquence on Sir Thomas Gates, and they "never left him" until at last he agreed to pardon Stephen Hopkins.[44] (Hopkins would eventually go back to England, and in 1620 he and his family would sail again to the New World—on the *Mayflower*.)

Winter dragged on. The Hopkins incident left a sour taste. Many people still harbored secret thoughts about staying in Bermuda, but now they knew they had better keep such thoughts to themselves. The women had a welcome distraction: helping John Rolfe's wife get ready for the birth of her first child. There were swaddling clothes to be made for the newborn, perhaps fashioned from some of their shifts and petticoats. Was there a midwife among them? No one knows. But the women helped young Mistress Rolfe to deliver a baby girl early in February. On Sunday, February 11, part of the religious service was the baptism of the Rolfes' daughter. She was christened—*Bermuda*. Her godparents were Mistress Horton, William Strachey, and Christopher Newport. But this happy event had a sad ending: a short time later, little Bermuda Rolfe died, as newborn infants often did in those days. They buried her in a place near the quarter, most likely in a graveyard already laid out. This winter may have been melancholy, as Strachey thought, because the bell tolled for other funerals besides Bermuda Rolfe's. He recorded the names of three men besides Edward Samuel who died in Bermuda, but did not note the dates or causes of their deaths. Jeffrey Briars, Richard Lewis, and William Hitchman were buried in Bermuda soil. Their lack of titles indicates that they were ordinary fellows, not gentry.

There was one other death and burial in Bermuda, but only one person knew the details. The grisly secret came out later in Virginia, and only John Smith wrote about it years later: "There were two savages . . . the one called Namontack, the other Matchumps, but some such differences fell between them, that Matchumps slew Namontack, and having made a hole to bury him, because it was too short, he cut off his legs and laid them by him, which murder he concealed till he was in Virginia." Who told John Smith this short but gruesome tale? Presumably Thomas Gates, or someone else who had been in Bermuda. Smith put it in his 1624 book, and Samuel Purchas has a marginal note in his 1625 *Purchas His Pilgrimes*, which he probably picked up from Smith: "Yet Namontack in his return was killed in Bermuda by another savage his fellow." A Dutch chronicler provided an intriguing detail: "During all this time they lost only four men, of whom one was a *cascike*, or son of a king in Virginia who had been in England and who had been killed by an Indian, his own servant." Namontack had served as a kind of liaison between his people and the English. Smith, who knew this young Indian in Virginia, called him a "trusty servant, and one of a shrewd, subtle capacity."[45] Namontack had helped with Powhatan's coronation, bargained with his people for corn for the hungry English colonists, and sailed with Newport to England in late 1608. He and Matchumps were going home to Virginia on the *Sea Venture*.

And what of Matchumps, the murderer? Like Namontack, he had spent time in England and knew some English. There is no record of his age, but it is safe to say he was a young man, and perhaps Namontack's servant. It was Matchumps who had told the English in Virginia in 1608 that he had seen stone houses and people who might be English survivors of the lost Roanoke colony. (They were never found.) What possessed him to kill Namontack? No one knows. The grave with a body and two amputated legs has never been found.

The murder of Namontack raises questions that have no answers: What quarrel between the two Indians was so bitter that it drove Matchumps to murder? And afterward, how did Matchumps explain Namontack's sudden absence to the other castaways? Was there an investigation? Besides these immediate questions, the murder raises others: What was the relationship between these two Indians? And how did they get along with the other castaways? Neither Jourdain nor Strachey mentions their presence aboard the *Sea Venture* or later in Bermuda. Did the two keep to themselves? Did they hunt and fish independently? Only John Smith, who read and listened to accounts from several castaways later, put Namontack and Matchumps into his narrative. Smith's account of the murder is frustratingly brief. What became of Matchumps, the murderer, when he later confessed his crime in Virginia? No one knows.

But in the winter of 1609 in Bermuda, other troubles were brewing. Perhaps it was the caulking of the pinnace in Frobisher's Building Bay that set some people thinking. In a few days, once its seams and joints were caulked and sealed, the pinnace that Gates and his company had so painstakingly built would be nearly ready to sail. And then the lieutenant-general and his loyal followers would pack up and leave Bermuda. But what if all of those followers were not keen on leaving? The time for decision was fast approaching. The caulking began in a celebratory manner, on February 26, recalling the laying of the pinnace's keel on August 28, just seven months earlier. Starting from nothing, they had built a two-masted, eighty-ton vessel from stem to stern. It was forty feet long and nineteen feet wide at the beam; it had a spacious 'tween-decks area, a great cabin, a roomy steerage, and a closed gallery. It could carry as many as eighty people and their provisions.

Lieutenant-General Gates's pinnace would soon be freighted with all the provisions they kept in the storehouse, and all supplies they had so laboriously salvaged from the wrecked *Sea Venture*. All of these were meant for Virginia, and Gates would take them there. Now hundreds of casks of precious meal would go to feed the hungry colonists at Jamestown. Muskets and pistols and powder and shot, axes and hoes and saws and shovels, cables and canvas and sails and oars would all soon be stowed aboard the new pinnace bound for Virginia.

What would be left behind for those who did not sail? Little or nothing. The time for action was at hand. There was no more time for discussions of liberty and authority, or arguments over staying in Bermuda. Push, as some said, had come to shove. Stephen Hopkins had been both the "Captaine, and the follower" of his one-man rebellion, but now there were many would-be rebels. Sometime in late February or early March, William Strachey wrote that after Stephen Hopkins had come "a worse practise, faction, and conjuration afoote, deadly and bloody, in which the life of our Governour, with many others were threatned."[46] The plot was to storm the storehouse in the quarter, remove all the supplies, and threaten to kill anyone who stood in the way. But before the appointed hour, one or more people thought better of it, went to Lieutenant-General Gates, and "discovered the whole order, and every Agent, and Actor thereof." Strachey wrote this, but did not name names. This time the rebels were scattered and not easily rounded up. Some were living in the quarter, but the rest—twenty or more—were with Somers on the main. The admiral's "whole company" (Strachey discreetly avoids naming the admiral himself) had joined the plot to sabotage Gates's plan to sail away with his loyal followers.

The rift between Gates and Somers was now a chasm. In the quarter, every man went about armed, with pistols loaded and muskets primed. Those who had swords buckled them about their waists. By Lieutenant-General Gates's orders, every man was "advised to stand upon his guard, his owne life not being in safety, whilest his next neighboor was not to be trusted."[47] Gates gave orders to double the number of sentinels guarding the storehouse. He also doubled the number of men assigned to night watches in the quarter.

On the night of March 13 a man named Henry Paine was called to take his turn at standing night watch. When the captain of the watch gave him his assignment, Paine struck him, swore at him, and declared he would not stand watch. He made fun of Gates's orders for doubling the watchmen's numbers. The watch captain told him that Lieutenant-General Gates would hear of this, and Paine answered him (as Strachey reported) "with a setled and bitter violence, and in such unreverent tearmes, as I should offend the modest ear too much to express it in his owne phrase." What Henry Paine said was that Gates had no authority over anyone there (Paine had obviously been talking to Stephen Hopkins). "*And therefore let the Governour* (said hee) *kisse, &c.*"[48] Strachey judged *kiss my arse* too vulgar an expression for his narrative, addressed to an aristocratic lady.

It was not too vulgar to be talked about in the quarter, and the next morning there must have been plenty of talk. Gates had the bell rung, and once again, as he had done for Stephen Hopkins, he called the entire company together. There the lieutenant-general took testimony from "many who were upon the watch" and had heard Paine's outburst. Gates listened grimly. Then, without hesitation, and without a trial, he condemned Henry Paine to be "instantly hanged." Before a stunned crowd, a makeshift gallows was rigged. But Henry Paine begged Gates not to string him up like a common criminal. He was a gentleman, he said, and he wished to be shot, not hanged. Gates grudgingly consented. Strachey wrote of Paine that "towards the evening he had his desire, the Sunne and his life setting together."[49]

Paine's execution took place on Tuesday, March 14, and the backlash came a few days later. Sunday, March 19, had long been set as the date when Somers would move his pinnace to join Gates's vessel in a sheltered mooring off St. George's Island. Before the two leaders had parted ways there had once been a plan for them to leave Bermuda together. In their new anchorage, both pinnaces would finish their tacking and rigging, load aboard their provisions, wait for a fair wind, and set sail for Virginia. But that plan had been made long ago. On March 19 Somers's pinnace did not move. Before the day was out, Somers's work crews—every last man of them—deserted the bay and hid in the woods.

The admiral's pinnace remained at Bailey's Bay, four miles away from Gates's vessel at Frobisher's Building Bay. When Somers's men had heard how Lieutenant-General Gates had treated Henry Paine, they were furious. They swore they would not take orders from Gates, and they aimed to stage their own rebellion. Even their beloved admiral could not reason with them.

The self-declared new outlaws sent a letter to Gates. It was, by Strachey's account, "an audacious and formal petition . . . subscribed with all their names and seals" (Strachey does not give any names). They wanted to stay in Bermuda, and they wanted Gates to give them permission to do so. And that was not all they wanted. As Strachey wrote, they requested "with great art" that Gates give each of them "two Sutes of Apparell" and a ration of meal for a year.[50] Up to now the castaways had been allowed rations of one and a half pounds of meal per person per week from the precious store they saved from the *Sea Venture*. The two suits of clothing—shirts and breeches, most likely—would have to come from a supply of clothing the *Sea Venture* had carried for the Jamestown colonists.

This petition was denied. Somers sulked. Gates fumed. Waves of discontent were eroding the lieutenant-general's authority like the sand on Bermuda's beaches at low tide. He dared not bend to these rebels.

Somers did nothing to dissuade his men. He and Gates had been at odds for a long time, and perhaps now was a time to part. Let Gates and his people leave, and Somers and his men would do as they pleased. There was plenty to eat, and they would have their own pinnace. They could sail home when they felt like it. Meanwhile, the admiral would content himself on the mainland with a few trusted companions and let the lieutenant-general make the next move. The admiral had not long to wait.

Back in the quarter on St. George's, Lt.-Gen. Sir Thomas Gates began composing a long, formal letter to Adm. Sir George Somers. Strachey must have read the letter, perhaps even helped to write it. He gives the gist of it in his narrative, and one can read between the lines. Gates began his letter by explaining that when they were first shipwrecked, he knew they could not build a vessel large enough to carry 150 people away from Bermuda. No one knew they were there, so they would have to help themselves. For this reason Gates confessed that he had secretly planned to take his pinnace and go for help himself. "But his purpose was not yet to forsake them so, as given up like Savages: but to leave them all things fitting to defend them from want and wretchednesse, as much at least as lay in his power . . . for one whole yeere or more" while they awaited the relief he would send. He was afraid that it might take a year, "so many hazards accompanying the Sea."[51]

Gates entreated Somers to get word to the rebels "if by any meanes he could learne where they were" and that he had never intended to abandon them. Obviously, there had been ugly rumors. The lieutenant-general went on to say that now the pinnace he had built was large enough to take them all. This was not true. Gates's pinnace could transport 70 or 80 people at most. But now Somers had a vessel that could carry the rest.

So the whole company, said Gates, must go on to Virginia, as it had been sent to do. He appealed to Somers to consider what King James I and the Virginia Company investors would think if this expedition broke apart and did not go on as one group to Virginia. He begged Somers to think "what an imputation and infamy it might be, to both their proper reputations, and honours, having each of them authoritie in their places" if they could not resolve their differences. And if the rebels were not brought in, "the blame would not lye upon the people (at all times wavering and insolent) but upon themselves [Gates and Somers] so weake and unworthy in their command."[52]

The lieutenant-general pleaded with the admiral to round up the rebels, "by any secret practice to apprehend them." Then Somers was to remind them of the "businesse for which they were sent out of England" and the expense laid out for them by the "Adventurers" (investors). Then a final plea: Gates asked Somers, "by the worthinesse of his (heretofore) well mayntayned reputation [the telling parenthesis implied Somers's reputation would be ruined if he did not comply], and by the powers of his owne judgement, and by the vertue of that ancient love and friendship, which had these many yeeres beene setled between them," to do his best to find the rebels and bring them in. If Somers could do that, Gates promised to pardon them all. Furthermore, he promised that "whatsoever they had sinisterly committed or practiced hitherto against the Lawes of dutie and honestie should not in any sort be imputed against them."[53]

A magnanimous and desperate offer. Would it work? If not, the Virginia Company's grand plan, long in the making, was a shambles. More than the *Sea Venture* would be wrecked in Bermuda.

4

THE STARVING TIME

IN SEVENTEENTH-CENTURY England, most people had enough to eat, however humble the fare. At home, even the poor had coarse bread or porridge, and now and then a bit of cheese or meat. It was not fine, but it was filling. Outside the cities, ordinary people grew their own food and butchered their own meat. Workers in towns and cities often had meals given them as part of their wages. In London, "cook shops" sold meat pies, sausages, and other comestibles. In England when hunger did occur, people perceived it (as one scholar has called it) as "an exception, a disruption, a corruption." It was not normal. To the English men and women who came to Virginia, constant hunger was an unfamiliar and unacceptable condition. To the Indians who lived in Virginia, on the other hand, hunger was a fact of life, depending on the time of year. As John Smith said, "It is strange to see how their bodies alter with their diet, even as the deer and wild beasts they seem fat and lean, strong and weak." The Indians ate well in the late summer and the fall, when they harvested their corn and hunted for game, but Edward Wingfield, writing about the Indians' habits, observed that he "never saw any of them gross [fat]." They grew thin in winter and early spring when game was scarce and their store of corn was used up. If food was scarce, they merely "girded up their bellies [pulled their belts tighter]."[1] Sparse diets in part of the year did not trouble them, because they looked forward to feasting later.[2] The English in Virginia did not want to be hungry at any time, but they were. After two years, they had yet to grow enough corn to feed themselves.

Besides gnawing hunger, there was other misery at Jamestown in the late summer of 1609. The weather was hot. Mosquitoes hummed. Flies buzzed, especially around the sick. Besides those with the calenture, fifty or more of the survivors in the ships from the *Sea Venture* fleet had come ashore with ship's fever, now known as typhus. Wracked with chills and nausea, the feverish, contagious sick (their body lice carried their disease) were crowded in among the well. Others came down sick. Someone had to clean up after them, empty their chamber pots, wash them, feed them, comfort them. Much of this work probably fell to the women.

There may have been as many as a hundred women in the nine-ship *Sea Venture* expedition, and an unknown number of them—sick and well— had been at Jamestown since August. At least two women were mourning the deaths of infants born at sea. Until they came, there had been only two Englishwomen in the fort: Anne Laydon and Mistress Forrest. The latter disappears from the records after 1608, so until now Anne Laydon, who was pregnant with her first child, may have been the only Englishwoman at Jamestown. Her joy at seeing other Englishwomen, many of them near her own age, can only be imagined. There was Temperance Yeardley, who had come on the *Falcon,* and Joan Pierce and her daughter, Jane, from the *Blessing,* and Thomasine Causey on the *Lion,* and others whose names are now lost. Thomasine's husband, Nathaniel, was there to greet her: he had been in Virginia a year. But Temperance's husband, George, and Joan's husband, William, were aboard the *Sea Venture* and presumed lost. Temperance, Joan, Thomasine, and the other women, if they were not themselves among the sick, would have taken their turns with others as nurses. Anne Laydon must have done all she could to help them. But she could not feed them or build houses for them.[3]

Housing inside the palisaded fort was still primitive and no doubt dismayed the newcomers. After two years, Jamestown's residences consisted of two long thatch-roofed, mud-walled barrackslike buildings and a scattering of small mostly one-room dwellings that were more like huts than houses. Archaeologists excavating the fort site have recently uncovered traces of the barracks: two structures fifty-five feet long and eighteen feet wide, each with two rooms, a cellar, and a fireplace. Along the fort's west wall, four pits may once have been the floors of crude lean-to houses. William Kelso, director of the Jamestown Rediscovery Project, believes that the original buildings inside the fort probably looked much like the replicas in the 2006 film *The New World.*[4]

During John Smith's presidency, the original triangle-shaped fort had been enlarged and more houses built. Smith wrote proudly that Jamestown was "strongly palisaded," with "fifty or sixty houses." Considering that the total population of Jamestown until the summer of 1609 had been no more than two hundred, that was about right. Three or four men could share a house, and a small one-room cabin was easy to build. It was just a matter of sinking four stout posts, putting a light wood framing on them, covering the walls, and thatching the roof. The colonists soon learned to do as the Indians did and cover their walls with bark. Sheets of tree bark they found to be "as durable and good proof against storms and winter weather as the best tile."[5]

There were houses inside the original one-and-a-half-acre fort and others close by outside, some, perhaps, in the newer palisaded extension. Who lived in these? No one knows. One of them may have belonged to George Percy, who had started building his house in 1608. A note written that year in London records expenses paid "to Mr. Melshawe for many necessaries which he delivered to Mr. Percy toward the building of a house in Virginia, 14s. [shillings]."[6] In the fall of 1609 Percy would follow Smith as the colony's president, with unfortunate results.

Jamestown now needed shelter—not to mention food—for five hundred people. But that number was steadily dropping. There was a graveyard about seven hundred feet west of the fort, and its population grew as the fort's numbers diminished. From August to October, when John Smith left, "one hundred sickened and half the number died."[7] That was only the beginning.

In late August John Smith was still upriver, trying to make peace between Francis West's men and Powhatan's Indians. He would soon be back, some people said, and things might get better. Others were not so sure.

When he did return, it was not in a manner that anyone expected. On that September afternoon when Smith's barge came into view on the river, people at Jamestown were shocked at what they saw—or, rather, what they did not see. Smith was always at the bow shouting orders when his barge came in. This time he was not there. As soon as the mooring was made fast, the reason for his absence at the bow was clear: he was "unable to stand, and neere bereft of his senses by reason of his torment."[8] Smith's sailors were preparing to carry their gravely wounded leader ashore on a makeshift litter. After the gunpowder accident, his men had brought him downriver as quickly as they could, but by now his untreated burns were hideously blistered and blackened. They oozed. Flies and gnats swarmed around them. People who saw John Smith lying helpless and crazed with pain shook their heads. What would become of Jamestown now?

Smith's enemies, John Ratcliffe, Gabriel Archer, and John Martin, were disappointed to see him still alive. Soon they and their confederates "plotted to have him murdered in his bed."[9] The story is not altogether clear, but it is mentioned in two of the existing sources: "The Proceedings of the English Colonie in Virginia," published in 1612, and Smith's own *Generall Historie of Virginia, New-England, and the Summer Isles,* published in 1624. The "Proceedings" was the work of at least eight authors—plus Smith, after he returned to London. The names of colonists William Phettiplace, Richard Potts, Nathaniel Powell, Dr. Walter Russell, Thomas Studley, Anas Todkill, and Richard Wyffin are listed on the title page, along with "divers other diligent observers, that were residents in Virginia." These men were all eyewitnesses to what had happened in Virginia. But about the attempted assassination of the wounded John Smith, the wording in both the "Proceedings" and the *Generall Historie* is identical and frustratingly brief: "But his hart did fail him that should have given fire to that mercilesse pistol."[10]

The details are missing in the *Generall Historie,* but the "Proceedings" supplies two names: "Coe and Dyer that should have murdered him." Thomas Coe and William Dyer each had a reason to hate John Smith. Once they had been his loyal companions on expeditions among the Indians. Thomas Coe was listed among the "gentlemen" who came to Jamestown in January 1608. When William Dyer arrived in Virginia is not recorded. Both their names appear on a partial list of men Smith chose to go with him and Christopher Newport on a visit to Powhatan in early 1608. Thomas Coe later went with Smith on another expedition upriver in December of that year. When Smith sent Coe and Richard Wyffin ashore to parley with Powhatan in his village, the Indian ruler was gone, and his men attacked Coe and Wyffin. They "were in great doubt how to escape with their lives."[11] As they fled, each of each of them must have been thinking of what these Indians—perhaps the very same ones—had done to George Cassen when he had gone ashore a few months earlier. Richard Wyffin (who had also risked his life to find Smith in December 1608) forgave him, but Thomas Coe did not. He could never forget that Smith had nearly cost him his life, and he would be glad to put an end to Capt. John Smith's.

William Dyer held a more recent grudge. Just this past summer, when the carefully hoarded corn in the storehouse was found to be rotten,

Dyer and a number of other people had wanted to give up and head for England. With Dyer as their leader, the malcontents had hatched a plan to take the pinnace *Discovery* under cover of darkness and abandon Jamestown. Smith found them out and "worthily punished" Dyer as the ringleader.[12] William Dyer, like Thomas Coe, nourished a healthy hatred for President Smith.

Was it Coe or was it Dyer whose heart "failed" him when the time came to shoot Smith? The record is silent. But one of these two had second thoughts about firing on Smith as he lay helpless on his pallet. Did Smith, feverish and wracked with pain, hear the click of a pistol being cocked and know at the time that someone had tried to kill him, or did he learn about it afterward? No one knows. And Coe and Dyer disappear from the records. Like Gabriel Archer, they may have died in the coming winter, the "Starving Time" at Jamestown.

After the assassination attempt, Smith's allies, his "old soldiers," the men who had been with him in his expeditions all over the Chesapeake, wanted revenge. They begged him to let them get rid of his enemies, "to take their heads that would resist his command." But John Smith had had enough. He was desperately weak and in excruciating pain from his burns. Most people—and perhaps Smith himself—did not expect that he would live. And so, as he and his coauthors wrote afterward, Smith's time in Virginia had come to a sad end.

> His commission [as president] to be suppressed he knew not why, himselfe and souldiers to be rewarded he knew not how, and a new commission graunted they knew not to whom.... [S]o grievous were his wounds, and so cruell his torment, few expected he could live, nor was hee able to follow his businesse to regaine what they had lost, suppresse those factions and range the countries for provision as he intended, and well he knew in those affaires his owne actions and presence was as requisite as his directions, which now could not be.[13]

If John Smith had not been wounded and had stayed in Virginia, hundreds of lives might have been saved.

With his remaining strength, Smith summoned the departing ships' captains and arranged to be transported back to England with them. One of the captains, a "Master Nellson," was very likely Smith's old friend

Francis Nelson, who had taken Smith's *True Relation* to London in 1608. Nelson was master of the *Falcon* now, and Smith would sail with him. But they did not sail for three more weeks.

Smith's enemies—Archer, Ratcliffe, and others—deliberately kept the ships moored at Jamestown while they gathered charges against him. Perhaps they hoped that he would die in the meantime. With the delay, food aboard the ships and on the land grew scarcer and scarcer. September dragged into October. Inside the fort, the stench of sickness and death hung like a foul miasma, and a festering discord made it worse. Hostility grew between the Smith loyalists—the ship captains and the soldiers—and Smith's enemies. The latter wanted Smith's reputation destroyed if they could not have him dead. "Perhaps you shall have it blazoned a mutinie by such as retaine old malice," Gabriel Archer wrote in a letter to London, "but Master West, Master Percie, and all the respected Gentlemen of worth in Virginia can and will testifie otherwise upon their oathes." John Ratcliffe wrote to the Earl of Salisbury on October 9 that Smith had governed "as sole governer without assistantes, and would at first admit of no councell but himselfe. This man is sent home to answer some misdemenors whereof I perswade me he can scarcely clear him selfe from great imputation of blame."[14]

But in his present state John Smith was unable to speak for himself, or to speak against his spiteful accusers. Neither Archer nor Ratcliffe gave any details of the charges against Smith, but the authors of the "Proceedings" included a summary of them:

> Now all those Smith had either whipped, punished, or any way disgraced, had free power and liberty to say or sweare anything, and from a whole armefull of their examinations this was concluded:
>
> The mutineers at the Falles, [Francis West and his men] complained hee caused the Salvages to assalt them, for that hee would not revenge their losse, they being but 120 and he 5 men and himselfe, and this they proved by the oath of one he had oft whipped for perjurie and pilfering. The dutch-men . . . swore he sent to poison them with rats bane. The prudent Councel, that he would not submit himselfe to their stoln authoritie. Coe and Dyer, that should have murdered him, were highly preferred [commended] for swearing they heard one say he heard Powhatan say, that he heard a man

say: if the king would not send that corne he had, he should not long enjoy his copper crowne, nor those robes he had sent him: yet those also swore he [Smith] might have had [traded] corne for tooles but would not. The truth was, Smith had no such engines as the king demanded, nor Powhatan any corne. Yet this argued he [Smith] would starve them. Others complained hee would not let them rest in the fort (to starve) but forced them to the oyster bankes, to live or starve, as he lived himselfe. For though hee had of his own private provisions sent from England, sufficient; yet hee gave it all away to the weak and sick.[15]

Some of Smith's enemies swore that he "would have made himselfe a king, by marrying Pocahontas, Powhatan's daughter." Smith's defenders wrote indignantly that such a "marriage could no way have intitled him by any right to the kingdome, nor was it ever suspected hee had ever such a thought."[16]

Smith's enemies outdid themselves in collecting information: "Some that knewe not any thing to say [against Smith], the Councel instructed, and advised what to sweare."[17] By early October the charges laid to John Smith were committed to paper, ready to send back to the Virginia Company officials in London. These documents are now lost, like the rest of the Virginia Company's records from 1607 to 1619. The ships of the *Sea Venture* expedition, carrying various letters, documents, and the wounded John Smith, were at last ready to sail for England. With the *Falcon,* which carried Smith, went the *Diamond, Unity, Blessing,* and *Lion.* The smaller *Swallow* stayed behind. Then a further disaster struck on the voyage to England. The little fleet lost two of its ships in a storm "entering into the narrow seas" off the coast of France.[18] But three vessels, including the *Falcon* with John Smith aboard, arrived safely in London by the end of November. Smith's injury took many months to heal. He would never return to Virginia.

George Percy, in poor health, had been planning to sail aboard one of the colony's departing ships, but he did not. Some of his friends begged him to stay and serve as the colony's interim president until they received further instructions. Percy accepted "within less than an howre."[19] Now one of Smith's old adversaries was in charge of the Virginia colony. Percy, like Smith, was a thirty-year-old bachelor, but, unlike Smith, he was not noted for his leadership. He was "easily highest in rank," but according to a Dutch chronicler, "no-one, either old [settler] or new comer would pay him much heed."[20] He took on the presidency of the Virginia colony reluctantly. He was not physically strong, and it is now believed that he suffered from epilepsy. George Percy was the eighth son of Henry Percy, the Earl of Northumberland. That meant, by English law, that George was a younger son who stood to inherit nothing and had to watch his eldest brother inherit everything. Percy was in fact the youngest son: he had seven older brothers. When Percy was five years old his father died, and his eldest brother, Henry Algernon Percy, at age twenty-one, became the ninth Earl of Northumberland. George grew up as his worshipful youngest brother and kept in close touch with him until Henry's death in 1632. George died the next year. During the time George Percy spent in Virginia his brother was spending time in the Tower of London, accused of conspiring in the Gunpowder Plot of 1605. Sir Henry Percy was not released until 1622, after he paid a fine of thirty thousand pounds.[21]

George Percy was not rich, and he was not handsome. A portrait painted in 1615, when he was thirty-five, shows a face with a grotesquely long nose that almost overshadows a minuscule mustache and thin, pursed lips. A fishlike gaze and a receding chin suggest an air of self-doubt, of uncertainty. While he was in Virginia he wrote regularly to his brother Henry, who sent him various supplies by Christopher Newport's return voyages in 1608: butter, cheese, books, paper, ink, sealing wax, soap, and starch for his ruff collars. One of the 1609 ships brought him a sword "hatched with gold." Percy sent home two small Virginia stones and one large one he wanted set into rings. He also ordered fabric for five taffeta-faced suits and a doublet, two hats with silk and gold bands, and a dozen Holland linen shirts with cambric bands (collars) and cuffs.[22] He believed in living grandly, even in a thatch-roofed hut in Virginia.

It was George Percy who presided at Jamestown during the winter of 1609–10, the infamous period that came to be known as the "Starving Time." That expression was not a metaphor. From October 1609 to May 1610, most of Jamestown's residents literally starved to death. Of about three hundred living there, all but sixty people died. What went wrong?

Scholars disagree to this very day. So do the existing eyewitness accounts. The men who wrote the 1612 "Proceedings" agreed with Smith's 1624 *Generall Historie* that there was food to last the winter, but

George Percy's "Trewe Relacyon" observed that the food supply was soon consumed, and people began to starve. The "Proceedings" and *Generall Historie* both provide a detailed list of supplies that should have kept Jamestown alive and well all winter until the next supply ship came: There were six mares and a horse (Gabriel Archer reported that he had brought "six mares and two horses" aboard the *Blessing*) and five or six hundred hogs (these, including a good number of piglets from the summer litters, would probably have been on Hog Island, three miles across the river from Jamestown). Besides the hogs there were "as many hens and chickens," plus an unspecified number of goats and sheep when Smith left. There were nets for fishing and tools of all kinds and a good supply of clothing. Besides all this, there were "3 ships [these were the pinnaces *Discovery* and *Virginia*, plus the larger *Swallow*], 7 boates, commodities ready to trade, the harvest newly gathered, 10 weekes provision in the store, 490 and odde persons, 24 peeces of ordnances, 300 muskets, snaphances and fire lockes [types of firearms], shot, powder, and match sufficient, cuirasses, pikes, swords, and moryons [helmets] more than men." To use these weapons if necessary there were a hundred trained soldiers who had been in Virginia long enough to know the Indians' habits and language.[23] What more could any settlement want? Were the authors of the "Proceedings" telling the truth? Smith's *Generall Historie* has the same account, but Smith was in no condition to take an inventory when he left in 1609. The "harvest newly gathered" meant corn from the thirty or forty acres Smith's colonists had proudly planted in the spring of 1609. At around twenty bushels per acre at most (this year, like others in the early 1600s in Virginia, was a drought year), that would mean a harvest of about five hundred to eight hundred bushels of corn, enough to feed a few hundred people for a few months. Was this harvest the "10 weeks' provision" in the storehouse? The "provision" was surely not from the *Sea Venture* ships. They had been at sea four weeks longer than they anticipated, and what provisions they brought in August, if any, would have been consumed by October.

Not only colonists but ships' crews had to eat, and the ships had stayed three weeks longer than their masters and crews had planned. They, too, were running low on provisions. In time the sailors' grumblings about meager rations at Jamestown reached the ears of Don Pedro de Zuñiga in London. In December 1609, after the ships had returned to England, the Spanish ambassador wrote to King Philip III, "They tell me that the sailors do not come very happy because [people] are suffering great hunger there."[24]

And what about the "490 persons" at Jamestown? The authors of the "Proceedings" had no reason to falsify or exaggerate the population of Jamestown, but their numbers do not add up. The men who were at Jamestown when Smith left, and Smith himself, did not have the time or the resources to take an accurate census of the colony. Not only would they have had to count everyone inside the fort, but they also would have had to travel miles upriver to count the men Smith had placed at the Falls and downriver to take an accounting of those at Nansemond and Point Comfort. Not to mention subtracting those who were constantly dying.

The number 490 was not the number of colonists Smith left in Virginia in October; it was the total number he remembered having to feed when the 300 newcomers from the *Sea Venture* expedition arrived in August. Since then, Indians had killed nearly half of Francis West's 100 men at the Falls and some of John Martin's men at Nansemond. At Jamestown at least 50 people had died of disease since August. The 30 "unruly youths" the Virginia Company had sent to Jamestown had been sent back to England, as "they were not wanted in Virginia." Some said that these boys "were suffered by stealth to get aboard the ships returning."[25] However they got aboard, they would be troublesome later in London, and they would spread tales of woe about Jamestown. At least 40 or 50 sailors also left when the ships left, but 17 more men came the day before they sailed: Capt. James Davis and the long-absent pinnace *Virginia* from the *Sea Venture* expedition docked at Jamestown.[26]

Considering these revised numbers, how many people were left in Virginia when Smith departed? There would have been around 300 mouths to feed, not 490 and not 500. So there should have been enough food to last through the winter: five hundred chickens (plus their eggs) and five hundred hogs, some goats (some of which no doubt gave milk) and sheep, not to mention the fish in the rivers, plus the provisions in the storehouse, should have fed 300 men, women, and children for six months or so, until a new supply ship came the next spring. But long before winter came, the "Starving Time" arrived.

George Percy (perhaps to make Smith's presidency look worse) picked up the inflated population figure and wrote years later, "Of fyve hundrethe men we had onely Lefte about sixty, The reste beinge either starved through famine or Cutt off by the salvages."[27] Percy should have known. He was there. He was the president, so why would he lie? Did it not occur to him that this catastrophe made his leadership look worse than incompetent? Or perhaps there is another explanation: in setting down on paper the grisly details of what happened at Jamestown on his own watch from October 1609 to May 1610, maybe George Percy was merely stupid. Percy did not write his account of his Virginia adventures until 1625, sixteen years later, as a rebuttal to Smith's 1624 *Generall Historie.* Percy had returned from Jamestown in 1612. He had suffered bouts of illness since then, as in 1615, when he wrote that "my fitts [perhaps epilepsy] here in England are more often, more longe, and more greevous." Percy's narrative did not see print in his lifetime. He dedicated it to his beloved brother Henry, the Earl of Northumberland, who may never have read it. It lay among family papers for nearly three centuries.[28]

In October 1609, during his first two weeks as president, Percy dispatched John Ratcliffe thirty-nine miles downriver to Point Comfort, at the edge of Chesapeake Bay, "for to Builde a foarte there." He chose that site because of "the plenty of the place for fisheinge" and for its location to sight any ships coming into the bay. The Virginia colonists lived in constant fear (with good reason) of a Spanish invasion. Percy named the new fort "Algernon's Fort" (Algernon was the middle name of both his father and his beloved eldest brother). Building Fort Algernon was a sensible decision—one of few in Percy's presidency. In fairness to him, however, it should be noted that he was not well. Around this time he was, according to Smith, "so sicke hee could neither goe nor stand."[29]

Percy's account of his presidency is a chronicle of disasters. Besides hunger and sickness and deaths in the fort, relations with the Indians outside it worsened. John Martin, whom Smith had sent with a contingent of men to live at Nansemond, across the James River from Point Comfort, left his men and fled to the relative safety of Jamestown because he feared "to be Surprysed by the Indians." He left "Lieutenant Sicklemore" in command. (This was probably Michael Sicklemore, who was not related to John Ratcliffe, alias Sicklemore.) But Sicklemore's men, living on an island in the Nansemond River, were frightened and hungry. Seventeen of them staged a "dangerous mutinie." They took a boat across the James River to the Indian town of Kecoughtan, about two miles north of Point

Comfort. At Kecoughtan, so Percy says, they hoped to trade "for victuals." They were never heard from again. Percy speculates that Sicklemore's mutineers were "in all lykelyhood cut off and slayne by the Salvages."[30]

A few days after these men left Nansemond, Lieutenant Sicklemore and "dyvers others were fownd also slayne with their mowthes stopped full of Breade." Virginia's Indians were not without a grisly sense of humor, not to mention a fine grasp of irony. Even Percy got their message. The stuffing of the corpses' mouths with bread, he said, was "don as it seemeth in Contempte and skorne, that others mighte expect the Lyke when they should come to seeke for breade and reliefe amongste them."[31] Who found the corpses? Percy does not say.

This happened in late October, perhaps early November. Because of the drought, it had been a poor year for corn, and the Indians were not about to trade what little they had. Winter was coming. Within the past four months, nearly three hundred more English colonists had come. When, the Indians surely wondered, would this all end?

At Jamestown the supplies were dwindling at an alarming rate. The survivors of Sicklemore's company at Nansemond came back to Jamestown as quickly as they could, "to feede," as Percy says, "upon the poore store we had lefte us." A short time later, Francis West and the remnants of his men came down from the Falls. They numbered perhaps fifty. West had "lost eleven men and a boate" on the way. At Jamestown the number of mouths to feed, President Percy says, was "increasinge" and the food supply "decreasinge for in Charety we could nott deny them [Sicklemore's and West's men] to participate with us. Whereupon I appointed Capteyne Tucker to Calculate and cast up our store . . . a poor alowanse of halfe a Cane of meal for a man a day."[32] What had become of all the hogs and hens and chickens, not to mention the sheep and the goats? Here Percy's leadership must surely be faulted. Granted, some or all of the hogs Smith had kept on Hog Island probably made roast pork an Indian delicacy that winter, but surely Percy could have rationed consumption of the poultry and livestock inside the fort. He did not, and starvation was the result.

Percy estimated the remaining half a can (a tin receptacle holding about four to eight ounces) of meal per person per day would last them three months. For a modern comparison, one cup (eight ounces) of oatmeal has three hundred calories. Adults need a minimum of fifteen hundred to two thousand calories per day to maintain a healthy body weight.

No wonder Jamestown's residents were starving. Their ration of meal was very likely from the "10 weeks' provision" mentioned earlier. Percy wrote proudly, "Yet Captain Tucker by his industry and Care caused the same to howlde outt four monthes." Daniel Tucker had some experience in the doling out of food supplies. His uncle had been the cape merchant, or supply officer, in Bartholomew Gosnold's expedition to New England in 1602, and Tucker was to have been the cape merchant for a short-lived colonizing venture there in 1606. He had come to Jamestown with the Second Supply in September 1608.[33] Eight years later he would be governor of Bermuda. But in Virginia, no matter how Daniel Tucker rationed it, half a can of meal a day was not enough to live on.

In desperate need of food, President Percy next turned to his close ally John Ratcliffe for help with the short rations at Jamestown. He sent Ratcliffe and fifty men upriver to see their old enemy, Powhatan, to "procure victuals by way of commerce and trade." But Ratcliffe and his men were careless, and Powhatan was crafty. He pretended friendship and promised help. He even allowed his son and daughter to go aboard the Englishmen's pinnace. In turn, Ratcliffe's men visited in some of the Indians' houses. About what happened next, Percy writes with justifiable anger of "Capteyne Ratliefe's Creduletie for Haveinge Powhatans sonne and dowghter aboard his pinesse freely suffered to departe ageine on shoare, whome if he had deteyned, might have bene a Sufficyentt pledge for his saffety." Instead, Powhatan, "the slye owlde kinge," waited for the right moment and killed all of Ratcliffe's men who had gone ashore except two, Jeffrey Shortridge and Henry Spelman. According to Smith's version of this episode in the *Generall Historie,* Shortridge somehow managed to escape and get back to the pinnace, and Pocahontas was able to save fourteen-year-old Henry Spelman. He "lived many years after, by her means, among the Patawomecks."[34] Spelman became a skilled interpreter and years later wrote his own brief narrative, "Relation of Virginia," but it was not published until 1872.

Capt. John Ratcliffe was not as fortunate as Shortridge and Spelman: he was captured alive and tortured to death. Percy describes the manner of his death in merciless detail: Ratcliffe was "bownd unto a tree naked with a fyer before, and by woemen his fleshe was skraped from his bones with Mussell shelles and, before his face throwne into the fyer; and so for wantt of Circumspection [here is a tinge of satisfaction] miserably perished."[35]

Meanwhile, in the pinnace riding at anchor in the river, Capt. William Phettiplace and sixteen men were horrified spectators of what went on ashore. They cast off as quickly as they could and set sail for Jamestown. Fifty men had set out; sixteen were coming back. There, said Percy, they related "the tragedy of Captain Ratcliffe, not bringing any relief with them either for themselves or us." Poor Jamestown. Poor Percy.

The president would try one more time to get food from the Indians. If Powhatan would not give them any, perhaps some other Indians would. But first Percy had to replace Ratcliffe as the commander of Algernon Fort, where thirty or forty colonists were now stationed. Fortunately, there was a seasoned officer available: Capt. James Davis, who had just arrived on the *Virginia* in October, was sent to the fort downriver sometime in late October or early November. Since Francis West was now returned from the Falls, Percy dispatched him and "about thirty-six" men to take the *Swallow* on a long voyage downriver to Chesapeake Bay and then up the coast northward to the Potomac River, where the sometimes-friendly Patawomecks lived. Though Percy and the others had no way of knowing, young Henry Spelman had been sent to live with the Patawomecks. But they, like the Indians at Nansemond and the Indians at Werowocomoco, had no food to spare. And if they did, they saw no point in giving it to foreigners whose numbers were growing. This fact, so obvious in hindsight, apparently never entered the minds of the first Englishmen in Virginia.

Twenty-four-year-old Francis West, like Percy, was a younger son of a titled family. His late father was Thomas West, Baron De La Warr, and his elder brother, also named Thomas West, now Lord De La Warr, was the newly appointed governor of Virginia. West reached the Patawomecks and somehow persuaded them to trade corn for trinkets, probably pieces of copper and glass beads. He loaded his ship "suffyciently yet used some harshe and Crewell dealinge by Cuttingeinge off two of the Salvages heads and other extremetyes."[36] What was he thinking?

Somehow West and his men aboard the *Swallow* escaped from the land of the Patawomecks without harm and with their load of corn intact. But when they sailed past Algernon Fort on their return voyage, something happened to change their course. Percy says that "Captain Davis did call to them acquainting them with our great wants, exhorting them to make all the speed they could to relieve us." Instead, West and his company "hoisted up sails and shaped their course directly for England." Whether this was West's decision, or whether his men forced him to do it, is not known. But as Percy writes sadly, they "left us in that extreme misery and wantte."[37]

The next part of Percy's narrative is too grim to be paraphrased. It deserves quoting in full:

> Now all of us at James Towne beginneinge to feele the sharp pricke of hunger, which noe man [can] trewly descrybe but he which hath Tasted the bitternesse thereof. A world of miseries insued . . . in so much that some to satisfye their hunger have Robbed the store [storehouse], for the which I Caused them to be executed. Then haveinge fedd upon horses and other beastes as longe as they Lasted [that would have been the horse and four mares, and the goats and sheep], we weare gladd to make shifte with vermin, as doggs, Catts Ratts, and myce all was fishe thatt Came to Nett to satisfye Crewell hunger, as to eat Bootes shoes or any other leather some could come by. And those being Spente and devoured, some were inforced to search the woodes and to feed upon Serpentts and snakes and to digge the earthe for wylde and unknowne Rootes, where many of our men weare Cutt off and slayne by the Salvages. And now famin beginneinge to Looke [so] ghastly and pale in every face, that notheinge was Spared to mainteyne Lyfe and to doe those things which seame incredible, as to digge up deade corpes outt of graves and to eate them. And some have Licked upp the Bloode which hathe fallen from their weake fellowes. And amongst the reste this was moste lamentable. Thatt one of our Colline murdered his wife, ripped the Childe out of her woambe and threwe itt into the River, and after Chopped the Mother in pieces and sallted her for his foode. The same not beinge discovered before he had eaten parte thereof. For the which Crewell and unhumane factt I adjudged him to be executed, the acknowledgment of the deed being inforced from him by torture, haveingee hung by the Thumbes with weightes at his feete a quarter of an howere before he would Confesse the same.[38]

It was John Smith who gave these horrors the name they have carried for four hundred years. "This was that time, which still to this day we called the Starving Time: it were too vile to say and scarce to be believed, what we endured."[39] Smith, of course, was not there. But when he wrote his *Generall Historie* years later, he took what he needed from the 1612

"Proceedings," written by some who had seen for themselves what happened in Virginia that terrible winter.

Percy was not exaggerating. Both the "Proceedings" and the *Generall Historie* describe in brief what he recounts in grisly detail. And the recent excavations at Jamestown give grim testimony to some of Percy's details. Did the starving colonists eat snakes, rats, and dogs? In the cellar pit of the barracks inside the fort archaeologists have unearthed the bones of poisonous snakes and musk turtles, butchered horse bones, the bones of the black rat, and dog and cat bones.[40] The dog bones are probably those of a mastiff, which the English used for hunting. In their desperate need, they killed and ate the dogs that might have hunted for game. But that assumes the hunters were not afraid to venture outside the fort. When the dogs and cats were gone, what was left to eat?

So far no one has uncovered any butchered human bones. But the excavations at Jamestown continue. Percy, Smith, and the other writers mention cannibalism without calling it by name. Percy supplies the details of the unfortunate man who murdered his pregnant wife and ate part of her remains, and Smith's *Generall Historie* elaborates on the consuming of at least one corpse: "So great was our famine, that a savage we slew, and buried, the poorer sort took him up again and ate him, and so did diverse one another boiled and stewed with roots and herbs." The last part of this sentence is not clear, but its implications are chilling: sometimes, when people died, their starving companions cooked and ate them. Horrific as it sounds, it is not impossible in a place where, as Percy says, people were so desperately hungry as to lick up the blood that had "fallen from their weake fellowes." Years later, another account of the Starving Time, also written by those who had lived through it, told of eating "vermin or carrion [what]soever we could light on, as also toadstools, jew's ears [*Auricularia auricula-judaea*, a small, ear-size tree fungus], or whatever else we found growing upon the ground that would fill either mouth or belly." They were also "driven through unsufferable hunger unnaturally to eat those things which nature most abhorred: the flesh and excrements of man." They ate these things "as of our own nation as [well as] of an Indian digged by some out of his grave after he had lain buried three days, and wholly devoured him. Others, envying the better state of body of any whom hunger had not yet so much wasted as their own, lay [in] wait and threatened to kill and eat them." Daniel Tucker, perhaps when the allotments of a half can of meal a day per person ran out, built a boat with his own hands, an occupation that, says Percy, "did keep us from killing one of an other To eate."[41]

Tales of the horrors at Jamestown eventually reached Don Alonso de Velasco, the new Spanish ambassador in London, who succeeded Don Pedro de Zuñiga in the summer of 1610. Zuñiga lingered in London and, as the archbishop of Canterbury wrote, conducted "secret business" and sent "scandalous reports of English affairs to Spain and Italy."[42] Ambassador Velasco wrote to King Philip about the Starving Time, saying that "the Indians hold the English surrounded in the strong place which they had erected there, having killed the larger part of them, and the others were left so entirely without provisions that they thought it impossible to escape, because the survivors eat the dead, and when one of the natives died fighting, they dug him up again, two days afterwards, to be eaten . . . and almost all who came . . . died from having eaten dogs, cat skins, and other vile stuff."[43]

The Starving Time was indeed, as Smith said, "scarce to be believed."[44] Should modern readers believe it? Historians have taken the various seventeenth-century accounts at face value, but these writers had their own reasons, perhaps, for distorting the truth. As one historian has recently observed, "Cannibalism may or may not have taken place during 1609–10; some evidence exists to suggest that it did, whereas other accounts might be cited to argue that it did not."[45] Evidence of cannibalism in the excavations at Jamestown might lay this argument to rest. But it is not unreasonable to believe that people crazed and sometimes mentally unbalanced by severe malnutrition and, ultimately, in many cases, starvation could turn to cannibalism.

As starvation took its toll on minds as well as bodies, conditions inside the log palisade at Jamestown can only be imagined. Percy wrote that some people ran away to live among the Indians. Who could blame them? How many people were there inside the fort? It is impossible to know. The number was anywhere from two to three hundred, living in an area of no more than two acres. As winter came and their meager rations dwindled, they dared not go outside the palisaded walls. Ratcliffe's horrible death by torture and the sixteen corpses with their mouths stuffed full of bread were grim reminders of what the Indians could do to the English. In the woods outside the fort there were squirrels and birds and other game, and there were fish in the river, but they might as well have been on the moon.

Inside the fort, people were not only desperately hungry but also literally starving. In a cruel paradox, the more they starved, the less they could digest food. Their stomachs cramped. Their digestive acids dried up. They grew paler and thinner by the day. They were listless. They were too tired even to chop firewood, and they were always cold. They began pulling down the frames of once-occupied houses and burning them to keep warm. People's skin dried and cracked and hung in ugly folds. Slight scratches turned into running sores that would not heal. Their ankles were often swollen, though their legs were pitifully thin. Besides, it was winter. Bone-chilling cold, on bones that had little flesh left on them.

How long does it take to starve to death? A modern medical study estimates that "complete starvation in adults leads to death within eight to 12 weeks." Death could come in a variety of guises: Hypothermia. Pneumonia. Anemia. Chronic diarrhea. "In the final stages of starvation, adult humans experience a variety of neurological and psychiatric symptoms, including hallucinations and convulsions, as well as severe muscle pain and disturbances in heart rhythm."[46]

Of more than two hundred people alive in October, only sixty survived until May. In the graveyard outside the fort, recent excavations have uncovered sixty-three graves. Some of the graves are crookedly dug in the otherwise straight rows of burial sites. Seventy-two people were buried here. The multiple burials and the misalignment suggest that at least some of these graves date from the Starving Time, when graves were dug in haste and grave diggers may have been too weak to dig multiple graves. Of the remains discovered so far, two men and one woman were buried in their clothes. This was highly unusual. In the preindustrial age, fabric was hand loomed and hand sewn, and clothing was too valuable to bury. But if the deceased happened to be diseased, their clothes might have been buried with them. The fifty skeletons examined so far are a poignant reminder of how fragile life was at Jamestown. The ages of the deceased range from infancy to late forties. Half were in their twenties. Seven were infants under the age of two.[47]

In one of the most puzzling mysteries of the Starving Time, while starvation stalked the Jamestown colonists, the thirty-odd residents of Algernon Fort, only thirty-nine miles downriver on Chesapeake Bay, had plenty to eat. In fact, they caught so many crabs that they fed the surplus to their hogs. Why didn't President George Percy contact Capt. James Davis and his people there at Algernon Fort? Why didn't Davis send someone upriver to find out what was happening to his countrymen at Jamestown? Perhaps the people at Algernon Fort did not want to know. Francis West had told them how desperate things were upriver and how hostile the Indians had become. Captain Davis, secure in his fort with plenty to eat, obviously made a decision to keep clear of Jamestown.

Why Percy and the others upriver did not try to reach Algernon Fort is more puzzling. And if some of them, according to Percy, ran away to live with the Indians, then why did not others take one of the boats and join their own people at Algernon Fort? For that matter, what became of the "7 boates" supposedly in the colony's supply when Smith left in October 1609? There were only two boats, one of them built by Daniel Tucker, in the winter of the Starving Time. Percy himself seems to have been ailing much of the time, but when it became clear that Jamestown was running out of food (and before starvation's ugly symptoms set in), why didn't someone go downriver to Algernon Fort in search of food? Part of the answer lies with the James River. It is an estuarial river (one whose currents reverse with the incoming and outgoing tides). When the tide rose in Chesapeake Bay, a boat sailing downriver had to stop and wait several hours to catch the outgoing tide again. Because of this, from Jamestown to Algernon Fort, nearly forty miles, was a sail of at least two, perhaps three, days. A boat on the river would be a sitting duck for Indians.

Another reason no one ventured downriver may be the lack of able-bodied men. Since Smith's departure in October, the Indians had killed at least a hundred at the Falls and Nansemond. Thirty or forty had been sent to Algernon Fort. Thirty-six had sailed to England with Francis West aboard the *Swallow*. An unknown number of others had died of disease or run away to live with the Indians. Inside the palisaded walls of Jamestown's fort, who was left? No one but a few able-bodied men, plus the weak, the sick, the ones too old or too young for military action—and the women. The women were another reason for not going downriver.

Of the unknown number of women who arrived at Jamestown to join young Anne Laydon (and maybe Mistress Forrest) in August 1609, how many were still alive? A handful of names are all that history has recorded. Anne Laydon and her infant daughter, Virginia (who was born sometime during that awful winter); Joan Pierce and her four-year-old daughter,

Jane; Temperance Yeardley; Thomasine Causey—all young women in their twenties. Anne Laydon's husband, John, and Thomasine Causey's husband, Nathaniel, were with them, but Temperance and Joan were *Sea Venture* widows. Besides these, there may have been fifteen or twenty other women and children.

Women and children, not to mention the sick, could not be left to fend for themselves while the men went downriver. What if the Indians killed the men on the way? What if the Indians attacked the fort while they were gone? A woman might load and fire a pistol, but a six-foot-long musket that had to have powder and wadding and a ball rammed down its barrel, another dose of powder in its firing pan, and a spark to ignite it to fire was not an easy weapon for a woman to lift and load.

And as for taking everyone at Jamestown to Algernon Fort, that was impossible. The two small boats remaining at Jamestown were not enough for sixty people. Francis West had taken the *Swallow* to England; Davis had the *Discovery* and the *Virginia* at his fort downriver.

And so the Jamestown people stayed inside the fort, waiting for death to claim them. One of the people who died at Jamestown that winter was John Smith's old enemy Gabriel Archer. Thomas Coe and William Dyer, his would-be assassins, may have died there as well.

Meanwhile, the ships that left Virginia in October had arrived in England by late November with the wounded John Smith and the news that the *Sea Venture* was lost. As these ships' crews talked to other sailors in pubs and inns, and as passengers told their stories to fascinated friends and families, rumors flew thick and fast. The rebellious "unruly youths" the Virginia Company had sent to Jamestown had come home full of horror stories—some all too true. One indignant critic wrote that these young toughs, "being of a most lewd and bad condition . . . are come for England again, giving out . . . most vile and scandalous reports, both of the country itself, and of the carriage of the business there."[48] The Virginia Company's great nine-ship expedition was a disaster beyond calculation.

Before 1609 ended the Virginia Company's desperate officials tried to put a good face on their misfortune. They put together a tract that would gladden the heart of any public relations expert. Titled *A True and Sincere Declaration of the purposes and ends of the plantation begun in Virginia,* a pamphlet available to London book buyers at a stall in St. Paul's churchyard, opened with a brief and glowing history of the Jamestown settlement from 1606 to the present. The *True and Sincere Declaration* was especially designed to answer the "imputations and aspersions with which ignorant rumor, virulent envy, or impious subtlety daily calumniate our industries and the success of it . . . to cool and assuage the curiosity of the jealous and suspicious, and to temper and convince the malignity of the false and treacherous."[49]

The truth, as set forth in this publication, was that when Samuel Argall had sailed to Virginia in the summer of 1609, he found "a want of victual" that was the fault of "misgovernment by the commanders, by dissension and ambition among themselves, and upon the idleness and bestial sloth of the common sort." But thanks to Argall, the colonists had undergone an amazing transformation: "By fishing only in few days, they were all recovered, grown hearty, able, and ready to undertake every action." Another account by a Dutch scholar in 1610 had a somewhat different view of conditions at Jamestown: The colonists there "had neglected their sowing-time, so their provisions had given out." The Indians, "seeing that the English were beginning to multiply, were determined to starve them and drive them out." According to the Dutch author, before Argall arrived in Virginia, the intrepid Englishman had caught "so many fish, mostly sturgeon, that he could have loaded his ship with them, if he had known how to salt or pickle them, for he had the misfortune that a man who knew how died on the way. He brought some caviar anyway, which is salted sturgeon's eggs."[50] Perhaps it was the caviar that helped the Jamestown colonists to recover so quickly.

The Virginia Company's *True Declaration* was doggedly cheerful, reporting that a few weeks after Argall arrived, the ships from the *Sea Venture* expedition came in (damaged and disease ridden). But according to the Virginia Company, "they landed in health near four hundred persons." Three hundred is more like it.[51] As for the lost flagship *Sea Venture* under the command of Adm. Sir George Somers, the company's pamphlet was optimistic: "We doubt not the mercy of God he is safe, with the pinnace which attended him, and shall both, or are by this time" (December 1609, six months since the June hurricane), "arrived at our colony." The pinnace was cut free in the storm and never seen again. As for the hurricane itself, "Who can avoid the hand of God, or dispute with Him? Is he fit to undertake any great action whose courage is shaken and

dissolved with one storm?" To make things right, the company was planning to send Lord De La Warr, the governor of its colony, and a "supply
of victual for one year." De La Warr was to leave London "by the last of
January."[52] De La Warr did not sail until April 1, 1610.

As the winter days at Jamestown warmed into spring, George Percy's
health improved, and he made a momentous decision: "By this Tyme
being Reasonable well recovered of my Sicknes, I did undertake a Jorney
unto Algernown's foarte." He did not go until early in May. He gave two
reasons for going (as if he needed any): one was to "understand how
things weare there ordered," and the other reason was to plan a revenge
on the Indians at nearby Kecoughtan who had killed John Martin's men
months before. President Percy says nothing about what should have
been his main concern: finding sustenance for the starving colonists at
Jamestown. That is a curious omission. He knew perfectly well that there
was food at Algernon Fort on Chesapeake Bay. One of the reasons he had
it built there was "the plenty of the place for fishing."[53]

Something is peculiar here. Percy pretends surprise about the plentiful
food downriver. And he blames them, not himself, for the terrible neglect:
"Our people [at Algernon Fort] I found in good case and well lykeinge,
haveinge concealed their plenty from us above att James Towne, Beinge
so well stored that the Crabb fishes wherewith they had fed their hoggs
would have bene a great relefe unto us and saved many of our Lyves. Butt
their intente was for to have keptt some of the better sorte alyve and with
their two pinnaces to have Retourned for England, not regarding our
miseries and wantts att all."[54]

After excoriating Captain Davis for keeping Algernon Fort's abundant
food a secret, President Percy proposed an illogical rescue plan: he would
"bringe halfe of our men from James Towne to be there releved." Half
would have been about thirty, or all that one of Davis's pinnaces would
hold. Then, as if Percy feared to impose too many hungry visitors at one
time on Captain Davis, Percy said he would "retourne them backe agaeine
[to Jamestown] and bring the reste to bee Sustayned there [at Algernon
Fort] also."[55]

How long did Percy think it took for starving people to be "relieved"?
One or two hearty meals? Neither George Percy nor anyone else knew
what modern medicine knows about the cure for starvation: "If the
degree of malnutrition is severe, the intestines may not tolerate a fully

balanced diet. They may, in fact, not be able to absorb adequate nutrition at all. . . . The treatment back to health is long and first begins with liquids. Gradually, solid foods are introduced and a daily diet providing 5,000 calories or more is instituted."[56] No colonist would see five thousand calories in a day at Jamestown for at least a decade.

But George Percy meant well. He had a Plan B: "And if all this [half at a time] would not serve to save our men's Lyves I purposed to bring them all unto Algernown's foarte." That would have meant sailing both of Davis's pinnaces upriver to transport the remaining men, women, and children, sixty or more severely malnourished people. There was not enough housing for sixty people at Algernon Fort. Did Captain Davis see a problem with this? Percy implies as much. He told Davis "that another towne or foarte mighte be erected and Builded, butt mens lyves once Loste could never be recovered." Evidently, Percy won out. He wrote that he planned to start for Jamestown "by the very next tide."[57] But that tide came and went, and Percy did not sail with it.

Before nightfall the lookouts at Algernon Fort who kept a watch on Chesapeake Bay sounded the alarm. Two vessels, their sails just barely visible on the horizon, were approaching Point Comfort. Captain Davis ordered an armed guard to stand watch all night. No one slept much. It looked as if the Spanish had come at last to attack the English in Virginia.

5

DELIVERANCE

IN THE EARLY SPRING of 1610 winter's biting winds were gone from Bermuda, but the castaways' worries hovered over them like sullen clouds. Would their two small ships ever leave Bermuda? No one could say what might happen if Somers rejected Gate's offer to make peace. Days turned to weeks as the two opposing groups sparred: Gates's loyal majority in the quarter on St. George's Island, and Somers's militant minority on the mainland. The end of March brought two events to lift spirits in the quarter at St. George's: the christening of a baby boy and the christening of the pinnace Gates had built. On Sunday, March 25, at the Reverend Richard Buck's service, the week-old son of Edward Eason and his wife was christened. The proud parents named him "Bermudas." William Strachey, Christopher Newport, and James Swift were godfathers.[1] If the Rolfes' infant daughter, christened Bermuda a few months before, had lived, little Bermudas Eason might have been a playmate for her. But he, too, probably died an untimely death. There is no record of Bermudas Eason after his christening.

On Friday, March 30, Lieutenant-General Gates ordered his lovingly built pinnace towed out from its birthplace in Frobisher's Building Bay. Gates's and Frobisher's helpers launched their pinnace unrigged, so as not to let its sails catch any damaging winds. As Strachey was careful to note, they sailed it "a little round the Iland, lying West-North West, and close aboord to the backe side of our Iland, both neerer the Ponds and Wels of some fresh water, as also from thence to make our way to the Sea the better, the Channell being there sufficient and deepe enough to lead her forth."[2] This was probably the channel leading into modern Castle Harbor, one of two places in Bermuda's waters where ships may safely navigate between the deadly reefs. As the pinnace was launched and "began to swimme," it had its christening. They dubbed it, for obvious reasons, *Deliverance*.

Once it was safely moored in the new location, Gates and his loyal followers left their old quarter at the southeastern tip of St. George's Island and moved to the western coast to be near their ship. They expected to be leaving Bermuda soon, with or without the Somers faction.

Meanwhile, Admiral Somers and his unrepentant rebels kept to themselves on the mainland, finishing their own vessel. At thirty tons, it was twenty-nine feet long and drew six feet of water, compared to the eighty-ton *Deliverance,* which was forty feet long and had a draft of eight feet. Somers and his company called their pinnace the *Patience.* Perhaps the hot-tempered admiral intended the name as a caution to himself.

Before deserting the quarter on St. George's Island where the castaways had lived for nearly ten months, Lieutenant-General Gates caused a marker to be put up in what had, in happier days, been called "Somers's Garden." On the trunk of a great cedar tree in the center of the garden, a cross fashioned from the wrecked *Sea Venture*'s timbers was attached with hand-hewn wooden trunnels. Gates ordered the tree's top branches lopped off to lessen the danger of its being uprooted by high winds. In the center of the cross Gates fastened a small silver coin worth twelve pence, which had the image of King James I on it. On a sheet of copper was an engraved inscription in Latin and English:

> In memory of our great Deliverance . . . wee have set up this to the honour of God. It is the spoyle of an English ship (of three hundred tunne) called the Sea Venture, bound with seven ships more (from which the storme divided us) to Virginia or Nova Brittania, in America. In it were two Knights, Sir Thomas Gates, Knight, Governour of the English forces and Colonie there: and Sir George Summers Knight, Admirall of the Seas. Her Captaine was Christopher Newport. Passengers and Mariners she had beside (which came all safe to Land) one hundred and fiftie. We were forced to runne her ashore (by reason of her leake) under a Point that bore South-east from the Northerne Point of the Iland, which wee discovered first the eight and twentieth of July 1609.[3]

It was now April 1610.

Unknown to the castaways in Bermuda, on April 1 three ships had set sail from the Isle of Wight off the English coast. Governor-Gen. Sir

Thomas West, Lord De La Warr, was at last bound for Virginia. On the way one of his ships, stopping at the Azores, met his younger brother, Francis West, aboard the *Swallow* on his way to England, fleeing Virginia. The news young West gave De La Warr's men about the hunger at Jamestown was not something they wanted to hear. And what did they say to the twenty-three-year-old Francis West, who had absconded with a ship belonging to the Virginia Company with a cargo of corn that could have fed its colonists? As one scholar has observed of this young aristocrat, "Had he not had Queen Anne Boleyn's sister for a great-grandmother and the Lord Lieutenant-General of Virginia for a brother, he would undoubtedly have been clamped in irons."[4] Instead, Francis West would soon be back in Virginia.

As the mild April days passed, Adm. Sir George Somers mulled over Gates's letter begging him to reunite with the rest of the company. At last he persuaded his rebellious sailors to give up their hideouts in the woods and accept Lieutenant-General Gates's pardon. All but two of them—Christopher Carter and Robert Waters—came back. Hearing of the two reluctant rebels, Somers ordered his other men to search for the two, to seize them "by any device or force." But Carter and Waters managed to hide from their would-be captors. Even with the threat of punishment if they surrendered themselves, why would these two choose to stay behind on one of the most remote islands in the world? It is possible that Sir George Somers himself told these two men to hide. They were devotedly loyal to him (he had saved Waters from hanging for the killing of a fellow sailor, Edward Samuel), and according to Nathaniel Butler's 1622 *Historye of the Bermudaes,* Somers gave these men a "direction of secretly stayeinge behind, makeing them a faithfull promise that he would speedily returne to their releife."[5] Sir George Somers, not looking forward to sharing power with Sir Thomas Gates in Virginia, may have had ideas of founding his own colony in Bermuda.[6]

By the end of April the last seams in Somers's pinnace had been caulked, its rigging and sails readied, and the newly christened *Patience* was launched. Somers sailed it from the sheltered bay on the north shore of the mainland, around St. George's, and into what is now Castle Harbor. Now the *Deliverance* and the *Patience* rode at anchor side by side, miraculously, peaceably, together. All that remained was to load them with provisions, board their passengers, and set sail for Virginia.

They had arrived with 150 people, but they were leaving with 135. Eight men had been lost at sea aboard the longboat with Henry Ravens. Edward Samuel and Namontack had been murdered, and 3 other men had died of unnamed causes during their ten-month stay. The two renegades, Robert Waters and Christopher Carter, skulked somewhere on the mainland. Strachey wrote that "we were faine to leave them behind."[7]

As for the castaways' departure, there must be enough food and water for 135 people—but for how long a voyage? No one could predict. Virginia was seven hundred miles away, and the *Deliverance* and the *Patience* were tiny two-masted vessels with little sail power. Ten days? Two weeks? For provisions Bermuda had food in abundance. Silvanus Jourdain wrote that they loaded a "store of Hoggess flesh" preserved with salt that Gates's men had boiled down from seawater during their stay. Their provisions included "a good portion of Tortoise oyle, which either for frying or baking did us very great pleasure, it being very sweete nourishing and wholesome."[8] They also loaded barrels of the dried, salted rockfish that Gates had laid by. A good supply of Bermuda cahows, also dried and salted, they took as well, along with what was left of the precious meal they had brought from England and salvaged from the *Sea Venture*. Besides, they believed that they needed only enough edibles to last them on the voyage. There would be food waiting for them in Virginia—or so they thought.

At long last, on the morning of May 10, all was in readiness. The castaways and their trunks and bundles and provisions were stowed aboard the two pinnaces, crowded into much smaller spaces than they had enjoyed on the three-hundred-ton *Sea Venture*. The eighty-ton *Deliverance* had a 'tween-deck space of four and a half feet, not enough room for an adult to stand upright, with a steerage five feet long and six feet high and a tiny gallery with two windows. The thirty-ton *Patience* had even less room.

To reach the open sea, first they had to navigate the channel between the reefs. Somers and Newport took their longboats and marked the narrow passage with two canoes as buoys to guide the pinnaces between the shoals on one side and the rocks on the other. Even so, disaster nearly struck. Despite the care of these experienced mariners, the *Deliverance*, being towed by one of the longboats, struck a rock near the buoy on the starboard side. As Strachey remembered, it was a "soft Rocke," and it miraculously gave way before the vessel's bow. From the longboat, coxswain Robert Walsingham was able to guide the *Deliverance* to deeper, safer water as all aboard held their breaths. Casting down the lead line for depth, at last they had a sounding of three fathoms, then three and a half fathoms. Finally, as Strachey wrote, "to the no little joy of us all we got cleere of the Ilands." All aboard shared Strachey's relief: if that rock had opened a gash in the *Deliverance*'s hull, "God knowes we might have been like enough, to have returned anew, and dwelt there, after tenne moneths of carefulness and great labour a longer time, but God was more mercifull to us."[9]

Now they were bound for Virginia. Ten months ago, so long ago it seemed a lifetime, they had sailed on the *Sea Venture* in convoy with their pinnace and seven other ships. Dare they hope that these had reached Virginia after the storm? But the ships had been scattered like flotsam and jetsam across the Atlantic, and everyone knew the odds of reaching a safe harbor. The castaways could hardly wait to hear. They had been nearly a year with no news from the outside world. The first two days of their voyage, the warm May wind blew fair. For seven more days they had "the wind sometimes fair, and sometimes scarce and contrary."[10] The *Deliverance* kept the *Patience* in view, but to do that it had to reduce its speed. On Captain Newport's orders the crew took in their main topsail and sometimes the forecourse sail as well. Even so, they lost Somers and the *Patience* twice. Some of them may have hoped they would not find him again.

Strachey kept a careful record of their approach to land: "The seventeenth of May we saw change of water and had much Rubbish swimme by our ship side, whereby wee knew wee were not far from Land." They began to take soundings with the "Dipsing Lead" (a line with a hollow plummet filled with tallow, to pick up sand or gravel from the seafloor) to check the ocean's depth at regular intervals. "The eighteenth about midnight wee sounded . . . and found thirtie seven fathoms (222 feet). The nineteenth in the morning we sounded, and had nineteene and an half fathom, stonie, and sandie ground. The twentieth about midnight, we had a marvelous sweet smell from the shoare . . . strong and pleasant, which did not a little glad us. In the morning, by day breake (as soon as one might well see from the fore top) one of the sailors descryed Land."[11] The rejoicing aboard both ships can scarcely be imagined. It was May 21, 1610.

Strachey himself clambered aloft and spied "two Hummockes to the Southward, from which (Northward all along) lay the Land, which wee were to coast to Cape Henrie." About seven in the morning a strong ebb tide and a light wind near Cape Henry at the entrance to Chesapeake Bay forced them to drop anchor until the next flood tide. But about noon a sudden strong gale allowed them to set sail again, and soon they were in Chesapeake Bay. "It is a goodly Bay," wrote Strachey, "and a fairer, not easily to be found."[12]

But when the pinnaces were within two miles of the mouth of the James River, they saw a puff of smoke and heard the report of a cannon. It came from the northern side of the river. Their Virginia Company instructions from last year mentioned nothing about a fort in that location. Their hearts sank. After all this time had the Spanish put an outpost in Virginia? They had no way of knowing. Gates cautiously sent a handful of men in the *Deliverance*'s little longboat to investigate, but told them that under no circumstances were they to set foot on shore.

On that shore, at Fort Algernon, Capt. James Davis, President Percy, and others had been keeping watch all night. When the two pinnaces were within range, Davis had fired the fort's cannon as a warning shot. In a little while those at Fort Algernon spied the longboat approaching and, as Percy remembered, "We haled them." Shouting back and forth across the water, he and his companions on shore "understood that Sir Thomas Gates and Sir George Somers weare come in these pinnesses which by their greate industry they had builded in the Bermudes with the remaynder of their wracktt shipp and other woode they found in the Country. Upon which newes we receved no small joye."[13] The lost were found. The dead were restored to life.

Jubilant shouts ashore, and then more news from shore to gladden the hearts of those in the longboat: all seven of the ships that sailed with the *Sea Venture* had reached Jamestown. The only one now lost was the little pinnace the *Sea Venture* had had to cut loose during the storm. Another piece of news confirmed what the Bermuda castaways had long feared: nothing had been seen in Virginia of Henry Ravens and the longboat that had left Bermuda last August. Gates's men in the longboat followed their orders and did not go ashore, but they rowed back to the *Deliverance* as quickly as their oars could pull through the water. They must soon have shouted out the good news: this fort was called Algernon Fort, and it was English, and all but one of the *Sea Venture* ships had reached Virginia.

Then it was the castaways' turn to rejoice. The *Deliverance* made fast its longboat, and with the *Patience* it prepared to draw closer to shore. As the two little ships sailed toward the fort, Strachey remembered how, "a mightie storme of Thunder, Lightning, and Raine gave us a shrewd and fearefull welcome."[14] It was an ominous sign.

Gates and Somers, anxious to see Jamestown, did not linger at Algernon Fort. By the next incoming tide the *Deliverance* and the *Patience* were on their way up the wide James River.

Percy had tried to warn the newcomers about what to expect at Jamestown, where he said they would

> Reade a lecture of miserie in our peoples faces, and perceve the skarsety of victewalles and understande the mallice of the Salvages, who knoweing our weaknes had diverse Tymes assawlted us withoutt [outside] the foarte. Fyndeinge of five hundrethe men we had onely Lefte about sixty, the rest being either starved throwe famine or Cutt off by the salvages, and those which weare Liveinge weare so maugre and Leane thatt itt was Lamentable to behowlde them, for many throwe extreme hunger have Runne outt of their naked bedds, being so Leane thatt they looked like anotannes [trees on which the old fruit clings until a new crop grows] Cryeinge owts we are starved. We are starved. Others going to bedd as we imagined in healthe weare fownd deade the next morneinge.[15]

Those aboard the *Patience* and the *Deliverance* had plenty of time to think about what Percy had told them. The voyage upriver took them two days. There was no breeze, and the air was as oppressive and heavy as their thoughts. Strachey wrote that "only by the helpe of Tydes (no winde stirring) wee plyed it sadly up the River."[16]

On May 23 they dropped anchor at Jamestown, no doubt throwing their mooring lines around trees at the water's edge, as was the custom. No longboats were needed to carry them to land: they were so close that men and women splashed solemnly, mournfully, ashore and trooped through the fort gate, whose massive log doors were hanging off their hinges. That was not a good sign. Worse yet, there was no one to greet them. An eerie stillness hung over the little fort, as if it were a haunted place. The barracks and storehouse and the church were still standing, but there was no sign of life around them, and no sounds within them. Most of the houses were in ruins. Bits of roof thatch and pieces of timber lay scattered like jackstraws on the ground. Had everyone died?

Lieutenant-General Gates, "much grieved," walked slowly with the Reverend Richard Buck straight to the desolate-looking little church in the fort's center. Spying the church bell, Gates asked that it be rung. Then he stepped inside, and the shocked castaways trooped into the small wooden structure after their leader. The deep, clangorous notes of the bell rang above their heads. After that, as Strachey remembered (he would soon become the colony's secretary), in a few moments "all such as were able to come forth of their houses repayred to Church."[17] Most of the people had taken to living in the barracks. Not many of the sixty men, women, and children at Jamestown were able to come forth. Those who did looked, as Percy had described them, as thin as bare trees.

But on that day, amid the horrors inside and outside the fort, there was inexpressible joy for a few. At least two Jamestown wives were reunited with husbands they had thought never to see again. Temperance and George Yeardley found each other. William Pierce embraced Joan and their four-year-old daughter, Jane. The young husbands' happiness was dimmed only by their loved ones' pitiful, malnourished conditions, by the sunken eyes in gray, gaunt faces, the once rounded bodies wasted to stick-figure shapes. Temperance Yeardley would not bear a child for eight years; Joan Pierce, never again.

In the church, the Reverend Richard Buck offered "a zealous and sorrowfull Prayer, finding all things so contrary to our expectations, so full of misery and misgovernment."[18] At the end of the service, Gates asked Strachey to read his commission as Jamestown's officially appointed lieutenant-general. Then George Percy handed over his own commission as president. Power had changed hands, but what was to be done? None of the newcomers had imagined conditions like this.

Strachey recorded what they found: "Viewing the Forte, we found the Pallisadoes torne downe, the Ports open, the Gates from off the hinges, and emptie houses (which Owners death had taken from them) rent up and burnt, rather than the dwellers would step into the Woods a stones cast off from them, to fetch other fire-wood; and it is true, the Indian killed as fast without, if our men stirred but beyond the bounds of their Block-house, as Famine and Pestilence did within."[19]

Strachey said that he had not have the heart to express the particulars—but Percy did. George Percy, the man who surely must share some blame for the pitiful conditions at Jamestown, did not hesitate to set down the ugly details. He wrote of a man named Hugh Pryse, "beinge pinched with extreme famin, in a furious distracted moode," who ran into the center of the marketplace, "blaspheameinge exclaimeinge and Cryeinge outt thatt there was noe god, alledgeinge thatt if there were a god he would not Suffer his Creatures whome he had made and framed, to indure those miseries and to perish for wante of food and Sustenance." Percy did not know that people in the last stages of starvation may become mentally disturbed and experience hallucinations. Poor Hugh Pryse. When Pryse and another colonist, "a Butcher, a Corpulentt fatt man," went into the woods to look for something to eat, the Indians killed them both. Percy wrote with some satisfaction that God had punished Pryse for his blasphemous talk, because his corpse was dismembered, perhaps by wolves, and his bowels torn out of his body. But the fat butcher, "not lyeing above six yardes from him, was fownd altogether untouched, onely by the salvages arrowes whereby he Received his deathe."[20]Guilt and pity aside, what was to be done? The Bermuda colonists had brought only enough provisions for themselves on the voyage. At Jamestown they had expected that there would be sturgeon and turkey and venison and Indian corn. Many of them had read the Virginia Company's promotional materials. Now the empty storehouse left them dumbfounded. Jamestown had literally nothing left to eat. Worse still, what the Bermuda voyagers had brought with them was nearly gone. The famished Jamestown residents (including at least one nursing mother and her infant, Anne Laydon and little Virginia) needed sustenance, and they needed it now. They were starving. By William Strachey's estimate, if the Bermuda castaways had arrived "but four days" later, the sixty Jamestown survivors "had doubtlesse bin the most part of them starved, for their best reliefe was onely Mushrums, and some hearbes, which stewed together, made but a thin and unsavory broath, and swelled them much."[21] Without the castaways from Bermuda and the food they had brought with them, Jamestown might not have survived.

The newcomers set to work at once, baking bread from the meal they had brought (perhaps using the "sweet and nourishing" tortoise oil they had left to enrich it). They shared salt pork and dried cahow and salted rockfish. For starving stomachs unable to tolerate solid food, they made broth. (Remains recently unearthed in Jamestown include cahow and fish bones, conch shells, and Bermuda limestone, the last probably used as ballast.)[22] But the Bermudians held back a precious reserve supply of meal they kept aboard the pinnaces.

Nothing was to be gotten from the Indians. Even if they had been disposed to do so, they had no food to share. Their meager winter store of corn was gone, and their new crop was just planted. As for fishing, the weakened residents of the fort had let their seines and nets rot. Perhaps that did not matter, since the river "had not now a Fish to be seene in it."[23] Gates sent his longboat and a crew downriver all the way to Point Comfort and into Chesapeake Bay in search of fish. They were gone for seven days and brought nothing back, barely catching enough to feed themselves.

Gates, Somers, Percy, and Newport held a grim consultation. With the castaways and the Jamestown people, they now had nearly two hundred people to feed, and sixty were nearly too weak to eat, much less to hunt or fish. There was still a small store of the meal the castaways had brought from Bermuda. By a careful rationing, they reckoned it could make two small cakes (baked bread) per person per day—for fourteen to sixteen days. Then what?

There was only one thing to do: abandon Jamestown as quickly as possible. They would take everyone. They would sail in four pinnaces—the Bermuda-built *Deliverance* and *Patience* and the Virginia-based *Discovery* and *Virginia*, parceling out their precious store of meal aboard each vessel. Barrels of water they could get from the well at Jamestown, one of the fort's few remaining amenities. They would make for Newfoundland, where the fishing season had begun, and plead with English ships to take them home. At least, that is what they thought.

Lt.-Gen. Sir Thomas Gates had another plan in mind. Or at least that is what he later told his superior officer, Capt.-Gen. Thomas West, Lord De La Warr. Gates said that he was not planning to abandon Jamestown immediately for Newfoundland. Instead, he secretly intended to "stay some ten days at Cape Comfort [Fort Algernon]" in case a relief expedition should arrive. Otherwise, he was set "to go for England, having but 30 days' victuals left him and his hungry company."[24] Evidently, Gates did not tell Somers or Newport, or Strachey, or Percy, or Davis of this plan. In secretly planning to delay leaving, Gates knew he was taking a great risk, and he seems to have kept his plans close to his chest. And most of all, he did not tell the colonists—nearly 250 of them, including Davis and the men at the fort—that he was planning to use up ten precious days' worth of food waiting at Algernon Fort in case a relief expedition showed up.

Did Gates, as he later told De La Warr, really have thirty days' worth of food left? Strachey thought they had, at most, sixteen days' supply left; Somers wrote that they had only fourteen. Someone was mistaken— or deliberately misrepresenting the truth. To say they had to abandon Jamestown because they had fourteen to sixteen days' worth of food left was reason beyond questioning. No one could fault such a decision. But thirty days' worth was another matter.

Lt.-Gen. Sir Thomas Gates must have felt the weight of the whole enterprise on his shoulders. The success or failure of England's only colony in the New World, a project that had taken years of work and thousands of pounds sterling to execute, now depended on the judgment of one man. Gates's own words to Somers in Bermuda must have echoed in his head as he anguished over what to do. During their quarrel he had reminded Somers of being answerable "to his Majestie for so many of his subjects . . . the Adventurers . . . in the businesse for which they were sent out of England."[25] What if they abandoned Jamestown when help was on the way? Ten days' wait, given the vagaries of transatlantic travel, was not a very long time. On the other hand, what if they stayed too long—and starved to death? Lt.-Gen. Sir Thomas Gates would have to make that choice.

At last the *Deliverance, Patience,* and *Discovery* were ready to set sail. The *Virginia* waited rigged and ready to join them at Point Comfort. Some people wanted to burn the log fort and its ramshackle contents as they left, but Gates craftily refused. "Lett the towne Stande," he said. "We know nott but thatt as honest men as ourselves may come and inhabitt here."[26] But they buried the cannons in the soft earth in front of the fort's gate. There was no point in providing artillery to the Spanish when they came, as most everyone thought they would. In case any die-hard malcontents disobeyed orders and tried to set fire to the fort, Gates ordered his company to remain ashore until everyone else had boarded the pinnaces, and he himself was the last to leave. With a "peale of small shot" to mark their departure, the pinnaces set sail about noon. By night, using the outgoing tide, they had sailed nearly four miles downriver and dropped anchor at Hog Island. It was June 7, 1610.

The next morning the little trio of pinnaces made their way six miles farther downriver to a point of land on the north shore. This place they had named Mulberry Island, though it, like Hog Island, was not really an island at all. It was named for its profusion of red mulberry trees. Here the James River was five miles across. They could see downriver a long way toward Kecoughtan and Nansemond, but there was nothing to see except the river, flowing between its leafy green banks. At Mulberry Island the pinnaces rode lazily at anchor in the warm afternoon sun, waiting for the tide to change. Since it was still mulberry season, some people may have ventured ashore in hopes of finding berries. Others took their ease on the decks. Some dozed. Many talked of what they would do once they got home to England.

Suddenly, an excited shout rang out across the water. There was a tiny speck on the horizon, far downriver. It looked like the mast of a ship. Even through the magnifying lens of a spyglass, it was hard to make out. At last they could see that it was a very small ship with one mast. In fact, it was a longboat, and it was coming toward them. They reckoned it was at least an hour away, but who was in it? As they waited for it to draw closer, there was much excited calling back and forth between the pinnaces. Who would be bringing a longboat fitted with a sail upriver to Jamestown? Captain Davis had left a light guard at Fort Algernon, but those men knew the pinnaces were coming down. There was no need for them to come upriver.

As the longboat came into shouting distance, they heard news that astounded them. Miracle of miracles: the longboat had come from Algernon Fort, where Lord De La Warr and his three ships had anchored the day before. As soon as De La Warr heard from Davis's men there what had happened at Jamestown, he dispatched Capt. Edward Brewster and the longboat to intercept the little fleet of pinnaces. Brewster brought official letters from Capt.-Gen. Thomas West, Lord De La Warr, to Lt.-Gen. Sir Thomas Gates, telling him of the three ships—the flagship *De La Warr, Blessing,* and *Hercules*—bearing 150 new colonists and "great store of victuals" for the Virginia colony.[27] Another letter, hastily written, ordered Gates and the whole company to return at once to Jamestown.

Adm. Sir George Somers said that De La Warr's coming "made our hearts very glad." William Strachey said that the arrival "gave us no little joyes."[28] What Thomas Gates thought, he did not say. He had kept the irate colonists from burning down the fort. It could be reclaimed. He had buried the cannons. They could be dug up again. He gave orders to sail for Jamestown.

Many people, then and later, saw this unexpected coincidence as a miracle. Back in London, the Reverend William Crashaw wrote that it was "the Hand of Heaven from above at the very instant sent in the Right Honorable La-War to meet them, even at the river's mouth with provision and comforts of all kind, who if he had stayed but two tides longer had come into Virginia and not found *one Englishman.*"[29]

John Smith wrote of two extraordinary coincidences: first, the arrival of the Bermuda ships and, second, De La Warr's coming. Smith believed these were the work of divine Providence:

> Never had any people more just cause, to cast themselves at the very foot-stoole of God, and to reverence his mercie, than this distressed Colonie; for if God had not sent Sir Thomas Gates from the Bermudas, within foure daies they had almost beene famished; if God had not directed the heart of that noble Knight to save the Fort from firing at their shipping, for many were very importunate to have burnt it, they had beene destitute of a present harbour and succour: if they had abandoned the Fort any longer time, and had not so soone returned, questionlesse the Indians would have destroied the Fort, which had beene the meanes of our safeties amongst them and a terror. If they had set saile sooner, and had launched into the vast Ocean, who would have promised they should have incountered the Fleet of the Lord la Ware, especially when they made for Newfoundland, as they intended, a course contrarie to our Navie approaching. If the Lord la Ware had not bought with him a yeeres provision, what comfort would those poore soules have received, to have beene relanded to a second distruction?[30]

Smith was right. The arrival of Lord De La Warr and his three ships just before Somers, Gates, and the four pinnaces sailed for Newfoundland was indeed a stroke of good luck, if not an act of Providence. It saved England's first settlement in North America. Three days later would have been too late. By that time the *Deliverance, Patience, Discovery,* and *Virginia* would have been at least a day's or maybe two days' sail up the coast, bound for Newfoundland.

Could one of De La Warr's ships have caught up with them? Not likely. Would De La Warr and his 150 new colonists have made a go of reviving Jamestown by themselves? Could De La Warr, who was not in good health (he was never to be really well while he was in Virginia) and a company of inexperienced newcomers who were ignorant of the Indians possibly succeed? Not likely.

Jamestown, once near death, was revived: with a fair wind at their backs (another act of Providence?) the little fleet of pinnaces sailed upriver, and by nightfall on June 8 they reached the fort they had abandoned just two days earlier. The relief expedition was close behind them. Two days later Lord De La Warr and his three ships with all their passengers and provisions dropped anchor at Jamestown fort.

With impressive pomp and ceremony Captain-General Lord De La Warr came ashore to assume his command. His own military escort under Capt. Edward Brewster formed a guard at the south palisade gate and stood with breastplates gleaming and pikes pointing skyward. William Strachey bore the captain-general's colors before him, and the new governor of Virginia, Sir Thomas West, Lord De La Warr, stepped ashore. No sooner had he set his elegant boots on Jamestown's marshy soil than he sank to his knees in a long, silent prayer. Then he and his company marched into the fort. Gates and Somers and all the rest were waiting for them, and everyone filed into the church. The Reverend Richard Buck gave a sermon. De La Warr's commission, making him captain-general and governor of Virginia for life, was read.

Then Lord De La Warr made a brief speech, perhaps not a well-thought one: he blamed the Virginia residents for their present pitiful state and told them they must work harder. (How the Jamestown colonists, so malnourished they were near death, received this speech is not recorded.) Lord De La Warr hoped that they would do better, "lest he should be compelled to draw the sword of justice to cut off such delinquents, which he had much rather, he protested, draw in their defense to protect them from injuries." At last (this must have been greeted with tears of joy and loud cheers) he told them that he had brought food enough to "serve foure hundred men for one whole yeare."[31]

But the new captain-general did not want to deplete the precious store of provisions too quickly, and he proposed to consult on the food supply with his newly appointed council (Gates, Somers, Percy, Newport, and Ferdinando Weinman, one of De La Warr's men), plus Strachey, who was now the secretary and recorder of the colony. For that position, Captain-General De La Warr could not have chosen better. Strachey, a diligent and eloquent writer, would chronicle not only what happened in Virginia but what had happened in Bermuda as well. His manuscript would eventually be titled "A True Reportory of the Wreck and Redemption of Sir Thomas Gates, Knight, upon and from the Islands of the Bermudas; his coming to Virginia, and the estate of that colony then, and after under the government of the Lord La Warr." Strachey's manuscript would reach England a year before its author, with consequences he never dreamed of.[32]

Consultation with the council on food proved a waste of time, except for Lord De La Warr and those with him who still had not come to terms with the depressing truth about Jamestown's food sources: there were none. The Indians, hostile since John Smith's leaving, had no food to trade, even if they had wanted to: it was early June, and their crops were barely in the ground. Admiral Somers noted that the Indians "had nothing to trade with but mulberries." And berries were not the best diet for delicate, malnourished digestions.

But what of the provisions Smith had left last year—the hogs, five of six hundred of them? Not one was left alive, and not "a hen nor chick in the fort." That was disappointing news, indeed. De La Warr and his provisioners had expected to find meat in Virginia, and so had brought none. Strachey wrote dispiritedly that the provisions that the captain-general had brought, "concerning any kinde of flesh, was little or nothing; in respect it was not dremt of by the Adventurers in England, that the Swine were destroyed."[33] Barrels of meal, dried beans perhaps, some oil and cheese they had, but no meat to stick to a hungry person's ribs. And there were in Jamestown at least sixty people whose ribs were in great need of fleshing out.

On June 10, just five days after De La Warr had taken command at Jamestown, the indomitable Admiral Somers had a plan to feed the colony: he would sail to Bermuda and bring back six months' worth of pork and fish and turtle meat. He wrote of this scheme in a letter to Robert Cecil, the Earl of Salisbury, saying, "I am in a good opinion to be back again before the Indians do gather their harvest [that would have been late August or early September]. Bermuda is the most plentiful place that ever I came to for fish, hogs, and fowl." Somers was also remembering the castaways who were left there: Christopher Carter and Robert Waters were no doubt hoping to see him again. He was eager to return "by reason of his promise to thoes two left behind, as [well as] upon an affection he carryed to the place it selfe."[34]

Somers sailed for Bermuda on June 19. He went in his own pinnace, the *Patience,* and with him went Samuel Argall in the *Discovery.* The residents of Jamestown watched hopefully and prayerfully as the two small ships "fell with the tide" downriver. By June 22 (as always, obliged to sail with the outgoing tides) they reached Chesapeake Bay and, as Strachey put it, "left the Bay, or Cape Henry, a sterne."[35]

Somers thought of going to Bermuda for food, but De La Warr took the credit for it. He wrote his own letter to the Earl of Salisbury after the admiral's departure: "I dispatched Sir George Sommers back again to the Barmudas, the good old gentleman [Somers was fifty-six; De La Warr was thirty-three at the time] out of his love and zeal not motioning [opposing], but most cheerfully and resolutely undertaking to perform so dangerous a voyage, and, if it please God he do safely return, he will store us with hog's flesh and fish enough to serve the whole colony this winter."[36]

Meanwhile, De La Warr set his men and others who were able-bodied to work. Some were put to cleaning up the debris of ruined houses inside the fort, others to making coal for the forges (blacksmiths were essential for making tools, weapons, and ammunition), still others to fish, but the latter, the captain-general noted with disappointment, "had ill success" in the James River. The starving residents of Jamestown had become too weak and too frightened of Indians to fish in the river, and they had let their nets—fourteen of them by one count—rot to pieces. The newcomers had some nets, but they had little luck in casting them. They hauled in their nets every day and night, "sometimes a dosen times one after the other," but they did not catch enough to feed even a fourth of the people who were there. Strachey wrote ruefully, "Notwithstanding the great store [of fish] we now saw daily in our River; but let the blame of this lye where it is, both upon our Nets, and the unskilfulnesse of our men to lay them."[37] Captain-General De La Warr sent some of his men in the pinnace *Virginia* to fish downriver and in Chesapeake Bay, but they returned by the end of June with nothing to show for their fishing trip.

In short, Jamestown's residents were still desperately hungry. They needed many more calories than normal if they were to recover from months of severe malnutrition. And many had simply lost heart. They no longer wanted to make an effort. Sir Thomas Gates was shocked to find that what little fish they managed to come by, they ate raw "rather than they would go a stones cast to fetch wood and dresse it."[38] Where was John Smith when they needed him?

The newly arrived English leaders had made no effort to understand the Indians or negotiate with them. But oddly enough, De La Warr had had a cordial meeting with Indians before he came to Jamestown, in fact on the very first day he set foot on Virginia soil. On June 6 De La Warr had arrived at Cape Henry and dropped anchor there to await one of his ships, the *Hercules,* which had lost contact with the others. He and his men went ashore and went fishing. While they were there, "diverse Indians" came out of the woods. As De La Warr wrote later, "With fair entreaty on both sides I gave unto them of such fish as we took, which was good store [a good amount] and was not unwelcome unto them, for indeed at this time of the year they live poor, their corn being newly put into the ground and their old store spent."[39]

Apparently, Lord De La Warr had dismissed that incident. Now he thought only of revenge. He was even more eager to wreak revenge on the Indians after what happened to one of Thomas Gates's men. On July 6 when Gates was on his way to Point Comfort, he found the Algernon Fort longboat drifting unmanned in the currents near the mouth of the Nansemond River. The boat had come loose from its moorings, and a strong north wind had blown the empty craft nearly eight miles across the water on the opposite side from the fort. Gates dispatched one of his men, a fellow named Humfrey Blunt, to take an "old canoe" (presumably one they carried on the pinnace) and recover the errant longboat. But before Blunt could lay hold of the longboat, the wind drove his canoe onto the shore, and "certaine Indians (watching the occasion) seised the poore fellow, and led him up into the Woods, and sacrificed him."[40]

These were no doubt Indians from the town of Nansemond. They had been friendly toward the English until a year earlier when James Martin and his men had captured their king and killed a number of them. The Indians had killed a number of English in return. Now they seized a chance for more revenge on this windfall of a solitary Englishman. How did they "sacrifice" him? Lieutenant-General Gates does not say. When he told the faithful recorder, Strachey, about this incident, he omitted the gory details. Strachey set down what he could. He did not say that Gates, helpless but safe aboard the pinnace, heard Humfrey Blunt's shouts for help and that they went unanswered. Perhaps Gates and his men could not risk shooting at the Indians for fear of hitting Blunt. Perhaps they could see the swiftness of the sacrifice left no time to rescue the victim. And so the men aboard the pinnace listened to their comrade's death screams and sailed away. But that was not the end of the story.

Gates, "being startled by this" (Blunt's capture and death by torture), "he well perceived, how little a faire and noble intreaie, workes upon a barbarous disposition, and therefore in some measure purposed to be revenged."[41] Perhaps Strachey left something out here. Thomas Gates had been in Virginia for seven weeks. During that time there is no record of his addressing any "faire and noble" entreaty to the Indians. He had seen them, yes, and he had seen the dead English bodies their forays left behind. It did not take the killing of Humfrey Blunt to put revenge on the veteran soldier Gates's agenda. But his and the other newcomers' ignorance of the Indians' ways, not to mention their various tribal groups and towns, could only lead to more disasters.

Three days later Lieutenant-General Gates took his revenge—on the wrong Indians, in the wrong place. He attacked the Indian town of Kecoughtan. It was on the opposite side of the James, nearly nine miles from Nansemond, where Humfrey Blunt had been killed. But Gates (according to Strachey, who was with him) "had soon taken it [Kecoughtan] without losse or hurt of any of his men." Kecoughtan's chief and his women fled, leaving their "poore baggage, and treasure to the spoyle of our Souldiers, which was only a few Baskets of old Wheate, and some other of Pease and Beanes, a little Tobacco, and some women's Girdles of Silke of the Grasse silke, not without art, and much neatness finely wrought."[42]

George Percy (ever one for sensational details) recorded the disturbing parts of this episode that Strachey left out. Upon coming to Kecoughtan, Gates, thinking to lure the Indians out, sent his taborer (drummer) into the center of the town to dance and beat upon his drum. When the Indians came wonderingly forth, eager to see and hear the drumming, Gates and his men attacked without warning. They "fell in upon them, putt fyve to the sworde, wownded many others, some of them beinge after fownde in the woods with such extreordinary large and mortall wownds that it seemed strange they could flye so far."[43]

Revenge was sweet. The English wanted more of it. When Powhatan (who was not pleased by the arrival of nearly three hundred more English in his domain) "returned proud and disdainful answers" to requests to return stolen English goods and English captives, Lord De La Warr became "much incensed." He ordered Capt. George Percy and seventy men "to take revenge upon the Paspaheans and Chiconomians." (Again, as in the case of Gates's attack on Kecoughtan, these were the wrong Indians, and they lived miles away from Powhatan and his people.) Percy himself tells the story of his attack on Paspahegh:

> And then we fell in upon them, put some fiftene or sixteene to the Sworde, and almost all the reste to flyghte. . . . My Lieutenant bringeinge with him the Quene and her Children and one Indiann prisoners for the which I taxed him because he had Spared them. His answer was, thatt having them now in my Custodie I might doe with them what I pleased. Upon the same I cawsed the Indian's head to be Cutt off. . . . [M]y sowldiers did begin to murmur becawse the quene and her Children were spared. So upon the same a Cowncell beinge called, it was agreed upon to putt the children to deathe, the which was effected by Throweinge them overboard and shoteinge outt their Braynes in the water.[44]

Percy claims that he tried to save their mother's life, but that Lord De La Warr, according to Captain Davis, wanted her burned to death. Percy replied that he had "seene so mutche Blood shedd thatt day, now in my Cold bloode I desyred to see noe more; and for to Burne her I did not howlde it fittinge, buttt either by shot or Sworde to give her a quicker dispatche." So Captain Davis "did take the quene with towe sowldiers a shoare and in the woods putt her to the Sworde."[45]

The manner of the queen's execution raises intriguing questions. That it took three men to handle her suggests that she did not go passively. Why take the trouble to remove her to a remote place? Why not simply shoot her, as they had her children? Did they feel that the wife of a king was entitled to a special death, or did her behavior infuriate the Englishmen? Was she swiftly run through, or was she savagely mutilated? English as well as Indians knew the meaning of vengeance, and both sides would keep a deadly seesaw of violence in motion until the end of the seventeenth century.

Shortly after his encounter with the Indians at Kecoughtan, Sir Thomas Gates left for England. He was dispatched aboard one of De La

Warr's ships, the *Blessing,* to deliver a much-needed report to the Virginia Company. It was a letter composed by the Council of Virginia: De La Warr, Gates, Weinman, Percy, and Strachey (who as recorder and secretary no doubt put it on paper). Somers, the remaining council member, was still on his errand to Bermuda. The letter offered some good news, and some not so good. But the authors did their best to be optimistic. The good news was that the land was fertile and promising. The not-so-good news was that the Indians were still dangerous and that as many as 150 of the 400-odd colonists were ill with "strange fluxes and agues" (including De La Warr himself, though he did not report it here).[46] Dr. Lawrence Boone, the physician De La Warr had brought with him, had "not above 3 weeks'" supply of medicine. This was July 7, 1610. They would run out long before a new supply ship could get there.

Meanwhile, in London the new Spanish ambassador, Don Alonso de Velasco, was following in his predecessor Zuñiga's footsteps, keeping a close watch on Virginia. In June 1610 he sent a long letter to King Philip, describing what he had heard of the death rate from starvation and Indian attacks at Jamestown. "Unless they succor them with some provisions in an English ship . . . they must have perished before this." Velasco did not know that De La Warr's ships had reached Virginia that month. But he concluded hopefully, "Thus it looks as if the zeal for this enterprise was [is] cooling off, and it would on that account be very easy to make an end of it altogether by sending out a few ships to finish what might be left in that place."[47]

An outpost perched on a point of land in Chesapeake Bay. A small log fort on the banks of the James River. Four hundred colonists, nearly half of them sick, many of them still feeble from months of near starvation. The Spanish ambassador was right: it would be easy to put an end to the English in Virginia. If the Spanish did not, the Indians would

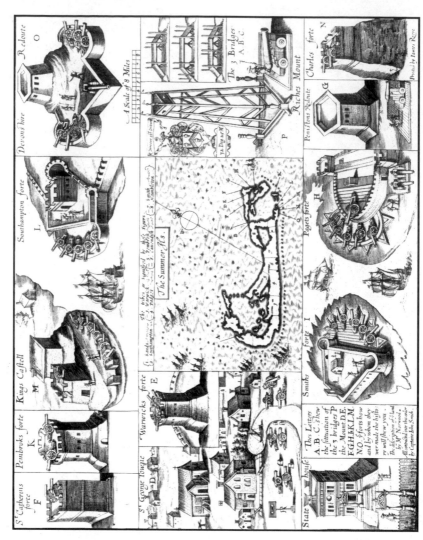

John Smith's map of Bermuda. *Courtesy of the National Museum of Bermuda.*

6

A TALE OF TWO COLONIES

WHEN ADM. SIR GEORGE SOMERS sailed away from Virginia on July 19, 1610, he left a colony perilously near collapse, but Bermuda's star was about to rise. But for the wreck of the *Sea Venture*, Bermuda might have remained what it had been for centuries: an uninhabited speck of land thought to be haunted by devils. But for the castaways' unlooked-for arrival at Jamestown, starvation would have killed many of Virginia's frail colonists. Both Bermuda's colonial begin nings and Virginia's continued survival were unexpected consequences of a fateful shipwreck in the summer of 1609. Within a decade, one of these colonies was giving "great contentment and incouragement," while the other was languishing from "misgovernment, idlenesse, and faction."[1] What happened to England's first two colonies in the New World is a tale of greed, deception, misunderstanding, espionage and incredible good fortune.

In September 1610, while Sir George Somers was battling rough seas on his way to Bermuda aboard the *Patience*, two of Lord De La Warr's ships, the *Blessing* and the *Hercules*, returned to England with unwelcome, disturbing news about Virginia. All of London was abuzz: after so much fanfare and so many pounds sterling, the Virginia Company's Jamestown settlement still was full of sick and hungry colonists, and, worse yet, there were no profits in sight. Investors looked in vain for their returns. Some grumbled that wealthy folks like Sir Thomas Smith, the Virginia Company's treasurer, and others like him could afford to wait for long-term gains, but ordinary people expected something sooner to show for their money.

The Spanish spy network in London was full of predictions that England's failing colony would soon be dead. On September 30 Ambassador Velasco wrote to King Philip about news he had from one of his key London sources, one "Guillermo Monco." This was Sir William Monson, former privateer, veteran of the battle of the Spanish Armada, onetime prisoner of the Spanish in Lisbon, and, since 1604, Admiral of the Narrow Seas (English Channel). He was also a spy, handsomely paid for leaking English plans to the Spanish ambassador. Monson told Velasco that the English were desperate to recoup their investments in Virginia and were planning to send another large expedition there early in 1611. Spain needed to move now to "drive out the few people that have remained there, and are so threatened by the Indians that they dare not leave the fort they have erected."[2]

Enclosed with Ambassador Velasco's letter was a Spanish translation of a report from an Irishman, one Francisco Maguel (McGill?), who purported to have been a spy in Virginia for eight months. Who was he? How did he get there? There is no name resembling his on any of the lists of Virginia colonists. But Maguel somehow found his way to Madrid and to a meeting with Florencio Conryo, who claimed to be the archbishop of Tuam, a town near Galway, Ireland. (Ireland was then under English control, and the Irish Catholics hoped to serve their cause by aiding Spain against their common enemy.) In Madrid Maguel's report was translated into Spanish, and he signed that document on July 1, 1610. The Irish spy's report gave a detailed account of Virginia's geography, including the best way to get there by sea. He described bays and rivers, the Jamestown fort, and the land's resources—but much of the account is sprinkled with falsehoods (there are pearls, coral, and perhaps diamonds in Virginia; the English plan to settle twenty or thirty thousand colonists there) and half-truths (Indians are devil worshipers). Maguel warned that the English "want nothing more than they want to make themselves masters of the South Sea, so as to have their share of the riches of the Indies and be in the way of the traffic of the King of Spain, and to seek other new worlds for themselves."[3] Whether the mysterious Francisco Maguel, who hoped "to serve his Catholic Majesty," ever did so is not known, but his report was enough to make Ambassador Velasco nervous. It had a similar effect on King Philip III. Before 1611 was out, Spanish authorities devised a plot to find out firsthand what the English were up to in Virginia, and in the summer of that year a Spanish caravel would sail into Chesapeake Bay.

Meanwhile, the Virginia Company's officials rushed to shine a good light on bad news. Lord De La Warr's ships had brought Thomas Gates and Christopher Newport back to London, and these two were scheduled to give firsthand reports to Sir Thomas Smith and the rest of the Virginia Company Council. Those hearings would be private, but the public could read a little pamphlet called *News from Virginia, of the happy arrival of that famous and worthy knight, Sir Thomas Gates, and well-reputed and valiant Captain Newport, into England.* It was in verse, composed by another of the Bermuda castaways, Robert Rich. This Robert Rich (not to be confused with his cousin of the same age, Sir Robert Rich) was twenty-three years old when he composed the verses celebrating Gates's and Newport's returns to England and recounting their adventures since the wreck of the *Sea Venture.* (It is interesting to note that Rich, who was probably a Gates loyalist, did not put Sir George Somers in the poem's title, though he was obliged to mention him as a member of the Virginia colony's council.) For its naive cheerfulness (its twenty-two stanzas neglect to mention the Indians) and wildly fanciful promises about Virginia, Rich's poem is worth quoting here in part:

> There is no fear of hunger here,

(Strachey described life at Jamestown as "cleannesse of teeth, famine, and death.")

> for corn much store here grows
> Much fish the gallant rivers yield—
> 'tis truth without suppose.

("The river . . . had not a fish to be seen in it."—Strachey)

> Great store of fowl, of venison,
> Of grapes and mulberries,

("Nothing to trade withal but mulberries."—Sir George Somers)

> Of chestnuts, walnuts, and suchlike,
> of fruits and strawberries
> There is indeed no want at all.
> But some, condition'd ill,
> That wish the work should not go on,
> with words do seem to kill.[4]

On November 8, 1610, another piece of propaganda, the Virginia Company's latest booklet, went on sale at the Black Bear in St. Paul's churchyard. It rushed into print the good parts of Thomas Gates's and Christopher Newport's testimony before the company's council. Its title is self-explanatory: *A True Declaration of the estate of the colony in Virginia, with a confutation of such scandalous reports as have tended to the disgrace of so worthy an enterprise.* It celebrated the safe return of Gates, Newport, and others from the *Sea Venture* expedition and did its best to dispel the worst of the Virginia reports, especially the "Starving Time" and the "tragical history of the man eating of his dead wife in Virginia." Sir Thomas Gates appeared before the Virginia Company Council and tried to set the record straight about the man who killed his wife. (Apparently, no one asked where Gates came by this information, since he himself was in Bermuda when the wife-butchering incident took place.) According to Gates, the man "mortally hated his wife." So he "secretly killed her, then cut her in pieces and hid her remains in divers parts of his house," the implication being that the husband did not kill his wife because he was starving—though he "fed daily upon her." As further proof that there was plenty to eat in Jamestown, Gates reported that besides the wife's dismembered body, the man's house contained "a good quantity of meal, oatmeal, beans, and peas."[5] Such a larder would have been news to the starving inhabitants inside the fort, who were existing on half a can of meal per day.

A True Declaration declared that all was well in Virginia, that Sir Thomas Gates liked it so much he was in a great hurry to go back there, and that Lord De La Warr wanted to stay there. Of these three items, only the second had a grain of truth in it.

About this time, Adm. Sir George Somers finally reached Bermuda on his errand to bring food to the hungry Virginians. The intrepid admiral and the *Patience* ran into "much foul and cross weather" on his voyage that summer of 1610. Due to the fierce winds, he soon lost contact with Samuel Argall and the *Discovery.* Argall, blown far off course, could not find Somers, and although Argall was an experienced sailor who had crossed the Atlantic several times, he could not find Bermuda, either. He finally wound up on the coast of what is now Maine, where he fished for cod and went back to Jamestown. The storm-tossed *Patience* did not drop anchor in Bermuda until well into the fall, perhaps in late October or early November. Somers's nephew Capt. Matthew Somers was with him, as well as a crew of his trusted sailors, but they had a difficult voyage.

Robert Waters and Christopher Carter, the two miscreants—once loyal Somers men—who had hidden themselves and refused to leave Bermuda in May, had been living by themselves for more than six months, wondering if and when a ship might appear. They may have spied the *Patience*'s sails from afar. Exactly how they met Somers and his crew is not known. The glad reunions and the swapping of stories, the feasting on Bermuda's tortoises and hogs and fish, must be left to the imagination, for there is no written account of it. But Waters and Carter, with another of Somers's sailors, would have major parts to play in the later colonization of Bermuda. Somers evidently talked of settling there himself. "It is well known," according to a contemporary who wrote a history of Bermuda, "that he [Somers] resolved upon a plantation, though it were by the purse and meanes of himself and his freinds."[6] If this account is true, Sir George Somers was planning to sever his ties with the Virginia Company and finance his own colony. He even selected a site and called it "Somers' seat," now called Somerset, a part of modern Sandys Parish, Bermuda.

Admiral Somers, never one to sit idle for long, soon set about doing what he had come to Bermuda for: hunting hogs and catching tortoises and fish to take back to Virginia. With Lord De La Warr's newcomers added to the *Sea Venture* castaways and the Starving Time survivors, there were four hundred people at Jamestown now. They were eagerly, hungrily awaiting his return. Besides, it would soon be December, and wintertime was not the best time to be sailing the Atlantic in a thirty-ton pinnace. And so Sir George and his sailors went to work. The admiral as usual seemed to be everywhere at once, directing, encouraging, and asking no one to do what he did not do himself. Perhaps he went at the hunting and fishing a bit too vigorously. He suddenly took ill. Perhaps it was a heart attack. "The strength of his body not answering the ever memorable courage of his minde," he was aware of the seriousness of his condition. "Finding his time but short," he told his nephew and his sailors to finish hunting and "with all expedition to return to Virginia."[7]

Sir George Somers died in Bermuda on November 9, 1610. Word of mouth, later set down by a London chronicler, said that he died "of a surfeit in eating of a pig."[8] The cause of Somers's death was probably more complicated than that, but after all, he had been on starvation rations in

Virginia and at sea for many weeks. Why should he not feast when he got to Bermuda? After the admiral's death, his nephew took command. Capt. Matthew Somers was determined to take his uncle's body home to England for burial, but there was a problem. According to the nautical wisdom of the time, sailing with a corpse aboard was "extreamely, prodigiously, ominous." Captain Somers dared not tell his crew, loyal though they had been to the admiral, that they were about to take his remains aboard for a long voyage. So the resourceful younger Somers had his uncle's body secretly packed in brine and concealed in a barrel. (After all, Captain Somers must have reasoned, they had been planning to take pork back to Jamestown in the same kinds of barrels.) But the *Patience* was not bound for Virginia. Despite the admiral's wishes, his pinnace set sail for England. Left behind once again in Bermuda at his own request was Christopher Carter, who believed that Somers "had taken some order with his friends in England, and had made some preparation for a plantation."[9] Robert Waters also remained, and Edward Chard, another of Somers's sailors, elected to throw in his lot with Carter and Waters. They would be alone in Bermuda for nearly two years. More than two hundred years later, their story fascinated Washington Irving, who wrote an essay called "Three Kings of Bermuda" in 1840.

Admiral Somers was going home in the cedar pinnace he himself had built. A time-hallowed Bermuda story has it that Somers's heart, at his own request, was buried in Bermuda. In a shady park in the modern town of St. George's there is a monument to him with an inscription that begins, "Near this spot in the year 1610 was buried the heart of the heroic Admiral Sir George Somers." The monument was put there by Bermuda's governor J. H. Lefroy in the 1870s. The site was first discovered in 1621 by another Bermuda governor, Nathaniel Butler, who "espied a great cross of wood pitched, sloping into the ground, in a by-place, all overgrown with bushes and rubbish." Butler was told that it was Sir George's "friends and followers" who had put the cross there. Thinking that "so noble a gentleman deserved a better monument," Butler put up a marble stone with an inscribed brass plate. Two centuries passed, and the stone disappeared. In 1819 the burial site supposedly containing the "heart and entrails" of Sir George Somers was opened, but nothing was found "except fragments of a glass vessel or bottle, the character of which is not recorded."[10]

In the small English town of Whitechurch Canonicorum in Dorsetshire, the admiral's body was entombed with full military honors. His untimely death was much talked of, and part of the talk, no doubt encouraged by the admiral's nephew and the men who had sailed with him, was that Bermuda would be a fine place to plant a colony.

In London some members of the Virginia Company, considering the ruinous state of their project at Jamestown, agreed. There was talk, and the vigilant Spanish heard it. In Madrid the president of the Board of Trade wrote to the Council of War that the *Sea Venture* survivors who had returned to London talked of "great wealth of pearls at that island, with the result that many people were minded to go and settle there, and a number had banded together for that very purpose." This same letter urged quick action to occupy Bermuda before the English did. If "the enemy has taken possession, efforts should be made to eject them from there before they can fortify themselves."[11]

In March the Virginia Company dispatched Sir Thomas Dale, a no-nonsense career military officer and veteran of the Dutch wars, to help bring order to Virginia. He left England with three ships and three hundred more colonists on March 17, 1611. Dale did not know it, but an ailing Lord De La Warr departed from Virginia en route to England a few days later, on March 28. Captain-General De La Warr had left a frail colony with only two hundred people, "most in health." (In other words, about fifty people had died in the past year, and of the living, not all were well.) Thomas West, Lord De La Warr, had some explaining to do. He had been appointed Virginia's governor for life in 1609. He did not set foot in Virginia until June 1610, when Jamestown came near to being abandoned. He had governed Virginia for less than a year, and now he was coming home.

As soon as he arrived in London, Lord De La Warr wrote a brief, hurried letter to the Earl of Salisbury, promising a detailed account of affairs in Virginia. He would, the captain-general said, give "full satisfaction to every doubt or scandal that lies upon that country, fearing [expecting] nothing less than an honorable and profitable end of all if now it be not let fall."[12] But the Virginia Company's funds were nearly gone, and investors were growing more and more anxious. Buying a few days' time, De La Warr sharpened his quill pens and set himself to composing a formal report for the Virginia Company Council, explaining his uncalled-for return to England. The captain-general was a master of excuses. His reason for leaving, he said, was very simple: he felt that he would die if he stayed longer in Virginia. But, he said, he had not intended to sail to England. His initial plan was to make for the island of Nevis in the West Indies and try the famous "wholesome baths" there. But contrary winds and bad weather forced him instead to the Azores. By the time his ship reached those islands, forty of the fifty-five men aboard the *De La Warr* were "neare sicke to death of the Scurvie, Callenture [ship's fever], and other diseases."[13] In the Azores they ate oranges, and most of them recovered within a few days. Then De La Warr considered sailing back to Virginia, but "was advised," he did not say specifically by whom, not to risk his frail health on such a long voyage. And so he had no choice but to sail for England. As further proof for the Virginia Company Council, Lord De La Warr described his many ailments: a "hot and violent ague" upon arrival in Virginia, then "the flux" (dysentery), "the cramp," after that an attack of the gout, and, finally, scurvy, which he described as a "sickness of slothfulness." Once in London, he claimed to be feeling better.[14]

Ambassador Velasco had another version of why De La Warr had left Virginia. Velasco notified King Philip of De La Warr's return, saying that he heard the English governor left Virginia "by stealth," fearing that if he told the colonists there, they would not have let him leave. De La Warr's report to the Virginia Company, said Velasco, was published in London "in order to excuse his return." Captain-General Lord De La Warr never set foot on Virginia soil again. He did sail for it seven years later, but he died on the way.

The latest talk about Bermuda made Ambassador Velasco very uneasy, and he wrote hurriedly to King Philip: "They now propose to erect a fort on the island of Bermuda . . . and although the coast of Bermuda is dangerous having no considerable port at all, still they will find shelter there for small vessels."[15] Velasco was not quite right: the English were not building a fort, but they were thinking about Bermuda.

In the various accounts of Virginia in that year of 1610, the most truth was to be found in an unpublished twenty-five-thousand-word manuscript sent to London by one of the colonists. William Strachey's meticulous, graceful narrative of the *Sea Venture* wreck, the castaways' adventures in Bermuda, and the events in Virginia through 1610 was in the form of a long letter addressed only to "Excellent Lady." Who was she? To this day, scholars have yet to identify her with certainty. She may have been Lucy, Countess of Bedford, or Dame Sara Smith, the wife of Virginia Company treasurer Sir Thomas Smith, or she may have been Lady Elizabeth Howard, wife of Lord Theophilus Howard of Walden. The Countess of Bedford was a patroness of the poet John Donne, who was also a friend of Strachey's.[16] Strachey may have hoped to win her favor with his letter. But Strachey was also hoping to further his career in the Virginia Company, so he may have chosen Smith's wife as his audience, knowing that his manuscript would reach her husband. On the other hand, the Howards of Walden were a family from his youth, and he could have chosen Lady Elizabeth for sentimental reasons. By all accounts, the "Excellent Lady" was not Strachey's wife, Frances. The long-suffering Frances and the couple's two sons were probably living at her family's home, Crowhurst, in Surrey. But perhaps a friend from London carried the news of Strachey's safe return and his many adventures to them. Or perhaps he sent a letter to them that has been lost.

Regardless of the addressee, Strachey's "True reportory" found its way to other fascinated readers—one of whom was William Shakespeare. As one scholar observed, "The shipwreck of Sir George Somers's relief expedition to Virginia upon the Bermudas in 1609 struck Shakespeare's imagination, and out of it came *The Tempest*."[17] This is not as far-fetched as it sounds. Shakespeare had friends connected to the Virginia Company, and Strachey had friends in London's literary circles (John Donne wrote of him as "Mr William Strachey allwayes my good friend").[18] Shakespeare may also have known Strachey. Unquestionably, Shakespeare knew, and was known to, several men connected to the Virginia Company. One was his patron, Sir Henry Wriothesley, Earl of Southampton, to whom Shakespeare had dedicated two poems in the 1590s. The earl was also a member of the Virginia Company Council. Another connection was Sir Dudley Digges, who may have helped to edit the company's pamphlet *A True Declaration*. Digges was the stepson of Shakespeare's Stratford friend Thomas Russell. Yet another contact was Sir Henry Rainsford, a Virginia Company Council member. Rainsford's physician was John Hall, Shakespeare's son-in-law.[19] If personal connections are not enough, further proof is in the text of *The Tempest*, a play about shipwrecked passengers on an enchanted island. In the play an ethereal creature named Ariel describes how he created havoc aboard the doomed ship before it was wrecked. Shakespeare's description closely mirrors Strachey's account of seeing Saint Elmo's fire aboard the *Sea Venture:*

> Now in the waist, the deck, in every cabin
> I flamed amazement. Sometime I'd divide
> And burn in many places—on the topmast,
> The yards and bowsprit would I flame distinctly,
> Then meet and join. Jove's lightning, the precursors
> O'th' dreadful thunderclaps, more momentary
> And sight-outrunning were not; the fire and cracks
> Of sulphurous roaring, the most mighty Neptune
> Seem to besiege and make his bold waves tremble,
> Yea, his dread trident shake.
>
> (*The Tempest,* 1.2)

Strachey wrote:

> An apparition of a little round light, like a faint Starre, trembling, and streaming along with a sparkeling blaze, halfe the height upon the Maine Mast, and shooting sometimes from Shroud to Shroud, tempting to settle as it were upon any of the foure Shrouds: and for three or foure houres together, or rather more, halfe the night it kept with us, running sometimes along the Mainyard to the very end, and then returning.[20]

In *The Tempest,* Ariel brings news of the shipwreck to the island magician, Prospero, and mentions Bermuda:

> Safely in harbour
> Is the King's ship, in the deep nook where once
> Thou called'st me up at midnight to fetch dew
> From the still-vexed Bermudas, there she's hid,
> The mariners all under hatches stowed,
> Who, with a charm joined to their summered labour,
> I have left asleep. And for the rest o'th' fleet,
> Which I dispersed, they all have met again,
> And are upon the Mediterranean float,
> Bound sadly home for Naples,

Supposing that they saw the King's ship wrecked
And his great person perish.

(*The Tempest*, 1.2)

A shipwreck (the *Sea Venture*) and the return of mariners (the remnants of the fleet) with "sad tales" of a lost king (Gates) who is later happily restored: a ready-made plot. What did Strachey think of it? He just might have seen *The Tempest* onstage.

The author of "A true reportory," for reasons unknown, traveled from Virginia to London in late October or early November 1611. He may have been sent for by the Virginia Company, he might have been ill or anxious to see his family—or both. *The Tempest* was first performed on November 1, 1611, in a special "Hallomas Night" or All Hallows' Eve performance before King James I at Whitehall. It is not impossible that William Strachey, who had sailed from Virginia on the *Prosperous* in September, was in the audience. He was living in London at that time in his old bachelor haunts, somewhere in the Blackfriars neighborhood.[21]

Strachey was using his legal training on a project for the Virginia Company: a compilation of laws titled *For the Colony in Virginea Britannia. Lawes Divine, Morall and Martiall, &c.* In its latest effort to improve conditions in Virginia, the company had decided to impose martial law. Gates, De La Warr, and Dale had gathered a body of laws for the colony, and it would be published in London in 1612. Sadly, this compilation would be William Strachey's only publication during his lifetime. He did it in hopes of advancing his career with the Virginia Company. One hopes that he also did it for money, which he would be in desperate need of for the rest of his life. In a lengthy dedication to the Virginia Company Council he wrote:

> For my paines, and gathering of them [the laws], as I know they will be right welcom to such young souldiers in the Colony who are desirous to learn and performe their duties, so I assure me, that by you [the Virginia Company Council] I shall be encouraged to go on in the discharge of greater offices by examining and favouring my good intention in this, and in what else my poore knowledge or faithfulnesse may enable me to be a servant in so beloved and sacred a business. . . .

At your best pleasures, either to returne unto the Colony, or to pray for the success of it heere.

William Strachey.[22]

In short, Strachey was looking for a job. He never got it. In London he worked on organizing and publishing his voluminous notes on Virginia—but John Smith got there first. Smith's *Map of Virginia, with a Description of the Country, the Commodities, People, Government, and Religion* was published in 1612.[23] The next year Silvanus Jourdain published the second version of his book about the Bermuda shipwreck. Strachey's *History of Travel into Virginia Britannia* was not published until 1849.

Strachey never went back to Virginia. In 1613 he was so badly in debt that he had to ask an unnamed friend for a quick loan: "Sir, Necessity, not my will, sends me unto you a borrower of 20s. if you may: this last dismal arrest, has taken from all my friends something, & from me all I had: & today I am to meet with some friends at dinner returned from Virginia, & God is witness with me I have not to pay for my dinner. All my things be at pawn."[24]

Who were the friends "returned from Virginia"? Did Strachey get the money to dine with them? No one knows. His life after his return to England fades into obscurity. His two sons were now grown. His wife Frances died sometime before 1615, when Strachey married a woman named Dorothy. How they lived and what he did until his death in 1621 is not known. He was buried at the church of St. Giles in Camberwell, in the London borough of Southwark—not far from Shakespeare's Globe Theater.[25] A copper-alloy signet ring with an eagle on its crest is among the artifacts recently unearthed at Jamestown. It is thought to have belonged to William Strachey.[26]

Laws Divine, Moral, and Martial went into effect under Deputy-Governor Thomas Dale's regime in Virginia—with emphasis on the "martial." A veteran of military service in Holland, he was a blunt middle-aged soldier known for his hot temper. He set sail for the Chesapeake with three ships in March 1611. Close behind him, a few months later, came Thomas Gates with six ships and three hundred colonists, including his wife and two daughters. Sadly, his wife died on the voyage, and a grieving Gates did not want to subject two motherless girls to the harshness of life in Virginia. They arrived in August, and Gates sent them back to England with Christopher Newport in December. That year Thomas Dale was busily making his own contributions to the harsh life in Virginia: under his regime, work gangs marched to and from work (building, farming) at the beat of a drum, and woe to him who shirked. Killing chickens or other livestock was punishable by death.[27] People who filched an ear of corn or a bunch of grapes could also be executed, as could anyone caught trading with the sailors on visiting ships. Punishments were unbelievably brutal. A man who stole some pints of oatmeal had a needle stuck through his tongue and was chained to a tree until he starved to death. Men who ran off to live with the Indians (as well they might!) were hanged, burned alive, or tortured to death on "wheels" (which broke their backs). The lucky ones were shot. Women were not exempted from punishment: Anne Laydon, pregnant with her second child, was whipped for "sewing shirts too short." She miscarried later that night.[28]

It was sometime in this first year of Thomas Dale's rule of martial law that the wife of the Reverend Richard Buck gave birth to a daughter. The scholarly clergyman named her Mara. In ancient Hebrew, *Mara* means *bitter.* In the Old Testament, Naomi takes the name *Mara* after the deaths of her husband and two sons. What personal anguish led Richard Buck to choose such a name for his first child born in Virginia can only be imagined. What did Thomas Gates, who had soldiered with Thomas Dale in the early 1600s when both served as English mercenaries for the Dutch war with Spain, think of his old companion's severe measures in Virginia? Whatever he thought, he left no written record of his opinions.

It was in the summer of 1611, when Thomas Dale had just taken charge in Virginia, and before Thomas Gates arrived to succeed him in August of that year, that the Spanish paid a surprise visit to Chesapeake Bay. Bungling on both sides—English and Spanish—would result in the deaths of two men and the imprisonment of two others. In June an unidentified caravel and a sloop came near Point Comfort, within cannon range of Fort Algernon. Capt. James Davis fired a warning shot and watched in some amazement as the sloop came nearer, dropped anchor, and three men waded onto the sandy shore. The visitors claimed to be searching for a lost Spanish munitions ship on the Virginia coast. Politely, they requested an English pilot to guide their waiting caravel into safe harbor. Captain

Davis, for reasons known only to himself, allowed John Clark, a skilled pilot, to go back with the sloop and board the Spanish caravel. But no sooner had Clark set foot on the caravel's deck than the Spaniards "hoysed upp their Sayles and Caryed the pilot quite away with them." They left the three Spaniards on shore. Davis quickly took them as prisoners and sent them upriver to Jamestown for questioning by Dale, Percy, and Strachey. The caravel sailed for Cuba with the English pilot, John Clark. He was to spend five years in Spanish jails in Havana and Madrid. On July 23, 1611, shortly after Clark's capture, officials in Havana questioned him at great length and made him sign a written deposition. The English pilot's statement gives a good idea of what the Spanish wanted most to know about Virginia: was there any gold there, and was it a base for English pirates? Clark said he had heard of gold but had not seen any. As for pirates, Clark first said he did not know if there were any, but later (perhaps under coercion) he said that "those who sail to these regions and gather there are abandoned people, who are accustomed to live by piracy."[29]

At the same time Clark was languishing behind bars in a Havana jail, the three Spaniards Captain Davis had taken into custody were being questioned in Virginia. One of them fell ill and died. The other two were held as prisoners, pending instructions from London. On December 24, 1611, Ambassador Velasco wrote to King Philip that his London sources had told him that King James was planning to return the three captives to Spanish soil by the next ship that came from Virginia. Velasco's sources were mistaken. Of the three Spaniards captured at Fort Algernon, one died in Virginia; one was held prisoner for three years, sent to England for further questioning, and finally returned to Spain in 1615; and the third Spanish prisoner was discovered to be an English pilot named Francis Limbrecke and hanged as a traitor by Thomas Dale in 1616.[30]

The Spanish visit, brief as it was, left Deputy-Governor Dale anxious. Virginia was too vulnerable to an attack by the Spanish. He wrote to the Earl of Salisbury on August 17 that he needed more support: Virginia could succeed only if it had about two thousand good men, and at present he had too many "disorder'd persons," who were profane, riotous, and likely to mutiny. Some were unfit, others sick, and of the three hundred he had brought with him, "not threescore may be called forth or employed upon any labor or service."[31] And worse yet, the Spanish now had full knowledge of Chesapeake Bay, Point Comfort, Virginia's coastal fortifications—and they had an English pilot as their prisoner. A Spanish attack could come at any time.

Meanwhile, Spain was having similar thoughts about the English. In December 1611 a caravel set out from Lisbon, supposedly bound for Cartagena, but the vessel's real orders, carried in a sealed dispatch from Philip III and not to be opened until the caravel was 40 leagues (120 miles) at sea, were to "reconnoitre Bermuda." On December 31, 1611, Ambassador Velasco wrote to King Philip about rumors of a new expedition to Virginia within the month, with "four ships, the Captain's ship of 250 tons, another of 150, and the other two of 120 each. They carry 300 men and the 60 with their wives, 8 ministers of their religion, 1000 arquebuses, 500 muskets, 30 corselets, 500 helmets, and a quantity of ammunition, all of which has been gotten ready with great secrecy, by order of the King." And, Velasco reminded Philip III, Virginia was only six days' sail from Havana.[32]

Early in 1612 the Virginia Company Council set about drafting a new charter, an expansion of the 1609 charter that would include Bermuda. One of the first records of it is the February 1612 letter of John Chamberlain, the diligent London letter writer (between 1597 and 1626 he wrote at least 179 letters, most of them to his good friend the diplomat Sir Dudley Carleton). Chamberlain was also a Virginia Company investor. The Virginia Company, Chamberlain wrote, had formed an "under companie for the trade of the Bermudes, which have changed theyre name twyse within this moneth, being first christned Virginiola . . . but now lately resolved to be called Sommer Ilands, as well in respect of the continual temporat ayre, as in remembrance of Sir George Sommers that died there."[33] But it would still be known as Bermuda.

On March 9, 1612, Sir John Digby, the English ambassador in Madrid, wrote anxiously to the Earl of Salisbury of Spanish plans to prevent a Bermuda settlement. They had recently sent a ship to reconnoiter there, but the captain reportedly could not find the islands. For his ineptitude, Capt. Diego de Avila was executed.[34] The king of Spain, said Digby, was resolved to "run any hazard with England rather than permit the English to settle in Virginia and Bermuda," and they were determined "to prevent the further growing of it."[35]

But grow Bermuda did, with its very first batch of colonists a month later. On April 28, 1612, Bermuda's appointed governor, a carpenter named

Richard Moore, set sail from England aboard the *Plough* with sixty settlers, including his wife and children. In June, while the *Plough* was under sail, Velasco wrote to King Philip that the English were sending three hundred men and sixty women to "establish a post in the Bermuda."[36] Not all of Velasco's London sources were reliable.

Governor Richard Moore and his band of colonists sighted Bermuda "betwixt nine and ten of the clock" on the morning of July 11, and by three o'clock that warm afternoon they had landed on the south side of Smith's Island, safe in Castle Harbor.[37] In about an hour Robert Waters, Christopher Carter, and Edward Chard, the three men who had stayed behind when Somers died, "came rowing down" and greeted the newcomers joyfully. They all sang a Psalm, said a prayer, "and went to supper."[38] There was plenty to eat: Bermuda's only three inhabitants until now had "an acre of good corne ripe and ready for the gatherour: numbers of pumpions, Indian beanes, many tortoises ready taken; and good store of hogge-flesh salted and made into flitches of bacon."[39]

There would be some shortages of food in the first few years, but there would be no Starving Time in this colony. And "not a man . . . sick or diseased." And no Indians. Henry Howard, the Earl of Northampton, wrote to King James in August 1612 that Bermuda's colonists would "grow more confident in the safe possession of a place which they have possessed so peaceably."[40]

As for Virginia, John Chamberlain wrote to Dudley Carleton that he feared the colony would soon "fall to the ground of itself." He blamed it on "the extreem beastly idleness of our nation, which (notwithstanding any cost or diligence used to support them) will rather die and starve than be brought to any labor or industrie to maintain themselves." Chamberlain had just heard that "two or three of the best ships that came thence bring nothing but discomfort, and that Sir Thomas Gates and Sir Thomas Dale are quite out of hart, and to mend the matter not past five dayes since, here arrived a ship with ten men who . . . fill the towne with ill reports."[41] The ship was the *Trial*, which arrived after a long and difficult voyage from Virginia. George Percy was among the passengers.

Virginia Company officials had even more reason to be "quite out of heart" in the fall of 1612, when a small book called *A Map of Virginia* appeared. It was put together, and in fact edited, by John Smith, who also wrote much of it. Friends and comrades who had been in Virginia with him and who had seen what happened there after he left wrote the rest, and, as Smith's biographer and editor, Philip Barbour, said, "Together they wrote the book telling their side of the story, and apparently against the wishes of the Virginia Company together they got it printed in Oxford."[42] There was nothing the Virginia Company could do about it. One of the most important books about Virginia ever printed, it contains, as the title promises, a historic map, with Smith's incomparable description of "the Country, the Commodities, People, Government, and Religion." But it also contains a narrative of the "Proceedings" of the colony, from the voyage of the *Susan Constant, Godspeed,* and *Discovery* in 1606 to the death of Sir George Somers in Bermuda in 1609. Here, for all of England to read, were firsthand accounts of the explorations, the confrontations with the Indians, the diseases and disasters, and the Starving Time with all its horrors. George Percy, newly returned from Virginia in the fall of 1612, must have been annoyed. He did not produce his narrative until 1625, and it was not published in his lifetime. *A Map of Virginia* made another account superfluous. William Strachey, who had been at work since 1609 on a long manuscript he called *A History of Travell into Virginia Britania,* a description of the land and the Native peoples, must have been devastated. His book by that title would not see print in his lifetime. It was published in 1849.

While Virginia languished, all London read *A Map of Virginia,* and Virginia Company officials fumed, Bermuda was about to turn a profit for its investors in its first year. At first, Robert Waters, Christopher Carter, and Edward Chard, the three men who had been the only residents of Bermuda since 1609, kept to themselves the news of something in their possession that was much more valuable than food: the three had stumbled upon "the greatest peece of Amber greece ever seen or heard of in one lumpe, being in weight fourescore [80] pound, besides divers other small peeces."[43] Ambergris, a substance produced in whales' stomachs and used in perfume making, was extremely rare and valuable. This huge lump was worth at least £9,000 sterling, at a time when an average English worker earned between £10 and £25 a year. (In present U.S. dollars, £9,000 is roughly $2,520,000.)

No wonder Waters, Carter, and Chard were not telling. They finally decided to confide in the captain of the *Plough,* Robert Davis, and the *Plough*'s master, whose name is not recorded. If the two mariners would take them and their ambergris to England, all would share in the profits. Then Christopher Carter had misgivings about this secret pact. He leaked it to Governor Moore, and things turned ugly: Moore seized the ship's master and Edward Chard and clapped them in irons. He could not do the same for Captain Davis, because the captain was aboard his ship. Moore may have let him alone because of his rank or because he happened to be a nephew of Sir Thomas Smith.[44] Whatever the reason, that was a mistake on Moore's part. Captain Davis rallied his sailors around him and declared he would free the prisoners, take the ambergris to share among themselves, and sail away. Governor Moore then gathered his colonists around him and prepared "to repulse force with force."[45]

What happened next is not recorded, but at last Governor Moore made peace with Captain Davis, the prisoners were freed, and all were reconciled. And the fortune in ambergris? John Smith's *Generall Historie* says that although Governor Moore took control of the greater part, "there was more of this Amber-greece imbeziled, than would have contented all the finders."[46] But there was more than enough to go around. Governor Moore shrewdly refrained from sending all of the ambergris at one time to England. When the Virginia Company sent another supply ship demanding a return cargo of ambergris, he refused, knowing that it was his "only lodestone to draw from England still more supplies." He doled out the ambergris in thirds over the next year, and the Virginia Company made a handsome profit from Bermuda. The ambergris sold from £3 to 32 shillings per ounce in London, for a total of £10,000 pounds sterling. One-third of this went to the company.[47] Since the early records of the Virginia Company are lost, no one knows the details, but the ambergris soon became the talk of London, not to mention Jamestown—and Madrid.

In May 1613 Diego de Molina, one of the Spanish prisoners at Jamestown, wrote to the Spanish ambassador in London that he had heard that the Bermudians had sent back to England a cargo worth "more than fifty thousand ducats." (A ducat was a twenty-four-carat gold Spanish coin.) In October that same year John Chamberlain wrote of "the greatest peece of amber [ambergris] in one lumpe that hath been heard of was found there this year, beeing as bigge as the body of a giant and answerable or resembling almost in all points saving for the want of the head and one arme: but they handled the matter so foolishly that they brake it in pieces, and the biggest they brought home was not above 68 ounces: which sells better by twelve or fifteen shillings in an ounce then that which is smaller."[48]

No more "fortunate finds" of ambergris were found, but Bermuda soon became a thriving colony, thanks to Governor Richard Moore. "Although he was but a carpenter, [these are John Smith's words] he was an excellent artist, a good gunner, very witty [clever] and industrious."[49] Moore quickly moved his colonists from Smith's Island to lay out what would become the modern town of St. George's, on the leeward side of St. George's Island. But until about 1619 the town was known as "New London."[50] Moore built a governor's residence, a "hansome house contrived into the fashion of a crosse," which "expressed him as an artist in that kind, as being nowe in his true element." He kept the precious ambergris there, and sometime during the first year the house caught fire. "The house and all that was in it, was in great danger to have bin burned to ashes, had not the governours wife herselfe (her husband being at the time abroad els wher), and some one or two more, nimbly bestirred themselves." As the number of people grew from sixty to nearly five hundred during his three-year term, Governor Moore "distributed and fitted everyone to his employment and labor." He failed to plant enough corn at first, but he managed. The worst that befell the colony was an infestation of rats in 1614, brought in a cargo of "Spanish meale" captured by a privateer named Daniel Elfrith, whose career would cause Bermuda more trouble a few years later.[51]

In Virginia, Governor Dale, planning new settlements called "hundreds" and desperately hoping to attract new "adventurers," named one of the first ones "Bermuda Hundred." Ralph Hamor thought that this project was "a business of the greatest hope, ever begun in our territories there." By 1613 there was a Bermuda City at the confluence of the James and Appomattox rivers, but it never grew into its name.[52] It is now part of the town of Hopewell, Virginia.

Bermuda's Governor Moore set the colonists there to hewing wood and sawing limestone into blocks, not just for houses but also for forts. Everyone was afraid of the Spanish: Moore, the colonists, and the Virginia Company backers all expected that a Spanish attack on Bermuda could come any day. During his three years in Bermuda, Governor Moore took no chances. He made plans for the construction of "eight or nine" forts, from one end of Bermuda to the other, to protect the islands from invaders.

By early October 1613 the first fort was ready, with "some guns," and there were "eighty persons both men and women" in residence in England's newest colony. As for Virginia, the Spanish ambassador had heard that the Virginia Company was "tired of spending so much money with no hope of profit, for the land has yielded none. They are seeking to remove the settlers to Bermuda or Ireland next spring."[53]

While Moore was building his forts, Spanish authorities were trying to get more information about Bermuda and Virginia. They moved the captive English pilot, John Clark, from Havana to Madrid for further questioning. They had interrogated him in Cuba in 1611, and now they wanted more details. In a deposition on February 18, 1613, Clark gave his Spanish captors information intended to frighten them. Virginia, he said, had a thousand men "capable of bearing arms." (It had barely four hundred people, and many of them were sick.) He also said that the English had come to Virginia to acquire land and build ships—and that with their ships "in fifteen days at most they can reach the Windward Islands [the southern islands of the Lesser Antilles, from which English ships could attack Spanish treasure fleets]." But Clark was exaggerating here, too: For a Virginia ship to reach these islands in fifteen days would mean a sail of about one hundred miles per day. Not likely. The Spanish, having extracted all they could from John Clark, decided he might still be useful. They did not release him until three years later. He returned to England in 1616. There he continued his seafaring career, and in 1620 he sailed as the master's mate aboard the *Mayflower*. Clark's Island in Duxbury Bay, Massachusetts, is named for him.[54]

At the same time Spanish officials were questioning John Clark, a great Spanish fleet was preparing to sail from Lisbon, and Sir John Digby, England's ambassador to Spain, was working diligently to find out what the Spanish intended to do about Bermuda and Virginia. He planned to send his own spies to infiltrate the Spanish navy to keep him informed. Rumors flew like seagulls: The fleet was to go to Bermuda; the fleet was bound for Virginia. Spain was seeking recruits from "all nations" except England, Scotland, and Holland.[55] These turned out to be nothing but rumors.

But in Madrid, Ambassador Digby continued to worry: on March 5, 1613, he wrote to James I that he now had doubts about Spain's ability to launch a large expedition against Virginia, but "it will be requisite that those of Virginia live in a continual expectation of being assailed, for first or last, the Spaniards will certainly attempt them." In August Digby reported that "I know both the Council of War and of State have set about the overthrowing of our plantation in the Bermudas." Digby was right about this: in June 1613 the Council of War warned King Philip that "new advices" had confirmed those that the council already had, to the effect that English pirates were fortifying themselves in Bermuda.[56] Philip rejected the Council of War's plan to send the fleet from Lisbon, but approved a voyage by Capt. Diego Ramirez to reconnoiter Bermuda and then to recommend action against it from Havana.

Ramirez already knew Bermuda well. He had spent twenty-two days there in 1603 when his treasure-laden galleon went aground. Ramirez had made a map of Bermuda and submitted a detailed description of the islands, but at the time, King Philip had seen no value in them. Now Ramirez was the expert on Bermuda, and best of all, he knew where it was.

In London the news from Virginia continued to be depressing. Ambassador Velasco relayed it to Madrid. On May 30, 1613, he wrote to King Philip that "hunger may have made an end of those people. . . . Thus they here are discouraged about this plan, on account of the heavy expenses they have incurred, and the disappointment, that there is no passage from there to the South Sea, as they had hoped, nor mines of gold or silver." Some of the bad news came from a Spanish prisoner at Jamestown. The unfortunate Don Diego de Molina, one of the Spanish mariners captured at Point Comfort in June 1611, managed to smuggle a letter to Ambassador Velasco in London. Molina wrote the letter in code and gave it to "a gentleman from Venice" at Jamestown (this person's identity remains unknown) to smuggle out in his shoe: "If you have the key to my cipher," Molina wrote to Velasco, "you can write to me in the same cipher. But this letter goes between the soles of a shoe, where it is sewed in."[57]

The letter carried in a shoe did reach Velasco, and he duly reported its contents to King Philip. It begins with a hope that Spain would soon snuff out the English colony in Virginia. There was a need "to cut short the advance of a Hydra in its infancy, since the [English] intention is the destruction of the whole West, by sea as well as on land, and I do not doubt that great results will follow, because the advantages of the place are such as to make it a rendezvous of all the pirates of Europe." Molina was also worried about Bermuda, "where it is said they have strong fortifications."

The colonists there "have little need of England, since they are . . . rich in amber [ambergris] and pearls." But in Virginia he says there was little but misery and hunger. Last year (1612) there were seven hundred people in the colony, "but only three hundred and fifty remain, because the hard work (and the scanty food) on public works kills them." Many had gone to live with the Indians. Molina was convinced that Virginia was ripe for the plucking: "And let a [Spanish] fleet come and give them a passage to that kingdom, not a single person will take up arms."[58] Molina, a ship captain himself, hoped to win his freedom and be "of some service" to his king and country. He would remain a prisoner for two more years.

In August 1613 a new Spanish ambassador took up his post in London. Don Diego Sarmiento de Acuña was wealthy, learned, and clever. At age forty-six, he was just a year younger than James I, and he soon ingratiated himself with the bookish English monarch. Acuña's portrait shows an unsmiling face with a high, round forehead, narrow jaw, and ferretlike eyes.[59] It could be the likeness of a villain, which he was, according to his enemies. For the next decade and more he would be a Machiavellian presence at the court of King James. Some said it was he who caused the beheading of Sir Walter Raleigh (for Raleigh's raids on Spain's New World lands) in 1618.

Acuña, who was made Count of Gondomar in 1617, worked tirelessly to undermine England's interests abroad, especially Bermuda and Virginia. He made good use of the "pensioners of Spain," the stable of paid English informants who fed Spain's ambassadors the latest reports and rumors. Robert Cecil, the Earl of Salisbury, had died the year before, but Acuña still had Henry Howard, the Earl of Northampton, Lady Suffolk (the wife of Thomas Howard, Earl of Suffolk, and the mother of Theophilus Howard, a member of the Virginia Company Council), Sir William Monson, and Mrs. Drummond, Queen Anne's lady-in-waiting.[60]

In Madrid Spanish officials continued to worry about Bermuda. In June 1613 Alonso Perez de Guzman, the Duke of Medina Sidonia, who had commanded Spain's fleet in the battle of the Armada, wrote that "to uproot them from that place is what is truly desirable." He told King Philip that "to cut this thread before the English take deeper root there, behooves mightily, because the place is what they may well desire, with very good havens, from which to overrun everything on the route of the fleets and armadas, because, although not within sight of this island, everything what comes from the Indies must pass to south or north of it." Another report stated that "the English who were in Virginia are seeking to settle and fortify that island [Bermuda] for obvious purposes. . . . [T]he day they establish a footing and fortify themselves there, being to windward of all the Indies, they can do very great damage in proportion to the strength they may possess."[61]

King Philip wrote a sharp reply to the reports about Bermuda: "It does surprise me that in all the years since the Indies have been discovered, no one should have thought to make certain of this island and that now so much importance is ascribed to it without even knowing for sure what enemies are there." The month of July had been proposed for sending the Duke of Sidonia's friend Ramirez to Bermuda, but that report was late in seeking royal approval, and when Philip wrote this short, undated response, July had come and gone. "Clearly, this won't do," he said. By September he received a long apology from the Council of War, which began: "Since the Indies were discovered it was always understood that Bermuda was an uninhabitable land—and its coast so dangerous, with such powerful currents and such heavy winds almost all the year round that not only has no one ventured to enter there but all have shunned the place."[62]

In an undated enclosure to another dispatch from the Council of War in the fall of 1613, a report carried disturbing news: the king of England was supposedly sending to Bermuda "twelve well equipped, strong vessels, and a great number of people, and the best guns that could be found. Engineers from England and Holland are going with them, to erect fortifications and castles." Another six vessels were going with "all sorts of live stock available in the kingdom of England." Twelve ships, plus six loaded with livestock? Ambassador Acuña's sources were not always reliable. Nonetheless, the news about Bermuda was alarming to the Spanish: "This has cheered them all and they are in high hopes that the island will be of great esteem, since nothing like this island has ever been discovered for any King of England."[63]

In London Acuña relied heavily on the letters of the Spanish spy Diego de Molina (whose release Acuña was supposed to be arranging). For example, the ambassador wrote to King Philip in October 1613 that there were only three hundred men in Virginia, "the majority sick and badly treated, because they have nothing to eat but bread of maize, with fish." That is very close to what Molina had written to Acuña's predecessor Velasco a few months earlier. But Acuña added his own flourish: "Nor do they [the Virginia colonists] drink anything but water—all of which is contrary to the nature of the English."[64]

Early the next year Acuña wrote to Philip III that the English planned to "abandon that colony [Virginia], and carry the people to Bermuda." The ambassador had heard that some members of the Virginia Company asked the king and council to "withdraw the people from there this spring, before the few survivors should die." Permission, said the ambassador, was not granted, because England looked on Virginia as a place to get rid of its unwanted population. Bermuda, on the other hand, was thriving: "Here they say that of old that country was called the land of the devils on account of the dangers of the sea, the coast and the harbour, but now this colony appears with great power." The ambassador wrote to King Philip that the island colony was prospering from "amber" (ambergris) and pearls, but he had heard that Bermuda had "certain fishes larger than dogs" that can "attack and at once, dispatch any man." But the English, he said, hoped to "catch them and clear the coast of them."[65] Bermuda had sharks. Virginia had Indians.

The Spanish Duke of Sidonia wrote to an unknown recipient in October 1613 that he had heard "from certain English masters who talked with those who came over in the vessel which reached London on August 15th from Bermuda and Virginia. They agree that there is nothing more there [in Virginia] and that the few people remaining are so dissatisfied that if they had the means to get away they would depart unquestionably."[66]

In response to London gossip about its Chesapeake colony, the Virginia Company published *Good News from Virginia* in 1613, a long sermon by the Reverend Alexander Whitaker, who painted a hopeful picture if Christian charity and hope prevailed. William Crashaw, the London clergyman, wrote a dedication to Whitaker's sermon that is almost as lengthy as the sermon. Whitaker was convinced of God's providence in the affairs of both Virginia and Bermuda, and he observed that Bermuda, "it is likely, will prove a matter of greater consequence than most men think of, and of more worth than any islands or continent discovered in our age."[67]

Later in 1613 John Chamberlain had heard some hopeful news about Virginia: "There is a ship come from Virginia with newes of theyre well dooing, which puts some life into that action, that before was almost at the last cast."[68] The ship was Thomas Dale's, and the news was that Virginia colonists had captured "the daughter of a king"—Pocahontas. In the spring of 1613 the daring Samuel Argall had sailed the *Treasurer* up the Potomac River and, with the help of another Indian king, tricked Pocahontas, now a young girl of sixteen or so, into coming aboard his ship. (Six years later Samuel Argall would take aboard the *Treasurer* another kind of captive: a contraband cargo of Africans, with even more fateful consequences for Virginia.) Argall confined Pocahontas aboard his ship and brought her back to Jamestown. With him as his interpreter was a grown-up Thomas Savage, whom Christopher Newport had given to Powhatan as a boy of fourteen in 1608 in exchange for the Indian Namontack. The plan was to hold Pocahontas for ransom: to get his daughter back, Powhatan must return all English captives and stolen weapons and throw in thirty baskets of corn besides. He did not buy into this offer.

What Pocahontas herself thought about her capture is not recorded. Argall merely refers to her as "my prisoner." But what someone else thought about her has become one of the most famous letters in American history. John Rolfe, age twenty-eight, widowed and lonely, fell in love with the captive Pocahontas. Sometime in 1614 he wrote a long letter confiding in Thomas Dale. Rolfe worried about his love for a non-Christian, "unbelieving creature," but he could not help himself. "Pocahontas," he wrote,

> To whom my hartie and best thoughts are, and have a long time bin so intangled, and inthralled in so intricate a laborinth, that I was even awearied to unwinde my selfe thereout. . . .
>
> To you therefore (most noble Sir) the patron and Father of us in this countrey doe I utter the effects of this my setled and long continued affection (which has made a mightie warre in my mediations) . . . which thus should provoke me to be in love with one whose education hath bin rude, her manners barbarous, her generation accursed, and so discrepant in all nurtriture from myselfe.[69]

But he loved her. And she wanted to become a Christian. Rolfe wrote of "her desire to be taught and instructed in the knowledge of God, her capablenesse of understanding, her aptnesse and willingnesse to receive anie good impression, and also the spirituall, besides her owne incitements stirring me up hereunto. What should I doe?"[70]

On April 5, 1614, John Rolfe and Pocahontas ("Little Mischief," her real name was Matoaka) were married. She had been baptized as a Christian and took the name Rebecca. Powhatan himself did not come to the wedding, but he must have given a grudging approval. Two of Pocahontas's brothers and "a old uncle" attended the ceremony at the Jamestown church, where Reverend Richard Buck presided.

Buck and his wife had another child sometime in 1614. This one, a boy, was Buck's first son. He named him Gershom, which in Hebrew means "stranger." It was the name of Moses's firstborn son, born in a foreign land. One wonders if Richard Buck ever hoped to see England again.

For a time, relations between the English and the Indians in Virginia took a decided turn for the better, and there was "friendly trade and commerce" with Powhatan and his subjects. For the first time in years, as John Rolfe wrote, "the people yerely plant and reape quietly; and travaile in the woodes a fowling and a hunting as freely and securely from feare of danger or treachery as in England." Thomas Dale tried to cement Indian-English relations further by asking to marry Powhatan's youngest daughter, age twelve. He sent Ralph Hamor to Powhatan with a delegation that included Thomas Savage as interpreter, to make the request. The shrewd old king refused. "His answer was, he loved his daughter as his life, and though hee had many children, hee delighted in none so much as shee, whom if he should not often behold, he could not possibly live." Powhatan's response also revealed his deep distrust of the English: if he gave another daughter to them, he could not visit her. That "he could not do, having resolved upon no termes to put himselfe into our hands, or come amongst us." He had refused to come to Jamestown for his coronation in 1608, and he did not attend Pocahontas's wedding in 1614. The emperor of the Chesapeake knew better than to put himself within the grasp of the English who were encroaching upon Virginia, his beloved *Tsenacommacah*. But he also knew better than to offend them unnecessarily. He cleverly couched his response to Deputy-Governor Dale in an old man's affection for his children: he had already given up Pocahontas, and he told Hamor to inform Dale that "I hold it not a brotherly part to desire to bereave me of my two children at once."[71]

On the occasion of this interview, Powhatan enjoyed a reunion with Thomas Savage, who was now about twenty years old. As a boy, Savage had lived with Powhatan and his people, learned their language, traveled with Newport to England, and returned to Virginia as a fluent interpreter. "My child," Powhatan said to him, "I gave you leave, being my boy, to goe see your friends, and these foure yeeres I have not seee you, nor heard of my owne man Namontack I sent to England, though many ships since have beene returned thence."[72] This conversation took place in May 1614. Somehow no one had thought to inform Powhatan that Namontack was dead, murdered by Matchumps in Bermuda in 1610. Ralph Hamor, who recorded this visit with Thomas Savage and Powhatan, and who was himself one of the Bermuda castaways, does not say what the response to Powhatan's plaintive inquiry was. Matchumps, who was now married to Powhatan's sister, was obviously not the one to tell his father-in-law what had become of Namontack. That story remains one of the small missing pieces of the Bermuda-Virginia narrative.

With the settlement of Thomas Dale's "hundreds," or privately sponsored settlements upriver at Henrico and elsewhere, colonists had moved away from the unhealthy, malaria-ridden Jamestown area, and the colony's appalling death rate went down for a time. But the Virginia enterprise was still dangerously near collapse. The problem was money, or, rather, the lack of it. The Virginia Company could not afford to keep sending supplies to a colony that sent nothing back. Seven years, no profits, and Virginia's colonists still could not be counted on to feed themselves.

In Bermuda fears of a Spanish invasion loomed larger than food supplies. Governor Richard Moore was frantically building forts to fend off Spanish ships. Spain might send them at any time. Three defense structures, all on the eastern end of Bermuda where gaps in the reefs left the land unprotected, were finished by 1614. Fortunately, Moore discovered that Bermuda had an ideal building material: limestone soft enough to be sawed into blocks that hardened after exposure to sun and air. Later on, Bermudians would build their houses of this same limestone. Moore's earliest fortifications consisted of Queen's Fort (later called Paget's Fort) on a point of land at the entrance to St. George's harbor (later called Castle Harbor), a cannon across the channel from it on Governor's Island (later Smith's Island), and "King's Castle," a platform with a cannon on Castle Island, facing the sea, the two cannons Moore had salvaged from the *Sea Venture* wreck. They were ready just in time.

On March 14, 1614, two Spanish ships appeared outside the channel to Castle Harbor on the southeast coast of Bermuda. From his newly built

King's Castle Fort, Governor Moore "himself (who was a very good gun-ner)" fired a shot, discovered that the ships were within range, and fired another shot. Then "both the shyps, cutting their maine-sayles, cast about and made quite awaye." The Bermuda colonists viewed this departure as the work of "divine providence for the good of the poore plantation" because they had "not above three quarters of a barrell of powder besides, and one onely shott." One of the ship captains, Domingo de Ulivari, later reported to his superiors that they had come upon Bermuda by accident on the way from Santo Domingo to Spain and, knowing King Philip's interest in the English in Bermuda, had thought to reconnoiter there. Captain Ulivari reported to Spain's Council of War on his visit, describing Bermuda's fortifications: "One of these looked new, built of masonry. The other, which is higher, is built of timber. They are about a hundred paces apart. In both there are some ten or twelve pieces of artillery." Ulivari had a slightly different version of his brief encounter with the Bermuda colonists: as one of his ships and a boat neared shore, "two launches of English came out to inspect them, and when they were about a musket shot off, they were invited to come aboard to talk. The English would not do so, nor would they go beyond the range of their fort's guns. The forts fired on our vessels, so they withdrew and continued their voyage."[73] Spain was still interested in Bermuda.

So were London investors. While the Virginia venture had cost forty-six thousand pounds and had yet to turn a profit, Bermuda cost twenty thousand pounds, and the ambergris found there had already brought in ten thousand pounds. More was expected. Bermuda had nearly 500 healthy colonists. Virginia had 350 colonists in 1615—but more than 900 had been buried there since its founding in 1607. In Bermuda, by con-trast, as a Bermuda clergyman, Lewis Hughes, exulted in 1615, "not one of all those threescore that beganne this Plantation was dead." Richard Norwood, one of the original Bermuda settlers, wrote proudly that Bermudians "built for themselves and their families, not tents or cabins, but more substantial houses; they cleared their grounds; and planted not only such things as would yield them their fruits in a year, or half a year, but all such, too, as would afford them a profit after certain years, &c." Virginia colonists lived in ramshackle houses and were still scrabbling to feed themselves. Bermuda was, by every measure, a success. In June 1615 a new joint-stock company called the Somers Islands Company was formed. It had 118 investors (many of whom were also Virginia Company backers) and a charter from the Crown.[74]

In the summer of 1615 the Virginia Company issued yet another publication designed to attract new investors and mollify old ones. It was called *A True Discourse of the Present Estate of Virginia, and the successe of the affaires there till the 18 of June, 1614. Together with a relation of the severall English Townes and forts, the assured hopes of that countrie and the peace concluded with the Indians. The Christening of Powhatan's Daughter and her marriage with an English-man.*[75] Who could resist such a title? Besides, a well-connected young Englishman was the author. Ralph Hamor, now age twenty-six, was the son of Ralph Hamor, a major player in the East India Company and the Merchant Tailors Company and one of the important backers of the Virginia Company. Young Hamor had impressive credentials: he was a *Sea Venture* survivor and a Jamestown resident and had succeeded William Strachey as the colony secretary. His presence on a visit to London no doubt boosted the sales of his *True Discourse.* It was reprinted twice that year. Hamor no doubt believed that the work's optimistic tone would spur investors to put their money into what had theretofore been perceived as a financial sinkhole. (He himself now had funds to invest: his wealthy father had died that year, and the younger Ralph was his only heir.)

A True Discourse began with a newsy narrative of Pocahontas's capture, courtship, and marriage (it appended a copy of John Rolfe's letter asking Thomas Dale what to do about marrying her). The second part of Hamor's work was a promotional tract describing Virginia's bounty. Peace with the Indians was a fact now that Powhatan's daughter was married to John Rolfe. To counter the "bruit of famine" rampant in London rumors about Virginia, Hamor launched into a catalog of edibles, from the deer "they kill as doe wee Beefes in England" to "wilde Turkeis, much bigger than our English," to sturgeon and porpoise in the rivers, not to mention carrots, parsnips, pumpkins, a variety of greens, and "wilde grapes in abundance al the woods over."[76]

Equally optimistic but less flowery was another Virginia report, John Rolfe's "True Relation of the State of Virginia," written in 1616 but not published during his lifetime. Its straightforward account (number of people in each of Virginia's six settlements, with a pathetic total of 351 persons) was not what the Virginia Company wanted to publicize. Rolfe probably brought it with him when he sailed to England that year with Pocahontas/Rebecca and their young son, Thomas.

Rolfe's report may not have been published, but his wife was celebrated all over London. Everyone wanted to see the "Indian princess." She and her husband dined in great houses and appeared at court. She had her portrait made, a solemn likeness in fine lace collar and richly embroidered bodice, like a proper Elizabethan lady. She had a poignant reunion with John Smith. But after this triumphal visit, she died on the way back to Virginia in March 1617. She and little Thomas and some of the others in her entourage were ill when they set sail, probably with colds or agues. Before the ship had left English waters, Pocahontas grew so ill, perhaps with pneumonia, that Rolfe asked that she be taken ashore. She drew her last breath at an inn in a small town near the waterfront. On March 21 they held a burial service for her in St. George's Church. The town was called Gravesend.

Pocahontas, the "Little Mischief," the carrier of messages, the converted Christian, Matoaka/Rebecca, the wife and mother, the liaison between English and Indian cultures, was gone. What would become of the English in Virginia now?

7

THE CONFLUENCE OF THREE CULTURES

IN THE SPRING OF 1616 the Somers Islands Company ordered Bermuda's governor, Daniel Tucker, to send to the West Indies for "negroes to dive for pearls."[1] Tucker (a former Virginia colonist and survivor of the Starving Time) gave the order, and the captain of the *Edwin* filled it as best he could: he brought back, as Nathaniel Butler noted, "one Indian and a Negro (the first thes Ilands ever had)."[2] But he was mistaken: the first African to set foot on Bermuda was a crew member of a Spanish ship captained by Diego Ramirez that was wrecked there in 1603. As Ramirez wrote in his journal, the ship's rudder was broken, and he sent a man ashore for wood to repair it:

> "Let Venturilla go ashore with an axe and cut a piece of cedar, for it must be made before we sleep." This man was a negro, and he carried a lantern. The moment he landed and went into the bush, he began to yell, so that I shouted, "The devil's carrying off the negro! Everybody ashore!" [The loud, catlike cries of Bermuda's cahow birds had long contributed to the island's reputation as the Isle of Devils.] The men jumped into the boat. At the negro's outcries and signals he made with the light and his hands, the clamour of the birds and of the men augmented. The birds, meanwhile, attracted by the light, dashed against him, so that he could not keep clear of them, even with a club. Neither could the men of the relief party.[3]

Who was Venturilla? All that Ramirez noted about him was that he was "a negro." Where was he from? Was he sent ashore at night on a dangerous mission because he was skillful and trustworthy—or because no one else could be forced to go ashore? But when Venturilla called for help, his comrades rushed to his aid, risking unknown danger themselves to save him. Nothing is known about Venturilla, but he is probably the first of his race to have set foot on Bermuda, which today has sixty-eight thousand people, about two-thirds of whom are of African ancestry. When Nathaniel Butler wrote his history of Bermuda, he had no way to know about Venturilla, and he was also unaware that two Indians, Namontack and Matchumps, had been among the 1609 Bermuda castaways. More Africans would soon arrive, and so would more Indians. Bermuda's multicultural history had begun. So had Virginia's.

In both Bermuda and Virginia, slavery was an unintended consequence, or, as one scholar called it, an "unthinking decision."[4] Its results would last for four hundred years. Spain and Portugal had been buying and selling Africans as slaves since the 1500s, but Bermuda was the first English colony in North America to import Africans as laborers. Virginia was the second. Spain's New World colonies in the Caribbean and on the mainland had been using Indians and Africans as slave laborers for more than a hundred years, since a 1503 Spanish decree allowed enslavement of the native Carib Indians.[5] Spanish traders soon began buying Africans as slaves and by 1600 had shipped as many as 150,000 of them to the plantations and mines of Spanish America.[6] By the early 1600s both Spanish and Portuguese traders were buying Africans by the thousands from native African dealers, with handsome profits for both sellers and buyers. Enslaved men, women, and children were packed into the holds of slave ships for the dreaded "Middle Passage," as the hellish voyage from Africa to America came to be called. The slave trade was on.

In the early 1600s slavery had not yet come to England's colonies, but tobacco as a money crop had. Virginians knew next to nothing about growing the leaf they saw the Indians smoking, but around 1611 John Rolfe (who was said to be an "ardent smoker") had begun experimenting with tobacco seeds from the West Indies, and by 1613 he was producing a milder tobacco that pleased the Virginians' tastes. (Among the thousands of artifacts excavated at the Jamestown fort site are numerous small clay pipes.)[7] Better yet, Virginia tobacco sold well in England. Virginia might yet turn a profit for its investors. Smoking soon became the rage in London, though King James hated it. He wrote a pamphlet called *A Counterblaste to Tobacco*, in which he said that "there cannot be a more base, and yet hurtful, corruption in a Country, than is the vile use (or other abuse) of taking Tobacco in this Kingdom, which hath moved me, shortly to discover the abuses thereof in this following little Pamphlet."

He called smoking "a custom loathsome to the eye, hateful to the nose, harmeful to the brain. dangerous to the lungs."[8] The French and Spanish had been puffing away since the 1560s. Thanks to the English market, and despite King James's dislike of smoking, tobacco growing was about to become a craze for the colonists in tiny Bermuda as well as in Virginia.

Eager Bermudians, urged by their first governor, Richard Moore, planted their first crop in 1613, when they had been there just one year and there were only one hundred men, women, and children in the entire colony. But the first tobacco harvest was disheartening: "By want of knowledge and skill in pruneinge, cureinge, and makeinge of it up," the crop was spoiled.[9] Within the next three years, practice made perfect, and by 1616 when Daniel Tucker took over as governor, Bermuda (now with five hundred colonists) produced its first sizable crop: thirty thousand pounds of marketable tobacco—and that market was growing. The tobacco boom was on.

Virginians began growing tobacco on every inch of land they could find. When Samuel Argall, Virginia's newly appointed governor, arrived at Jamestown in 1617, he was shocked to find "the market-place, and streets, and all other spare places planted with Tobacco." Jamestown's buildings had been sorely neglected in the frenzy of tobacco planting. Argall found "but five or six houses, the Church downe, the Palizado's broken, the Bridge in pieces, the Well of fresh water spoiled; the Store-house they used for the Church."[10] By 1619 the Virginians turned out twenty thousand pounds of tobacco—but they doubled that the very next year.[11] The fragrant leaf that Columbus had found the Indians smoking in the Caribbean islands was now selling in England for 18 pence to 3 shillings per pound. For ordinary folks the profits were mind-boggling. One man could work four acres by himself, and four acres of tobacco would yield fifteen hundred to two thousand pounds of tobacco. That meant a year's income of £225 to £300, at a time when the average year's income for a farmer in England was about £10 to £20. No wonder tobacco took off. If one man working a small plot alone could reap profits beyond his dreams, what could a man with more land and more workers reap? The key ingredient was workers. Where would they come from? The answer to that question was already apparent to some landowners, and it was about to open up a chapter in the histories of Bermuda and Virginia that would not close for centuries.

The coming of the first Africans to England's New World colonies can be traced in part to the activities of one man, the energetic and dashing Sir Robert Rich. At age sixteen he was made a knight of the Order of the Bath at James I's coronation, and in 1619, at age thirty-two, he became the second Earl of Warwick.[12] The Riches were aptly named: their family had one of the greatest fortunes in England. Robert Rich and his cousin Nathaniel were major players in the Virginia Company and the Somers Islands Company, and they were the largest landowners in Bermuda. When the island colony was settled, the Riches put Nathaniel's younger brother, also named Robert, in charge of the family's acreage in the new colony. This Robert Rich, a sort of poor relation, had sailed on the *Sea Venture*, spent ten months as a castaway in Bermuda, made it to Virginia in 1610, published a poem called "News from Virginia," and was now back in Bermuda, still hoping to make his fortune. He had 250 acres of his own as a gift from his brother Nathaniel. Both Sir Robert and Sir Nathaniel had interests in the Somers Islands Company, but it was the ambitious, charming Sir Robert who would devote much of his energies and fortune to colonizing activities in Bermuda and elsewhere. He would soon have a hand in the founding of Plymouth and other Puritan colonies in New England and Providence Island in the Caribbean. A staunch Puritan and member of Parliament, he would later command Parliament's fleet in the English Civil War. Sir Robert Rich was also a privateer.[13]

Like many good Englishmen, Rich passionately hated the Spanish, and to nourish that hatred he secretly paid privateers to prey on Spanish shipping. But there was a problem: England had been at peace with Spain since 1604. Privateering—the practice of issuing a commission to a ship authorizing it to attack and plunder another country's vessels at sea—was no longer permissible against Spain. But others besides Robert Rich still did it, and James I enriched his royal coffers by issuing licenses authorizing ships to capture pirates. This was a handy cover for privateers. Licensing was, as the diplomat Sir Thomas Roe wryly observed, "a common pretense of being pirates."[14] But piracy and privateering were too tempting: Spanish ships still carried fortunes in gold and silver from mines in the Americas, and now they carried another treasure from Africa to America: Africans to sell as slaves. English privateers could make a handsome profit on both kinds of cargo.

Since much of what Sir Robert Rich did to acquire Africans was illegal, the records of his involvement are sketchy. In May 1617, for example, the younger Rich, tending the family's lands in Bermuda, wrote to his elder brother Nathaniel that the colony now had "good store of neggars which Mr. Powell brought from the West Indies."[15] This was only a year after the first African and Indian had arrived in Bermuda. How many was a "good store"? The number of Africans now had clearly grown. "Mr. Powell" was John Powell, a ship captain the Riches paid to carry supplies to Bermuda, but he was also a privateer with a commission from the Dutch (who, like the English, still hated the Spanish). Powell raided Spanish ships and captured Africans, an undetermined number of whom he deposited in Bermuda. They were not the only ones. Robert Rich, the second Earl of Warwick, had other privateers in his employ, and they soon delivered other Africans to Bermuda.

Tobacco was a labor-intensive crop, and the laborers who knew best how to grow it were the Africans who had grown it in the West Indies—where Spanish slave ships had sold them to the islands' planters. There they were slaves, but once captured and taken to Bermuda, an English colony where slavery did not yet exist, what were they? Apparently, the Riches and others who used these Africans as laborers did not worry much about their workers' status. What mattered was their labor. Young Robert Rich wrote to Nathaniel in February 1618 that he planned to put one of the Africans on Nathaniel's land to plant "west endy [West Indies] plants, wherein he has good skill." In the same letter Robert Rich also asked his brother to bargain with the privateer Powell for an African named Francisco. Said Rich, "His judgment in the curing of tobacco is such that I had rather have him than all the other Negroes that be here."[16]

The histories of Bermuda's first Africans are sparse but suggestive of what lay in store for those who came after them. Francisco would soon be working on Nathaniel Rich's land, but Francisco was a servant, not a slave. By the spring of 1618 he and two other Africans—Anthony and James—were laborers on Sir Nathaniel Rich's land. Their names appear at the bottom of a list of nineteen workers that young Robert Rich sent to his brother. The Africans are the only men without surnames. They were clearly perceived as different from the white laborers, but they were not enslaved. In the summer of 1619 more Africans were about to join them.

In that same summer, one of Warwick's privateers also left some Africans in Virginia, with fateful and unintended consequences.

For many decades, scholars believed that slavery in North America began when a Dutch ship sold "20. and odd Negroes," as John Rolfe wrote, in Virginia in August 1619.[17] Nearly three hundred years later, at least one scholar had doubts: in 1898 Alexander Brown, in his history of early Virginia, wrote, "I do not know that these negroes were the first brought to the colony."[18] Brown was absolutely right. They were not the first.

The coming of the very first Africans to Virginia is still a puzzle, but some of the missing pieces have now been found. Nearly a hundred years after Brown's work, a scholar named William Thorndale discovered a 1619/20 census for the Virginia colony that lists a total of 978 people—32 of whom were Africans. This census of March 1620 shows that 32 Africans were living and working in Virginia, including the now-famous 20 who arrived in August 1619.[19] How did the others get there? How long had they been there? No records have yet been found, but as Alexander Brown reasoned quite sensibly, "The accounts which we have even of the voyages of the [Virginia] company's ships are very incomplete, and we have scarcely any idea of the private trading voyages which would have been most apt to bring such 'purchas' to Virginia."[20] In short, no one knows how or when these Africans got there or where they came from. They were part of the colony's English population in 1620: 670 able men, 119 women, 39 "serviceable" boys, and 57 younger children. Besides the 32 Africans (15 men and 17 women), there were also 4 Indians. All of them were listed as "Others not Christians in the Service of the English." All of them were "in the service of several planters."[21] Virginia's multicultural labor force had begun about the same time as Bermuda's.

What happened in 1619 once again entwines the histories of Bermuda and Virginia. The story begins in 1617, when the Virginia Company rewarded one of its loyal employees with the deputy-governorship of Virginia. The ambitious Samuel Argall, who had sailed a shorter route across the Atlantic in 1612 and was said to be "a good mariner, and a very civil gentleman," who had kidnapped Pocahontas in 1613, and who had traded up and down the coast in the *Treasurer* for the company, may also have been trading a little on the side for Samuel Argall when he was governing Virginia. The unexpected arrivals of certain Africans in Virginia and Bermuda in 1619 involved Argall in a complicated tale of three ships—the *San Juan Bautista, White Lion,* and *Treasurer*—and their illicit cargoes. Deputy-Governor Argall was now a part owner of the 130-ton *Treasurer* (Sir Robert Rich was the other owner). In 1618 Argall was supposed to send this ship up the coast to fish and trade for the Virginia colony. Instead, Samuel Argall secretly dispatched the *Treasurer* on another expedition.

Sometime in 1618 Argall sent the *Treasurer,* under the command of Capt. Daniel Elfrith, to the West Indies in search of Spanish plunder. Elfrith apparently went by way of Bermuda. He arrived there early in 1619, just as Bermuda's outgoing governor, Daniel Tucker, was leaving the islands. Tucker had served as Bermuda's governor since 1616. He was suspicious of Elfrith, who arrived unexpectedly in the *Treasurer,* supposedly "sent from Virginia to trade." Tucker warned Bermuda's deputy-governor, Miles Kendall, "to have a care of all things and beware of too much acquaintance with this ship, which hee suspected was bound for the West Indies."²² It was.

Governor Tucker was not the only one who harbored suspicions about the *Treasurer.* Argall's successor as Virginia's governor in 1619 was the former Bermuda castaway George Yeardley, and Yeardley had instructions from the Virginia Company to investigate the *Treasurer,* along with Samuel Argall's alleged mishandling of company resources. If Argall's behavior is any indication, he may have had something to hide. In April 1619 he left Virginia in some haste before Yeardley arrived. It was rumored that the Earl of Warwick (Argall's partner in ownership of the *Treasurer*) had sent a small, fast ship, the brig *Eleanor,* to help Argall escape before Yeardley arrived to question him. Yeardley's ship dropped anchor in Virginia waters on April 18, 1619, which was "but ten or twelve daies" after Argall had left.²³

Capt. George Yeardley, the young military officer who was cast away on Bermuda in 1609 and reunited with his wife at Jamestown in 1610, was now the newly knighted Sir George Yeardley, governor of Virginia. As soon as he reached Virginia he wrote to his mentor, Sir Edwin Sandys, a powerful member of both the Virginia and the Somers Islands companies, that there were rumors in Virginia that the *Treasurer* "had gone to rob the King of Spaynes Subjects by seeking Pillage in the West Indyes and that this was done by direction from my Lord of Warwick."²⁴ Yeardley was right, and his letters were about to set off a firestorm across the Atlantic.

On June 21, 1619, Sir Edwin Sandys dispatched a letter to Yeardley, praising him for sending the information about the *Treasurer* and ordering him to detain it in Virginia as soon as it returned.[25]

Meanwhile, the *Treasurer* was on the high seas, and there, in the summer of 1619, is when some pieces of the African-arrival puzzle fall into place. The *Treasurer* met another privateer, a Dutch warship called the *White Lion,* under the command of one Captain Jope. The two ships met and decided to sail in consort to hunt for Spanish ships. What very likely happened after that is documented in a long-unnoticed account book in the Spanish archives. The book contains a record of a shipment of 2,000 Africans from Portuguese Angola to Vera Cruz, Mexico, in June 1619. There were six ships, and one of them, the *San Juan Bautista,* was attacked in late July or early August 1619 by "English corsairs" (pirate ships) off the Bay of Campeche in Mexico. The attackers boarded the vessel and found no gold, but a shipment of 350 Africans. According to the account book, the English ships left *San Juan Bautista* "with only 147 [Africans]." It is impossible to say how many Africans the English raiders took, for "there were many sick aboard, and many had already died."[26]

Were these "English corsairs" the *Treasurer* and the *White Lion*? The evidence is compelling: Spanish records for 1618–22 show that only one slave ship of those bound for Vera Cruz from Angola was attacked by corsairs. It was the *San Juan Bautista.* The corsairs' captains (Elfrith and Jope) divided what they could take of the Spanish slaver's lucrative human cargo between them and made for Chesapeake Bay. The *Treasurer* stopped at Point Comfort, and the *White Lion* sailed upriver to Jamestown. There the "dutch ship" (the *White Lion*) brought "twenty Negroes." At least, that was the only mention of this transaction in Rolfe's report a few months later.

In 1619 John Rolfe had many things on his mind. Pocahontas had been dead for two years, and the Rolfes' young son, Thomas, now four years old, was still being cared for by Rolfe's brother in England. (John Rolfe, who died in 1622, never saw his son again.) Sometime in 1619 Rolfe, the thirty-four-year-old widower, took a new wife who was less than half his age: she was Jane Pierce, the daughter of William and Joan Pierce. Jane and her mother had come to Virginia in 1609, when Jane was four years old. Now she was fourteen, perhaps fifteen. Her father had arrived with the Bermuda castaways in 1610. A young bride was not all John

Rolfe had to think about. In 1619 representative government came to Virginia: the General Assembly, the first legislature in the New World, met at Jamestown for the first time from July 30 to August 4. The legislators—two men elected from each of eleven settlements plus Governor Yeardley and six council members—used the Jamestown church for a legislative chamber. On the opening day, July 30, the Reverend Richard Buck, who had performed the wedding ceremony for Pocahontas and John Rolfe, offered the first prayers for the first representative government in the New World.

Richard Buck had a son born in 1616, whom he named Benoni, which means "son of my sorrow." In the Old Testament the dying Rachel gives that name to her newborn son. Buck's wife may have been near death at the time. Either she recovered or Buck remarried after her death, for the record shows another child born in 1620. This one was named Peleg, after the son born to Eber in the book of Genesis. The name means "division." Perhaps the quarrels that began in the Virginia Company in 1620 prompted the choice of that name.[27] Early in 1620, besides his new wife and the new legislature, John Rolfe was also concerned about something else, and he wrote a letter about it. That letter has become one of the most quoted and most studied documents in American history. It was addressed to Sir Edwin Sandys, who had replaced Sir Thomas Smith as the treasurer of the financially troubled Virginia Company, and it described the arrival of some Africans in Virginia:

> About the latter end of August [1619], a Dutch man of war of the burden of 160 tons arrived at Point Comfort, the commander's name Capt Jope, his pilot for the West Indies one Mr. Marmaduke an Englishman. They met with the Treasurer in the West Indies, and determined to hold consort . . . but in their passage lost one the other. He [Jope] brought not any thing but 20. and odd Negroes, which the governor and cape merchant [George Yeardley and Abraham Piersey] bought for victuals (whereof he was in great need as he pretended) at the best and easiest rate they could. He had a large and ample commission from his Excellency [Maurice, the Count of Nassau and commander of the Dutch army], to range and to take purchase [that is, to attack Spanish ships] in the West Indies.
>
> Three or four days after [afterward] the *Treasurer* arrived.[28]

Rolfe was not telling the whole story here. He failed to mention that the *Treasurer* also carried Africans—but these passengers were ill-gotten gain. This ship had been licensed as a privateer under a commission from the Italian Duke of Savoy, but the duke had recently settled his differences with Spain, so the *Treasurer*'s commission as a privateer was no longer valid. Now the *Treasurer,* captained by Daniel Elfrith, owned by Robert Rich, Earl of Warwick, and Capt. Samuel Argall, former deputy-governor of Virginia, was sailing as an unlicensed privateer in the service of Sir Robert Rich. Governor Yeardley, Sir Edwin Sandys, and other members of the Virginia Company Council wanted an investigation.

Once the *Treasurer* reached Virginia, Captain Elfrith did not sail upriver to Jamestown. Instead, he cautiously sent word to the deputy-governor, whom he expected to be Samuel Argall. (Elfrith had been at sea since April 1619 and had no way of knowing that Argall was no longer in charge.) At this point Governor Yeardley dispatched John Rolfe, along with Rolfe's father-in-law, William Pierce, and another planter, William Evans, to summon Elfrith to Jamestown. Meanwhile, the *Treasurer* (whose reputation apparently had preceded it) received a cool welcome downriver at Point Comfort, where "they would not offer them a vessel of water." "Before we got down," said Rolfe, "he [Elfrith] had set sail and was gone."[29] Rolfe was not telling the whole truth here, either.

The *Treasurer* departed from Point Comfort "in a very distressed state." The exact date is not known and the records are nonexistent, but there is evidence that Elfrith sold some of his Africans in Virginia before he left. William Pierce numbered among his servants an African woman who was still in his household six years later. Her name was Angelo, and in a census of 1625 she was listed as having come on the *Treasurer.* But the *Treasurer,* battered by years of wind and waves and privateering, did not put out to sea after 1620, so Angelo must have arrived on or before that date. Angelo was very likely not the only African who arrived on the *Treasurer.* The 1625 census record shows that William Tucker, the commander at Point Comfort, had in his household a young African couple, William and Isabel, and their child, William. There is, unfortunately, no record of the ship that brought them or the date they arrived. But Tucker was commander at Point Comfort when the *Treasurer* stopped there in 1619.[30]

A few weeks after Daniel Elfrith and the *Treasurer* left Virginia, Temperance Yeardley's cousin John Pory, who succeeded John Rolfe as secretary of Virginia under Yeardley's governorship, wrote to the English diplomat Sir Dudley Carleton on September 30, 1619, mentioning the August visits of the Dutch ship and the *Treasurer*: but like Rolfe, Pory was careful not to reveal too much. He did not say a word about any Africans. Pory was also careful to place the blame for the *Treasurer*'s doings firmly on Samuel Argall: "He [Argall] more for love of gain the root of all evil, than for any true love he bore to this plantation, victualled and manned her [the *Treasurer*] anew, and sent her . . . to ravage the Indies."[31] Pory did not mention the involvement of the rich and powerful Earl of Warwick—but that was soon to become an issue that split the Virginia Company.

Samuel Argall, meanwhile, was back in England, hoping to clear his name. Sometime in 1620 Temperance, Lady Yeardley, gave birth to the couple's first son, and his proud parents named him Argall. The relationship between George Yeardley and Samuel Argall is something of a mystery, but it obviously had once been a close one. Now Samuel Argall's reputation was in danger on both sides of the Atlantic.

When Captain Elfrith left Virginia in August 1619, he made for Bermuda, arriving at an unknown date in the fall of that year. In January 1620 John Dutton, a newly hired Bermuda employee of Sir Robert Rich, wrote to his employer that Elfrith had brought "29 Negroes, 2 chests of grain, 2 chests of wax, a small quantity of tallow, little worth." These "29 Negroes" were very likely the remaining contraband Africans that Elfrith had captured from the *San Juan Bautista*. It fell to John Dutton to dispose of these Africans. (The younger Robert Rich, who ordinarily would have been the one to take charge, was then in England, where he had just married Dutton's sister, Elizabeth. The newlyweds came back to Bermuda in 1620, but Robert Rich became ill of "some form of pestilence" on the voyage. He died in Bermuda in September or October 1620, leaving his young wife and an infant son named Nathaniel.)[32]

Dutton's letter to the Earl of Warwick goes on to say that the Africans Elfrith brought were "all disposed of, for this yeere to the use of the [Somers Islands] Companie, till truly knowne in whom the right lyeth." Here was a can of worms indeed: these were contraband Africans, stolen from a Spanish ship by an English vessel owned by the Earl of Warwick. To cover for his employer, the clever Dutton proposed to blame the *Treasurer*'s part owner Samuel Argall instead. Dutton says that "I, dealinge with Elfred and the Purser . . . found plainely how your Lordship was ingaiged in the

bussines, which though I sawe, I spaireingly confessed how easy a matter it might be, for Cap. Argall . . . to abuse so noble a nature."[33] In short,
Dutton proposed to keep the Earl of Warwick's name out of it.

So did Sir Nathaniel Rich, the earl's cousin. Sir Robert Rich's involvement with the stealing of Spanish property must be kept secret at all costs
if he was to stay clear of the Tower of London—or worse. And most of all,
no one wanted the Spanish ambassador to find out. But everyone knew
that Don Diego de Acuña, Count Gondomar, had secret English sources.
For several months in 1620 Warwick's fate hung by a thread: too many
people knew about his connection with the *Treasurer*. Bermuda's governor, Nathaniel Butler, wrote to the earl in October 1620 that members of
the *Treasurer*'s crew were still in Bermuda. Butler said that he would like
to send them home, but if they were not paid well, they threatened to "go
to the Spanish ambassador and tell all."[34]

In the end it was not the sailors from the *Treasurer* but Sir Edwin
Sandys who told. He had received Governor Yeardley's incriminating
documents accusing Warwick of piracy, and as the newly elected chief
officer of the Virginia Company, Sandys could hardly conceal them from
the other members of the company's council. But before he submitted the
documents, he did what he could: he "blotted my Lord of Warwicks name
out of these letters and anything that might directly touch him."[35]

When the Virginia Company's council met, charges and counter-
charges flew, and corporate chicanery at the highest levels prevailed. Sir
Edwin Sandys argued that the Privy Council must be informed that an
English ship had been engaged in piracy against the Spanish. Both Sir
Robert Rich and Sir Nathaniel Rich conferred with Sandys. They con-
sulted others at the London house of Henry Wriothesley, the Earl of
Southampton. Wriothesley was a member of both the Virginia Company
Council (he would become treasurer in 1620) and the Privy Council. He
promised to work privately with other members of the Privy Council "so
to quiett any further search or stirring in the business."[36]

If the accusations against Robert Rich, Earl of Warwick, were made
public, the damage to him and to the Virginia Company would be immea-
surable. But Sir Edwin Sandys argued that not only the Privy Council but
also the "Spanish Agent," as he referred to Ambassador Gondomar, must
be informed. The company's council, at odds over policy and finances
even before the *Treasurer* issue, split into hostile camps: the Sandys faction

and those loyal to the Riches and former treasurer Sir Thomas Smith. The Rich cousins closed ranks against Sandys, and Sir Nathaniel Rich used his lawyer's skill to write a long defense of the Earl of Warwick. Sir Nathaniel shrewdly skirted the issue of his cousin's guilt or innocence. Instead, he placed the blame on treasurer Sandys—for mishandling the whole affair.

After weeks of acrimonious wrangling, the matter was finally settled, complete with the cover-up. The involvement of Sir Robert Rich, Earl of Warwick, privateer, was concealed. On March 7, 1620, the Privy Council's register noted:

> This day Sir Edwin Sandys Governor and others of the Virginia Company represented unto this Board—That whereas a ship called The Treasurer sent out to the West Indies at such time as Captain Argall was Governor of Virginia, and had committed offences against the Spaniards, and that by public letters from that colony that act was by them disavowed. So likewise the Council and Company of Virginia here joined in the letter disclaiming of the same of which their especial care to give unto his Majesties friends and allies no offence their letters gave good allowance and approbation. It appeared also by the letters produced at the Board, that the Spanish Agent [Count Gondomar] here residing hath received satisfaction for the offence aforesaid.[37]

If the matter had not been laid to rest, as Sir Nathaniel Rich wrote, the Earl of Warwick would "have ben brought under the clutches of the King of Spayn, which perhaps would not have ben remooved till he had crusht him to peices." Then, in a pointed allusion to the Spanish ambassador and his circle of paid informers, Sir Nathaniel continued: "For God deliver me from the clemencye of the Spanyard and from them that would enforme for him, especially without giving any warning."[38]

Warwick was safe, and, as it turned out, so was Argall, but hostilities in the Virginia Company remained at a dangerous level. The Riches and their supporters hated the Sandys faction, and vice versa. Sandys hated the Riches and claimed that Bermuda was infested with pirates: "Now as the case stands the Somers Islands are much frequented with men of war and pirates, with whom the inhabitants there are grown in great liking, by reason of the commodities they bring unto them. . . . And the ship called the *Treasurer* belonging to Captain Argall, after her robbing of the

Spaniard, is there entertained and diverse men of war set out to the same end are there refreshed."[39] Sandys was telling the truth, and he feared that Spain would retaliate against Bermuda and Virginia.

Sir Edwin Sandys was not alone in his concerns: John Pory wrote to Dudley Carleton that Virginians were afraid of "some attempte of the Spaniard upon us, either by waye of revenge, or by way of prevention." But the powerful Rich family and others who hated Spain looked upon piracy as a legitimate and profitable pursuit. The pro-Warwick Earl of Southampton replaced Sandys as treasurer of the Virginia Company in the summer of 1620, but the change was nominal: Sandys and his supporters continued as a strong force on the company's council. Bermuda's governor, Nathaniel Butler, wrote to Nathaniel Rich in October 1620 complaining of "the continuall brangles and perpetuall disputes you have amongst you in your Courts."[40] Butler could afford to be condescending, since Bermuda was controlled by the Somers Islands Company, not the Virginia Company.

Even before the *Treasurer* controversy, troubles in Virginia were causing troubles in the Virginia Company. The colony founded in 1607 had yet to produce a return for its investors, and long after the Starving Time, people were still desperately hungry. When Sir Edwin Sandys replaced Sir Thomas Smith in 1619 as the company's treasurer, conditions in Virginia grew worse. To revive the fragile colony, Sandys's idea was to send more colonists—but not necessarily more supplies and food. He saw to it that company publications promised a new life of peace and plenty for all who went there and convinced hundreds of people to emigrate. From 1619 to 1623 under Sandys's leadership, four thousand hopeful new colonists set sail for Virginia. Nearly three thousand of them died there. Sir Edwin Sandys was said to be "a popular man, a great speaker, and of wise estimation," but his judgment about Virginia led to disaster. Sandys's opponents in the Virginia Company accused him of sending thousands of people to their deaths by false propaganda and "cozening ballads." Sandys, in turn, claimed that Virginia's enemies (the anti-Sandys faction in the Virginia Company) had spread rumors "to stain and blemish that country, as being barren and unprofitable."[41] A recent biography defends Sandys: "He may often have been misguided, and toward the end of his tenure his behavior was shabby, but one cannot denigrate the high-mindedness of his aims and hopes."⁴² But aims and hopes did not keep Virginia colonists from dying by the hundreds.

The strife in the Virginia Company affected another colonizing venture: a group of English Puritans in Holland had begun negotiations with the Virginia Company to arrange a migration to America. They received a patent from the company in June 1619, but that was before the storm over the *Treasurer*. In May 1620 one of the Holland Puritans' agents came to London, only to discover that no progress had been made. He wrote disappointedly that the cause was the factional quarrels within the company, "which are such that ever since we came up no business could by them be dispatched."⁴³ William Bradford and others had to seek support elsewhere, and the *Mayflower* did not sail for America until September 6, 1620. Its master's mate and pilot was John Clark, who had spent five years in Spanish jails after he was captured at Jamestown in 1611. Among the *Mayflower*'s 102 passengers was Stephen Hopkins, the Bermuda castaway who had tried to start a mutiny against Sir Thomas Gates. Hopkins had spent two years in Virginia, found it not to his liking, and now was casting his lot with the Pilgrims. His first wife, Mary, and one of his daughters, Elizabeth, had died, and he was sailing with his second wife, Elizabeth (she would give birth to a son named Oceanus on the voyage), and his three children. The older ones, Constance, now fourteen, and Giles, twelve, were with him in Bermuda. They had a little half-sister named Damaris, about a year old.⁴⁴ After trying Bermuda and Virginia, the hard-to-please Stephen Hopkins made a life for himself and his family in New England. He died there in 1644 at age sixty-three.

As the 1620s began, there were troubles brewing in Virginia as well as in London. Pocahontas and Powhatan were both dead (she in 1617 and her father the year after), and, though the English did not realize it, an era had ended. Opechancanough, whom John Smith had once held by the hair, was now the emperor of the Chesapeake tribes, and he was secretly planning a daring attack upon the English. On the surface, peace and friendship reigned. In 1621 the Virginia Company officials noted that the Virginia colonists "all write so confidently of their assured peace with the Salvages, there is now no more feare nor danger either of their power or trechery, so that every man planteth himselfe where he pleaseth, and followeth his business securely." Indians came freely into Jamestown and visited outlying settlements, bringing produce and deerskins to trade for trinkets and metal tools. Now proficient with English muskets, some Indians even hunted game for the colonists. Opechancanough had an English-style house with a front door that locked with a key. It pleased him no end, and he was fond of locking and unlocking it "a hundred times a day." As for the residents of Jamestown and the settlements scattered up and down the James River, the Indians were "as frequent in their houses as themselves."[45]

In London John Smith, who knew the Indians better than most Englishmen, scented danger. He let the Virginia Company officials know that it disturbed him to hear how the Indians had been "taught the use of our armes, and imploied in hunting and fowling with our fowling pieces," while the English colonists rooted in the ground after tobacco "like Swine." Smith worried that "the Salvages that doe little but continually exercise their bow and arrows, should dwell and lie so familiarly amongst our men," while the colonists, he observed, "practised little but the Spade." Planting tobacco and thinking of little else, the English in Virginia had let down their guard against the Indians, "being so farr asunder, and in such small parties dispersed, and neither Fort, exercise of armes used, Ordnances mounted, Courts of guard, nor any preparation nor provision."[46] The Virginia colony, Smith thought, was asking for trouble.

The Virginia Company, meanwhile, may also have unknowingly angered Opechancanough with a scheme to start a fur trade with Indians living near the "De La Ware River" at the north of Chesapeake Bay. The ruler of most of Virginia's Indians preferred to keep trade with the English among his people and within his bounds, not to share it with distant Indians such as the powerful Susquehannas to the north. Such trade was a distinct threat to his power. News of the new fur-trade plan reached the Virginia colony (and Opechancanough) in 1621 and early 1622. It was one more reason for the ruler of the Chesapeake to plot against the English.[47]

On the morning of March 22, 1622, the Indian attack that John Smith had worried about in 1619 came to pass: Opechancanough launched an audacious Indian uprising in Virginia that surprised and killed nearly four hundred men, women, and children.

> On the Friday morning that fatall day, . . . as at other times they
> came unarmed into our houses, with Deere, Turkies, Fish, Fruits, and
> other provisions to sell us, yea in some places sat downe at breakfast

with our people whom immediately with their owne tools they slew most barbarously, not sparing either age or sex, man woman or childe, so sudden in their execution, that few or none discerned the weapon or blow that brought them to destruction. . . . [N]ot being content with their lives, they fell again upon the dead bodies, making as well as they could a fresh murder, defacing, dragging, and mangling their dead carkases into many peeces, and carrying some parts away in decision, with base and brutish triumph.[48]

March 22, 1622, marked the end of peaceful relations between English and Indians in Virginia for generations. A report prepared that year for the Virginia Company said of the Indians: "Now we have just cause to destroy them by all means possible."[49] Before 1622 had ended, John Smith proposed to the Virginia Company that he take a hundred soldiers and thirty sailors to the devastated colony and either persuade the Indians to "leave the country" or "bring them into fear and subjection."[50] The company refused. They had no funds for such a project. The Indians and the English in Virginia would not be at peace for another half century.

Indians were not the only problem for the Virginia Company. By now it was clear that Sir Thomas Smith's leadership from 1607 to 1619 had been a financial disaster. One of Smith's most vociferous critics was Governor Nathaniel Butler of Bermuda, who wrote about the Virginia colony's long history of "slack and lame supplyes of former times (which always came droopeingly on)." Two public lotteries in 1613 and 1615 had failed to bolster the company's finances. Funds were unaccounted for, and by the 1620s the company was nearing bankruptcy. Sir Edwin Sandys's leadership made matters worse: the more people the company sent to Virginia, the more people died. Hostilities between Sandys and his supporters and the Thomas Smith contingent rankled, and accusations flew. As Nathaniel Butler said of the company, "All their meetings and consultations seemed rather cockpits than courts." Many people thought, as John Smith wrote, that "if there be such defects in the government, and distress in the colony, it is thought by many it has been too long concealed."[51] Since the change in leadership in 1619, company officials had tried in vain to account for expenses during Sir Thomas Smith's tenure. Some records had evidently been lost—perhaps deliberately. The Virginia Company's days were numbered.

In 1623 Nathaniel Butler, who had just ended his term as governor of Bermuda, visited Virginia on his way back to England and wrote a scathing exposé of conditions in the colony. "The Unmasked Face of Our Colony in Virginia" declared that disease and death ravaged the place. Conditions there were so awful, he said, that people died "under hedges" and were left unburied. Butler's vitriolic attack provoked more charges and countercharges, one of which claimed that Butler was lying, because there was "no hedge in all Virginia."[52] Besides all this, the warring factions had not forgotten their enmity over the *Treasurer*.[53] Some people wanted James I to take over the Virginia Company and make Virginia a royal colony. One of them was Count Gondomar, who tried to use his influence with the Lords of Trade to ask the Virginia Company to surrender its patent.

In the midst of this controversy, to criticize the Smith administration of the Virginia Company, some of the Virginia colonists, many of whom had been there since 1607, wrote their own history of what had happened during those twelve years. The Virginia Assembly's document contained a shocking catalog of the horrors that had taken place in the Starving Time: Many people "digged holes in the earth and there hid themselves till they famished." Others turned to cannibalism. The story of the man who killed and ate his wife was only one instance. "Many besides fedd on the Corps of dead men, and one who had gotten unsatiable, out of custome to that food could not be restrayned untill such time as he was executed for it."[54] This report was signed by Governor Francis Wyatt, the six council members, and the twenty-two members of the assembly.

On November 17, 1623, an ominous move was made in London: the royal commissioners for Virginia ordered the Virginia Company to surrender a "locked trunk" that contained all of the company's records. But Nicholas Ferrar, a member of Parliament and brother of the Virginia Company's deputy treasurer, John Ferrar, had anticipated this seizure. Six months earlier he had hired a clerk and set him to copying all of the records.[55] Ferrar gave the copies to the Earl of Southampton in midsummer 1624, but they disappeared. Some of the documents wound up in Thomas Jefferson's library at Monticello, and when he sold his collections to the Library of Congress in 1815, they were preserved there for future scholars. The original records of the Virginia Company from 1606 to 1619 have never been found.

Meanwhile, Bermuda officials were conducting a search of a different kind, to locate all of the Africans who had been illegally brought there. Besides the twenty-nine Africans Elfrith left in Bermuda in 1619 and the fourteen others that acting governor Miles Kendall claimed were found "floating on the seas," an unknown number of other Africans were living in Bermuda in the 1620s, most probably brought in by the Earl of Warwick. They were much prized as workers, and Governor Butler wrote with satisfaction that they were "a most necessary commoditie for these Ilands." Like their counterparts in Virginia, they left few footprints in the historical record. But as late as 1623 the new governor, John Harrison, ordered the islands' sheriff to "make diligent search for all those Negroes that belong unto the Earl of Warwick which have been brought unto these parts by Capt Kirby and Capt Elfrey [Elfrith]."[56] Where were they? They were supposed to be working on English lands, growing tobacco.

These Africans numbered more than forty, and they were the reason for the first law dealing with Africans in the English colonies. Bermuda had its own representative government a year after Virginia's (its first session was August 1, 1620), and in 1623 the Bermuda Assembly passed the first law in the English colonies concerning Africans. It was entitled "An Act to restrain the insolencies of the Negroes." "Insolencies." Not a word about slavery.[57]

The law was obviously a response to existing conditions, and it strongly suggested that the Africans in Bermuda were doing as they pleased. They were stealing "pigs, potatoes, poultry and other fruit and things." One imagines them feasting merrily, if furtively, on the incriminating evidence. Even bolder, they were arming themselves to "prevent such as should pursue to apprehend them." The law accused them of carrying "cudgels and other weapons and working tools, very dangerous." Armed Africans were clearly intimidating to other colonists. Besides, these Africans were competitors in commerce: they were trading tobacco for other goods, perhaps with sailors from visiting ships, and with other Bermudians. To control these "insolencies," the law penalized masters, not servants: the act made masters responsible for any "negro" who wore "any weapon" in the daytime, was discovered walking "abroad at any undue hour in the night time," or ventured onto land other than his place of residence. Masters would have to make "full recompense" for goods stolen or damages done by an African in their employ. This law also forbade Africans to trade without the consent of a master. And the punishment for the guilty party? It was to be "corporal punishment" of an unspecified nature, inflicted "as the law requires" or as the officer in charge should "think fit." The punishments apparently did little to prevent the crimes: this 1623 law, with minor changes in wording, would be periodically reenacted by Bermuda's lawmakers for the next hundred years.

In a few more decades colonial officials in Bermuda and in Virginia would have to adapt to a system that no one had foreseen. As more Africans came, they eventually became servants—not for seven or ten years—but for life. Slavery in North America did not happen overnight; it evolved gradually, and by the opening years of the eighteenth century, slavery in Bermuda and Virginia, as well as in England's other colonies, would be locked into law. But Virginia and Bermuda were where it began.[58]

In the 1620s an unknown number of Africans were living and working in both Bermuda and Virginia, but they were not slaves. There were no laws defining them as such, and they were not referred to as slaves. They lived and worked among other servants in English fields and gardens, houses, and barns. In the larger society the first few years of relationships between Africans and English in both Bermuda and Virginia are mostly undocumented. The earliest public records are Bermuda's 1623 law about "insolencies" and the Virginia census surveys of 1619 and 1625. In 1619 there were thirty-two Africans, but in 1625 there were only twenty-three. What became of the nine who were missing? No one knows. There is no record of any Africans being killed in the Indian uprising of 1622.

In the census of Virginia households in 1625 the colony's African population numbered eleven men, ten women, and two children, all in the households of some of the colony's wealthiest planters.[59] The lives of these Africans, the first of thousands who would come to the English colonies in America, are mostly unrecorded. Some of them have names noted in the census; most do not. The household of Abraham Piersey, the cape merchant who, with Governor Yeardley, had accepted the twenty Africans from the Dutch ship in August 1619, had forty servants in all in 1625. They included seven Africans: "4 Negro Men, 1 Negro Woman, 1 Negro Woman and a young child of hers." No diaries, no letters, exist to tell later generations what their lives were like.

Eight Africans—three men and five women—were in the service of Governor Yeardley in James City. These, like those belonging to

Abraham Piersey, probably came from the Dutch ship. Their names are not recorded.

William Tucker, the commander at Point Comfort, had eighteen servants in 1625, including three Africans and an Indian—who are named and listed as "baptized": "Anthony Negro," "Isabell Negro: and William their child," and "William Crashaw an Indian." He must have been given that name in honor of the English clergyman William Crashaw. No record of him exists apart from this census, and he was the only Indian listed in the service of an English household in 1625. Was he also among the four unnamed Indians who were listed as servants in planter households in the census of 1619? Like the lives of Virginia's first Africans, the lives of these Indian servants are without documentation.

The 1625 census yields only scraps of information about Africans in the other households: William and Joan Pierce, John Rolfe's in-laws, had seventeen servants in all, but "Angelo a Negro Woman in the Treasurer" was their only African servant in 1625. Lord De La Warr's younger brother, Francis West, who was now age thirty-six, had come back to live in Virginia after absconding to England with a boat during the Starving Time. He was living on Virginia Company land at Elizabeth City, and he had six servants, five men and a woman. Among them was "John Pedro, a Negro aged 30" who came on the *Swan* in 1623. Richard Kingsmill, who lived near Jamestown, had four servants, three men and a woman. One of the men was "Edward a Negro." How and when Edward came to Jamestown is not known. Edward Bennett, who lived at Warraskoyack, near Nansemond, had twelve servants, including "Antonio a Negro" who had come to Virginia aboard the *James* in 1621. The next year "Mary a Negro Woman" arrived on the *Margaret & John*.

These are tantalizing scraps of information about twenty-three people. Only eight of them had names listed in the census. Only Angelo, Antony, Mary, and John Pedro had records with information about when they arrived in Virginia. But it is clear that the *Treasurer* and the *White Lion* were not the only ships bringing Africans to the colony by the 1620s. The two children, little William on the Tucker plantation and the unnamed child in the Piersey household, were very likely born in Virginia. What became of these people? No one knows. There is one exception: Antonio and Mary on Edward Bennett's plantation, a couple whose story has been told over and over.[60]

Antonio was lucky enough to find a wife a year after he began work on Bennett's plantation. Perhaps Bennett bought Mary with that in mind. Antonio and Mary eventually had four children. Somehow the couple acquired their freedom, and Antonio became Anthony Johnson, a free man and a landowner. By the 1650s he owned 250 acres in Northampton County, Virginia. Even more remarkable for an African in Virginia at the time, he had at least one servant—an African man named John Casor. Was Anthony Johnson's experience common, or were there others like him? If so, their stories have been lost. Legal records account for Anthony Johnson's presence in Virginia's history, and the path he cleared from servant to landowner proves that such a thing was possible: there was a brief window of time before slavery drew the lines between those who were free and those who were not.

How many Africans were in Bermuda by the 1620s is impossible to say. A census taken in 1622 lists a total population of 806 people (413 men and 393 women), but it does not include "the Negroes" or the servants working on the public lands.[61] A true accounting of the number of servants, both white and black, would have revealed to the Somers Islands Company the numbers of Africans illegally brought there by Warwick and others. Among the Africans were Francisco and James, who had been working on Nathaniel Rich's land since 1617. In the 1620s they both had wives, and they were living and working independently as tenants, just as white servants did, turning over the tobacco they raised to their landlords. In 1629 Francisco and his wife, Antonia, were working for the Somers Islands Company and earning wages. They worked for a master, but they were not slaves. There is no evidence to indicate that they were slaves or that they were any less free than Bermuda's white indentured servants. Like Anthony and Mary in Virginia, Francisco and James and their wives managed to make a life for themselves and to enjoy limited access to a legal system that would eventually close them in.[62]

In the first generation of contact between English and Africans, the Africans in service to planters in Virginia and in Bermuda ate and slept and worked alongside English servants, and both groups may have received much the same treatment. All were indentured, or bound, to serve a master for a certain length of time, but there was one crucial difference: the English servants had written contracts, "indentures," promising them freedom in a certain number of years, usually seven to ten; the

Africans in Virginia had none. In Bermuda some Africans and Indians did have indentures, but theirs were different. The earliest are in a collection of indentures ranging from 1636 to 1661. The wording is similar to those for other servants, with one telling, fateful difference: for most Africans and Indians, the specified length of servitude in Bermuda was "4 score and 19"—or ninety-nine years. But under the letter of the law, they were not enslaved.

In the 1620s there were no laws that used the word *slavery* in Virginia or in Bermuda. Bermuda's earliest legal records show that the word *slave* was applied without regard to race. In 1617 a white man was sentenced to be "a slave unto the colony" for aiding a faction critical of Governor Daniel Tucker, and at that same assize court, "Symon, the Negro" was "condemned to be a slave to the Colony during the Governor's pleasure" for assaulting a child whose race is not specified.⁶³ Here the word *slave* meant a laborer who was obliged to work for the governor on the public lands. Governor Nathaniel Butler used the word *slave* when he wrote to Nathaniel Rich in 1621, referring to the contraband Africans left there in 1619: "Thes Slaves are the most proper and cheape instruments for this plantation that can be, and not safe to be any wher but under the Governour's eye."⁶⁴ Or Butler may have been using *slave* in a figurative sense, in the way that Shakespeare had Hamlet call himself a "rogue and peasant slave." Other laborers—English, African, and Indian—were servants bound or hired to serve a certain master, but they were not enslaved. In Virginia, as in Bermuda, a legal definition of slavery was slow in evolving, and the gate to freedom was ajar. In both colonies the fateful transition from servitude to slavery would not begin until the second generation of contact between English, Africans, and Indians.⁶⁵

The seventeenth-century convergence of Indian, African, and English cultures in Bermuda and Virginia ended in death for some, slavery for others, and racism that refused to die. But as the years passed, that same convergence inspired some to study, some to seek freedom, and some to work for justice.

In 1624 the Virginia Company was dissolved, and Virginia became a royal colony. Bermuda remained under the control of the Somers Islands Company until 1684, when it, like Virginia, became a royal colony. Unlike Virginia, Bermuda kept its ties to Great Britain. Today it is a member of the British Commonwealth. In less than a hundred years, Virginia and twelve other English colonies in North America would declare their independence from England's royal government and become the United States of America.

Slavery ended in Bermuda in 1834, when slavery was abolished in all of Great Britain's possessions. Slavery ended in the United States in 1865, when the Civil War was over.

In the early 1600s, for nearly two decades, Virginia and Bermuda were the only English colonies in the New World. Here, for the first time, English, Indians, and Africans had to learn to live together. After four hundred years, there is still much to learn.

NOTES

INTRODUCTION

1. Lorri Glover and Daniel Blake Smith, *The Shipwreck That Saved Jamestown: The "Sea Venture" Castaways and the Fate of America* (New York: Henry Holt, 2008); Hobson Woodward, *A Brave Vessel: The True Tale of the Castaways Who Rescued Jamestown and Inspired Shakespeare's "The Tempest"* (New York: Viking, 2009); Kieran Doherty, *"Sea Venture": Shipwreck, Survival, and the Salvation of the First English Colony in the New World* (New York: St. Martin's Press, 2007).

1. THE WRECK OF THE *SEA VENTURE*

1. On the changing Atlantic world and the race for colonization, see Bernard Bailyn, *Atlantic History: Concepts and Contours* (Cambridge: Harvard University Press, 2006); Robert Applebaum and John Wood Sweet, eds., *Envisioning an English Empire: Jamestown and the Making of the North Atlantic World* (Philadelphia: University of Pennsylvania Press, 2005); David Armitage and Michael J. Braddick, eds., *The British Atlantic World, 1500–1800* (Basingstoke and New York: Palgrave Macmillan, 2002); and Peter Mancall, ed., *The Atlantic World and Virginia, 1550–1624* (Chapel Hill: University of North Carolina Press, 2007). See also E. K. Chatterton, *English Seamen and the Colonization of America* (London: Arrowsmith, 1930); April Lee Hatfield, *Atlantic Virginia: Intercolonial Relations in the Seventeenth Century* (Philadelphia: University of Pennsylvania Press, 2004); and Karen Ordahl Kupperman, *The Jamestown Project* (Cambridge: Harvard University Press, Belknap Press, 2007).

2. Don Pedro de Zuñiga to King Philip III, March 28, 1608, in *The Genesis of the United States,* by Alexander Brown, 2 vols. (1890; reprint, New York: Russell and Russell, 1964), 1:147.

3. Paul C. Allen, *Philip III and the Pax Hispanica, 1598–1621* (New Haven: Yale University Press, 2000), 10 (quote), 150. See also Charlotte Andrews, "Spanish Connections . . . ," *Maritimes: The Magazine of the Bermuda Maritime Museum* 19, no. 1 (2006): 3–4.

4. For a biographical sketch of Zuñiga, see Brown, *Genesis,* 2:1067.

5. Irene A. Wright, "Spanish Policy toward Virginia, 1606–1612: Jamestown, Ecija, and John Clark of the *Mayflower,*" *American Historical Review* 25, no. 3 (1920): 448n1.

6. Henry Wilkinson, ed., "Spanish Intentions for Bermuda, 1603–1615, As Revealed by Records in the Archives of the Indies, Seville, Spain," *Bermuda Historical Quarterly* 7, no. 2 (1950): 52; Brown, *Genesis,* 1:44.

7. Zuñiga to King Philip III, January 24, 1607, in *The Jamestown Voyages under the First Charter, 1606–1609,* ed. Philip L. Barbour, 2 vols. (Cambridge: Hakluyt Society, 1969), 1:70.

8. Allen, *Philip III,* 3.

9. Philip III to Zuñiga, June 1607, in *Genesis,* by Brown, 1:103; Zuñiga to Philip III, October 8, 1607, ibid., 1:121.

10. Quoted in William M. Kelso, *Jamestown: The Buried Truth* (Charlottesville: University Press of Virginia, 2006), 41.

11. Zuñiga to Philip III, June 26, 1608, in *Genesis,* by Brown, 1:172.

12. On Newport, see Kenneth R. Andrews, "Christopher Newport of Limehouse, Mariner," *William and Mary Quarterly,* 3rd ser., 11 (1954): 28–41; and David B. Quinn, "Christopher Newport in 1590," *North Carolina Historical Review* 29 (1952): 305–16.

13. John Smith, *A True Relation of such occurrences and accidents of note, as hath happened in Virginia since the first planting of that Collony, which is now resident in the South part thereof, till the last returne* (London, 1608), in *The Complete Works of Captain John Smith,* ed. Philip L. Barbour, 3 vols. (Chapel Hill: University of North Carolina Press, 1986), 1:33, 47.

14. Brown, *Genesis,* 1:184 (quote); Russell Shorto, *The Island at the Center of the World: The Epic Story of Dutch Manhattan and the Forgotten Colony That Shaped America* (New York: Doubleday, 2004), 22–23, 31.

15. Zuñiga to Philip III, September 10, 1608, in *Genesis,* by Brown, 1:195. For more on this map and a color illustration of it, see Kelso, *Jamestown: The Buried Truth,* 11–12. See also Philip L. Barbour, "The Earliest Reconnaissance of the Chesapeake Bay Area: Captain John Smith's Map and Indian Vocabulary," *Virginia Magazine of History and Biography* 79 (1971): 280–302.

16. Wright, "Spanish Policy," 450; Philip III to Zuñiga September 23, 1608, and Zuñiga to Philip III, November 8, 1608, in *Genesis,* by Brown, 1:196.

17. George Chapman, Ben Jonson, and John Marston, *Eastward, Ho!* (London, 1605), in *English Drama, 1580–1642,* ed. C. F. Tucker Brooke and Nathaniel Burton Paradise (Boston: D. C. Heath, 1933), 416 (3.3); Sir Walter Cope to Lord Salisbury, August 12, 1607, in *Jamestown Voyages,* ed. Barbour, 1:108; Zuñiga to Philip III, March 5, 1609, in *Genesis,* by Brown, 1:243–47 (quote on 246).

18. John Smith, *The Generall Historie of Virginia, New-England, and the Summer Isles . . . ,* in *Complete Works of John Smith,* ed. Barbour, 2:191, 187.

19. London Council, "Instructions given by way of Advice," between November 20 and December 19, 1606, in *Jamestown Voyages,* ed. Barbour, 1:52; Nathaniel Butler, *The Historye of the Bermudaes or Summer Islands,* ed. J. H. Lefroy (London: Hakluyt Society, 1882), 11. The original is an unsigned manuscript at the British Museum (Sloan MS, no. 750). It was written by Nathaniel Butler, governor

of Bermuda from 1620 to 1622. For a new edition, see C. F. E. Hollis Hallett, ed., Butler's "Historye of the Bermudas": A Contemporary Account of Bermuda's Earliest Government (Bermuda: Bermuda Maritime Museum Press, 2007).

20. For the portrait and biographical sketch of Thomas Smith, see Vernon A. Ives, ed., The Rich Papers: Letters from Bermuda, 1615–1646: Eyewitness Accounts Sent by the Early Colonists to Sir Nathaniel Rich (Toronto: University of Toronto Press, 1984), 392–93.

21. Nova Britannia: Offering Most Excellent Fruites by Planting in Virginia (London, 1609), http://etext.lib.virginia.edu/etcbin/jamestown-browse?id=J1051, 21, 23. On Symonds, Crashaw, and the Virginia Company's 1609 public relations campaign, see James Horn, A Land as God Made It: Jamestown and the Birth of America (New York: Basic Books, 2005), 138–41.

22. Broadside copy enclosed in Zuñiga's letter to Philip III, March 5, 1609, in Genesis, by Brown, 1:248–49. Brown says, "I doubt if a single original [of the broadside] remains" (249n).

23. Zuñiga to Philip III, March 15, 1609, in Jamestown Voyages, ed. Barbour, 2:254–55. See also Kelso, Jamestown: The Buried Truth, 41.

24. Zuñiga to Philip III, April 1, 12, 1609, in Jamestown Voyages, ed. Barbour, 2:258, 259.

25. "The Second Charter," in Genesis, by Brown, 1:228n.

26. Gabriel Archer, "The description of the now-discovered river and country of Virginia, with the likelihood of ensuing riches by England's aid and industry," Public Record Office, London, CO1/1-53, printed in Jamestown Narratives, Eyewitness Accounts of the Virginia Colony: The First Decade 1607–1617, ed. Edward Wright Haile (Champlain, Va.: Roundhouse, 1998), 119–21.

27. S. G. Culliford, William Strachey, 1571–1621 (Charlottesville: University Press of Virginia, 1965), 100–101.

28. Ibid., 93–94. Strachey borrowed thirty pounds in June 1608. But in 1609 he lacked "present money" to lend to a friend in debt. On Strachey, see also Woodward, Brave Vessel (see introduction, n. 1).

29. William Strachey, "A true reportory of the wracke, and redemption of Sir Thomas Gates Knight; upon, and from the Ilands of the Bermudas: His comming to Virginia, and the estate of that Colonie then, and after, under the government of the Lord La Warre, July 15, 1610, written by William Strachey, Esquire," in Captain John Smith with Other Narratives of Roanoke, Jamestown, and the First English Settlement of America, ed. James Horn (New York: Library of America, 2007), 979–1037.

30. Virginia Company letter to Capt. Thomas Holcroft, May 29, 1609, in Genesis, by Brown, 1:317; Council of Virginia, A True and Sincere Declaration of the purposes and ends of the plantation begun in Virginia . . . (London, 1609 or 1610), ibid., 1:345; Zuñiga to Philip III, March 15, 1609, in Jamestown Voyages, ed. Barbour, 2:255.

31. For a biographical sketch of Gates, see Haile, Jamestown Narratives, 46–47.

His portrait is reproduced on 380. For Somers, see 61–62 and his portrait on 444.

32. Henry Wilkinson, *Adventurers of Bermuda: A History of the Island from Its Discovery until the Dissolution of the Somers Island Company in 1684* (London: Oxford University Press, 1933), 42.

33. "Gabriel Archer, from Virginia, to an unknown friend, 31 August 1609," in *Jamestown Voyages*, ed. Barbour, 2:279.

34. Wilkinson, *Adventurers of Bermuda*, 50.

35. John Stowe, *Annales; or, A Generale Chronicle of England from Brute until the present yeare of Christ 1580*, ed. Edmond Howes (London, reprinted in 1592, 1601, 1605, 1615, and 1631), quoted in Wilkinson, *Adventurers of Bermuda*, 40. In 1621 the Virginia Company gave Newport's widow thirty-five hundred acres in Virginia. See Brown, *Genesis*, 2:958.

36. Strachey, "A true reportory," 979. Unless otherwise noted, the rest of the quotations from Strachey in this chapter are to be found in "A true reportory," 979–87.

37. Ibid., 979.

38. This account of the fleet's voyage is in a lengthy Council of Virginia document hastily assembled in the fall of 1609, when news of the *Sea Venture*'s loss reached London: *A True and Sincere Declaration of the purposes and ends of the plantation begun in Virginia . . .* , in *Jamestown Narratives*, ed. Haile, 356–71 (quote on 364).

39. Strachey, "A true reportory," 979.

40. Thomas Gates's report is quoted in Council of Virginia, *A True Declaration of the estate of the colony in Virginia, with a confutation of such scandalous reports as have tended to the disgrace of so worthy an enterprise* (London, 1610), in *Jamestown Narratives*, ed. Haile, 468–77 (quote on 471).

41. Strachey, "A true reportory," 980.

42. Letter to the British Admiralty in 1628, quoted in Samuel Eliot Morison, *The European Discovery of America: The Northern Voyages, A.D. 500–160* (New York: Oxford University Press, 1972), 131–32.

43. Thomas J. Oertling, *Ships' Bilge Pumps: A History of Their Development, 1500–1900* (College Station: Texas A&M University Press, 1996), 6–7.

44. Strachey, "A true reportory," 980.

45. Haile, *Jamestown Narratives*, 350; Strachey, "A true reportory," 980. Strachey says they towed the pinnace astern until the storm came. Gabriel Archer wrote that an unnamed pinnace left the fleet six days out from England and that Michael Philes was its master. Gabriel Archer has him as "Matthew Fitch." See "31 August 1609. Gabriel Archer, from Virginia, to an unknown friend," in *Jamestown Voyages*, ed. Barbour, 1:280.

46. Strachey, "A true reportory," 980.

47. Silvanus Jourdain, *A discovery of the Barmudas, otherwise called the Ile of Divels, by Sir Thomas Gates, Sir George Summers, and Captayne Christopher Newport, with Divers others, set forth for the love of my country and also for the Good of the plantation in Virginia,* in *Memorials of the Discovery and Early Settlement of the Bermudas or*

Somers Islands, 1515–1685, by J. H. Lefroy, 2 vols. (1877; reprint, Toronto: University of Toronto Press, 1981), 1:14–21. Lefroy's *Memorials,* a two-volume collection of letters, journals, minutes, and court records dating from the 1500s through the 1680s, has become the essential source for early Bermuda's history.

48. Smith, *Generall Historie,* 2:347.

49. Strachey, "A true reportory," 983.

50. Ibid., 986. Somers refers to "140 men & woemen." Jourdain has "150 men." See Lefroy, *Memorials,* 1:10, 16.

51. Strachey, "A true reportory," 981–84.

52. Ibid., 985.

53. Jourdain, *A discovery of the Barmudas,* 1:15; Strachey, "A true reportory," 986.

54. Herrera's narrative, quoted in Wilkinson, *Adventurers of Bermuda,* 24; Jourdain, *A discovery of the Barmudas,* 1:15.

55. Smith, *Generall Historie,* 2:348.

56. Strachey, "A true reportory," 990, 986.

57. On the *Sea Venture* wreck, see A. J. Wingood, "*Sea Venture:* An Interim Report on an Early 17th Century Shipwreck Lost in 1609," *International Journal of Nautical Bermuda* (1990); *Navigational Chart, North Atlantic Ocean: Bermuda Islands* (London: Admiralty Charts and Publications, 1996); and J. Maxwell Greene, "Bermuda (Alias Somers Islands): Historical Sketch," *Bulletin of the American Geographical Society* 33, no. 3 (1901): 220–42. For a native Bermudian's account of the *Sea Venture* wreck and other hurricanes in Bermuda, see Terry Tucker, *Beware the Hurricane!* (Bermuda: Island Press, 1966). See also W. S. Zuill, *The Story of Bermuda and Her People,* 3rd ed. (London and Basingstoke: Macmillan Education, 1999).

2. Bad Blood at Jamestown

1. A. L. Rowse, *The Expansion of Elizabethan England* (London: Macmillan, 1955), 229.

2. James P. C. Southall, "Captain John Martin of Brandon on the James," *Virginia Magazine of History and Biography* 54 (January 1946): 21–67; Samuel M. Bemis, "John Martin, Ancient Adventurer," *Virginia Magazine of History and Biography* 65, no. 2 (1957): 209–21.

3. For the council members' qualifications compared to Smith's, see Barbour, *Complete Works of John Smith,* 1:lxvii (see chap. 1, n. 13).

4. Philip L. Barbour, *The Three Worlds of Captain John Smith* (Boston: Houghton Mifflin, 1964), 109.

5. John Smith, "The Proceedings of the English Colonie in Virginia, [1606–1612]," in *Complete Works of John Smith,* ed. Barbour, 1:207. For an account of the authorship of this document, see 1:193–97.

6. Smith's own version is in *The True Travels, Adventures, and Observations of Captaine John Smith* (1630), ibid., 3:123–241 (quote on 236). See also Alden T. Vaughan, *American Genesis: Captain John Smith and the Founding of Virginia* (Boston: Little, Brown, 1975), 25–26; and Kelso, *Jamestown: The Buried Truth*, 131 (see chap. 1, n. 10).

7. Smith, "Proceedings of the English Colonie," 1:205–7, 2:139n2.

8. The fort is described in Kelso, *Jamestown: The Buried Truth*, 55–78.

9. Ibid., 55.

10. Smith, "Proceedings of the English Colonie," 1:209–10; Vaughan, *American Genesis*, 31.

11. Percy, "Observations gathered out of a discourse of the plantation of the southern colony in Virginia by the English, 1606, Written by that honorable gentleman, Master George Percy," in *Captain John Smith*, ed. Horn, 933 (see chap. 1, n. 29).

12. Kelso, *Jamestown: The Buried Truth*, 123–39.

13. Barbour, *Three Worlds*, 104.

14. Edward Wingfield, "A Discourse of Virginia," in *Captain John Smith*, ed. Horn, 960.

15. Smith's letter of fall 1608 was added to his *Generall Historie*, published in 1624. The original is not extant. Scholars disagree on whether the published letter was a copy or a rewritten version. Barbour, *Complete Works of John Smith*, 2:187–90.

16. Smith, *True Relation*, 1:47 (see chap. 1, n. 13).

17. Smith, "Proceedings of the English Colonie," 1:175n10.

18. Smith, *Generall Historie*, 2:150 (see chap. 1, n. 18).

19. Ibid., 1:150–51. See also A. J. Leo Lemay, *Did Pocahontas Save John Smith?* (Athens: University of Georgia Press, 1992).

20. Pocahontas descriptions are in Smith, *True Relation*, 1:93; William Strachey, "The Indians of Virginia," an excerpt from Strachey's *Historie of Travell into Virginia Britania*, in *Captain John Smith*, ed. Horn, 1030.

21. Daniel K. Richter, "Tsenacommacah and the Atlantic World," in *Atlantic World and Virginia*, ed. Mancall, 31n3 (see chap. 1, n. 1); Applebaum and Sweet, *Envisioning an English Empire*, 75 (see chap. 1, n. 1). On Smith's Virginia voyages, see Helen C. Rountree, Wayne E. Clark, and Kent Mountford, eds., *John Smith's Chesapeake Voyages, 1607–1609* (Charlottesville: University Press of Virginia, 2007).

22. Smith, *Generall Historie*, 2:114–15. The literature on Indians and English colonists is abundant. See, for example, James Axtell, *Natives and Newcomers: The Cultural Origins of North America* (New York and Oxford: Oxford University Press, 2001); Karen Ordahl Kupperman, *Indians and English: Facing Off in Early America* (Ithaca: Cornell University Press, 2000); Daniel K. Richter, *Facing East from Indian Country: A Native History of Early America* (Cambridge: Harvard University Press, 2001); Frederic W. Gleach, *Powhatan's World and Colonial*

Virginia: A Conflict of Cultures (Lincoln: University of Nebraska Press, 1997); Rountree, Clark, and Mountford, *John Smith's Jamestown Voyages;* Helen Rountree, *Pocahontas, Powhatan, Opechancanough: Three Indian Lives Changed by Jamestown* (Charlottesville: University Press of Virginia, 2005); and Helen Rountree and E. Randolph Turner III, *Before and After Jamestown: Virginia's Powhatans and Their Predecessors* (Gainesville: University Press of Florida, 2002).

23. Brown, *Genesis,* 1:184–85.

24. Strachey, "The Indians of Virginia," 1087. Strachey believed that Powhatan had killed the surviving Roanoke colonists. On the "lost" colonists, see Helen Rountree, *Pocahontas's People: The Powhatan Indians of Virginia through Four Centuries* (Norman: University of Oklahoma Press, 1990), 20–22; and Michael Leroy Oberg, *Dominion and Civility: English Imperialism and Native America, 1585–1685* (Ithaca: Cornell University Press, 1999), 55–56.

25. Smith, "Proceedings of the English Colonie," 1:216.

26. Ibid., 219.

27. Smith, *Generall Historie,* 2:186.

28. Ibid., 187n3.

29. The text of Smith's letter is in *Generall Historie,* 2:187–90.

30. Smith, "Proceedings of the English Colonie," 1:237.

31. Alden T. Vaughan, *Transatlantic Encounters: American Indians in Britain, 1500–1776* (Cambridge: Cambridge University Press, 2006), 126n27.

32. Smith, *Generall Historie,* 2:192.

33. Ibid., 192–99, narrative of Smith's voyage through Pocahontas's rescue of him and his men.

34. Ibid., 196.

35. Ibid.

36. Ibid., 198–99.

37. Ibid.

38. Ibid., 201–6, for Smith's visit to Opechancanough.

39. Ibid., 201.

40. Ibid., 208.

41. Ibid., 208, 212. On the well and other construction, see Kelso, *Jamestown: The Buried Truth,* 19.

42. Smith, *Generall Historie,* 2:210.

43. Ibid.

44. Ibid., 211; Kelso, *Jamestown: The Buried Truth,* 99.

45. Smith, *Generall Historie,* 2:211.

46. Ibid., 213.

47. Ibid., 212.

48. Ibid.

49. Ibid., 213.

50. Ibid., 214.

51. Kelso, *Jamestown: The Buried Truth,* 95.

52. Smith, *Generall Historie,* 2:213.

53. Ibid., 216.

54. Ibid., 216–17.

55. "Gabriel Archer to an unknown friend, August 31, 1609," in *Jamestown Voyages,* ed. Barbour, 1:281, 282.

56. Ibid., 282.

57. Council of Virginia, *True and Sincere Declaration,* 360 (see chap. 1, n. 30).

58. "Gabriel Archer to an unknown friend," 1:282.

59. Smith, *Generall Historie,* 2:221.

60. Ibid.

61. Ibid., 222, 223.

62. Smith, "Proceedings of the English Colonie," 1:272. This account was published in London in 1612 and in Smith's *Generall Historie* in 1624. See Barbour, *Complete Works of John Smith,* 2:223. The accounts of the accident are identical. The distance by water from Powhatan Village to Jamestown was sixty-eight miles, according to Lyon G. Tyler, ed., *Narratives of Early Virginia, 1605–1625* (New York: Charles Scribner's Sons, 1907), 196n1.

63. George Percy, "A Trewe Relacyon," in *Captain John Smith,* ed. Horn, 1096–97. See also William L. Shea, *The Virginia Militia in the Seventeenth Century* (Baton Rouge: Louisiana State University Press, 1983).

64. David S. Shields, "The Genius of Ancient Britain," in *Atlantic World and Virginia,* ed. Mancall, 489–509 (quote on 403). Shields argues that Smith, so severely injured that he was unable to father children, turned to writing instead.

65. Brad Bowden, M.D., in response to the author's medical query about Smith's accident, said, "The inguinal area is full of nerves, blood vessels and lymph glands. It is also possible to injure the intestines and bladder in that area. The explosion would cause physical destruction of tissue in addition to the thermal burn. No doubt the tissue destruction and subsequent scarring would have been disfiguring, making relations embarrassing or difficult. It quite possibly could have made him unable to function sexually or, at least, infertile."

66. John Smith, *New England's Trials* (1622), in *Complete Works of John Smith,* ed. Barbour, 1:434.

3. Troubles in Paradise

1. Barbour, *Jamestown Voyages,* 1:58n (see chap. 1, n. 7).

2. Jourdain, *A discovery of the Barmudas,* 1:16 (see chap. 1, n. 47).

3. Smith, *Generall Historie,* 2:348 (see chap. 1, n. 18).

4. Strachey, "A true reportory," 992–93 (see chap. 1, n. 29).

5. The account of the murder, ibid., 1008–9.

6. Smith, *Generall Historie,* 2:349; Butler, *Historye of the Bermudaes,* 14 (see chap. 1, n. 19).

7. Smith, *Generall Historie,* 2:347; Silvanus Jourdain, *A Plaine description of the Barmodas now called sommer Ilands . . . with an addition of more ample relation of divers other remarkeable matters concerning those Ilands . . . lately sent from thence by one of the Colonie . . .* (London, 1613).

8. Strachey, "A true repertory," 1000.

9. Jourdain, *A discovery of the Barmudas,* 1:16.

10. Strachey, "A true repertory," 995.

11. Ibid., 995–96.

12. Jourdain, *A discovery of the Barmudas,* 1:17; Strachey, "A true repertory," 993, 996.

13. Jourdain, *A discovery of the Barmudas,* 1:19; Strachey, "A true repertory," 992–93.

14. Strachey, "A true repertory," 991–92 (on the palmetto trees); Jourdain, *A discovery of the Barmudas,* 1:17.

15. Strachey, "A true repertory," 993.

16. Smith, *Generall Historie,* 2:348; G. Daniel Blagg, *Bermuda Atlas and Gazetteer* (Dover, Del.: G. Daniel Blagg, 1997), 89.

17. Smith, *Generall Historie,* 2:349; Strachey, "A true repertory," 994.

18. Strachey, "A true repertory," 996–97.

19. Jourdain, *A discovery of the Barmudas,* 1:17.

20. Strachey, "A true repertory," 994–95.

21. Smith, *Generall Historie,* 2:342.

22. Strachey, "A true repertory," 995.

23. Jourdain, *A discovery of the Barmudas,* 18.

24. Strachey, "A true repertory," 991.

25. Ibid., 997.

26. Smith, *Generall Historie,* 2:349.

27. Strachey, "A true repertory," 990.

28. Ibid., 1008.

29. Smith, *Generall Historie,* 2:339, 344; Strachey, "A true repertory," 990.

30. Jourdain, *A discovery of the Barmudas,* 1:20. On Bermuda's undersea terrain and harbors, see Edward C. Harris, *Bermuda Forts, 1612–1957* (The Keep, the Old Royal Naval Dockyard, Bermuda: Bermuda Maritime Museum Press, 1997), 37–40; David B. Quinn, "Bermuda in the Age of Exploration," *Bermuda Journal of Archaeology and Maritime History* 1 (1989): 4; U.S. Coast Guard and Naval Historical Center, "Bermuda Triangle Fact Sheet," August 12, 1996, http://www.sartori.com/nhc/frames/faqs/faq8–1.html; and Margaret Palmer, *The Mapping of Bermuda: A Bibliography of Printed Maps and Charts, 1548–1970,* ed. R. V. Tooley, 3rd ed. (London: Holland Press Cartographica, 1983).

31. Strachey, "A true repertory," 1001–2.

32. Ibid., 1008.

33. Ibid., 990.

34. Ibid., 1000.

35. Jourdain, *A discovery of the Barmudas,* 1:19.

36. Blagg, *Bermuda Atlas and Gazetteer,* 101.

37. Jourdain, *A discovery of the Barmudas,* 1:20–21.

38. Butler, *Historye of the Bermudaes,* 9; Strachey, "A true reportory," 989.

39. Strachey, "A true reportory," 1008.

40. Ibid., 1009–10.

41. Ibid., 1002.

42. Ibid., 1001–2.

43. Ibid., 1000.

44. The account of Stephen Hopkins's trial, ibid., 1002–3.

45. Smith, *Generall Historie,* 2:350; Purchas, *Hakluytus Posthumus,* 4:1771 (see chap. 1, n. 29); Van Meterin's *Historie,* quoted in Woodward, *Brave Vessel,* 208 (see introduction, n. 1); Smith, "Proceedings of the English Colonie," 1:216 (see chap. 2, n. 5).

46. The account of this conspiracy is in Strachey, "A true reportory," 1003–5.

47. Ibid., 1004.

48. Ibid., 1005.

49. Ibid.

50. Ibid., 1006.

51. Ibid.

52. Ibid., 1007.

53. Ibid.

4. The Starving Time

1. Robert Applebaum, "Hunger in Early Virginia: Indians and English Facing Off over Excess, Want, and Need," in *Envisioning an English Empire,* ed. Applebaum and Sweet, 209 (see chap. 1, n. 1); John Smith, "A Map of Virginia," in *Complete Works of John Smith,* ed. Barbour, 1:162–63 (see chap. 1, n. 13); excerpt from a lost document by Edward Wingfield, in Purchas, *Hakluytus Posthumus,* quoted in Haile, *Jamestown Narratives,* 202 (see chap. 1, n. 26); Robert Beverly, *History,* quoted in Helen Rountree, *The Powhatan Indians of Virginia: Their Traditional Culture* (Norman: University of Oklahoma Press, 1989), 50.

2. Applebaum, "Hunger in Early Virginia," 216.

3. For an account of the known women at Jamestown, see Virginia Bernhard, "'Men, Women, and Children' at Jamestown: Population and Gender in Early Virginia," *Journal of Southern History* 58, no. 4 (1992): 599–618.

4. Kelso, *Jamestown: The Buried Truth,* 80–81 (see chap. 1, n. 10).

5. Smith, *Generall Historie,* 2:225 (see chap. 1, n. 18); Strachey quoted in Kelso, *Jamestown: The Buried Truth,* 25.

6. "Memoranda of Henry Percy in 1607–1608," quoted in Brown, *Genesis of the United States,* 1:178 (see chap. 1, n. 2). See also John W. Shirley, "George Percy at Jamestown, 1607–1612," *Virginia Magazine of History and Biography* 17, no. 3 (1949): 227–43.

7. Alexander Brown, *The First Republic in America* (Boston: Houghton Mifflin, 1898), 97.

8. Smith, *Generall Historie,* 2:223.

9. Ibid.

10. Smith, "Proceedings of the English Colonie," 1:197–98, 272 (see chap. 2, n. 5); Smith, *Generall Historie,* 2:223.

11. Smith, "Proceedings of the English Colonie," 1:274; Smith, *Generall Historie,* 2:206.

12. Smith, "Proceedings of the English Colonie," 1:264; Smith, *Generall Historie,* 2:213.

13. Smith, "Proceedings of the English Colonie," 1:272.

14. Gabriel Archer, "Letter," in *Jamestown Voyages,* ed. Barbour, 2:283 (see chap. 1, n. 7); John Ratcliffe, "Letter to Salisbury, 4 October 1609," ibid., 284.

15. Smith, "Proceedings of the English Colonie," 1:273–74.

16. Ibid., 274.

17. Ibid.

18. Barbour, *Jamestown Voyages,* 2:253; Zuñiga to Philip III, December 10, 1609, ibid., 286.

19. Smith, "Proceedings of the English Colonie," 1:272.

20. Emmanuel van Meteren, *Historical Commentaries relating to the Netherlands* (London, 1610), quoted in Barbour, *Jamestown Voyages,* 2:278.

21. For biographical information about George Percy, see Mark Nicholls, "George Percy's 'Trewe Relacyon': A Primary Source for the Jamestown Settlement," *Virginia Magazine of History and Biography* 113, no. 3 (2005): 214–19. There were rumors that Percy married a woman named Anne Floyd while he was at Jamestown, but no evidence of such a woman or a marriage has been found.

22. Seymour V. Connor, "Sir Samuel Argall: A Biographical Sketch," *Virginia Magazine of History and Biography* 59 (April 1951): 236, 238.

23. On the food supply and starvation at Jamestown, see Smith, "Proceedings of the English Colonie," 1:273, 275–76; Smith, *Generall Historie,* 2:225, 232–33; and Percy, "A Trewe Relacyon," 1099–1100 (see chap. 2, n. 63).

24. Zuñiga to Philip III, December 10, 1609, in *Jamestown Voyages,* ed. Barbour, 2:286.

25. Brown, *First Republic,* 109; Brown, *Genesis of the United States,* 1:354.

26. Smith, *Generall Historie,* 2:231.

27. Percy, "A Trewe Relacyon," 1101. Percy's narrative did not see print until 1922, when it appeared in *Tyler's Quarterly Historical and Genealogical Magazine* 3 (April 1922): 59–82. In 2005 a carefully transcribed version supplanted the 1922 publication. Nicholls's "George Percy's 'Trewe Relacyon,'" 212–75, is based on the

original manuscript in the Elkins Collection of the Free Library of Philadelphia. The Nicholls transcription is the one used by James Horn in the work cited above and in this book.

28. Quoted in Nicholls, "George Percy's 'Trewe Relacyon,'" 219. George Percy died in 1633.

29. Smith, *Generall Historie*, 2:232.

30. Percy, "A Trewe Relacyon," 1097, 1098.

31. Ibid., 1098.

32. Ibid.

33. Wilkinson, *Adventurers of Bermuda*, 46 (see chap. 1, n. 32); Smith, *Generall Historie*, 2:190.

34. Smith, *Generall Historie*, 2:232.

35. Percy, "A Trewe Relacyon," 1099.

36. Ibid.

37. Ibid.

38. Ibid., 1099–1100.

39. Smith, *Generall Historie*, 2:233.

40. Kelso, *Jamestown: The Buried Truth*, 89–90, 92.

41. Smith, *Generall Historie*, 2:232; "A Brief Declaration of the plantation of Virginia during the first twelve years, when Sir Thomas Smith was governor of the Company, and down to this present time. By the Ancient Planters now remaining alive in Virginia" (1624), in *Jamestown Narratives*, ed. Haile, 895–96; Percy, "A Trewe Relacyon," 1100.

42. Biographical sketch, quoted in Brown, *Genesis of the United States*, 2:1037.

43. Velasco to Philip III, June 14, 1610, ibid., 1:392.

44. John Smith's account of the Starving Time, *Generall Historie*, 2:232–33 (quote on 233).

45. Rachel B. Hermann, "'The tragicall historie': Cannibalism and Abundance in Colonial Jamestown," *William and Mary Quarterly*, 3rd ser., 68, no. 1 (2011): 49.

46. Medical information about starvation may be found at http://www.healthatoz.com/healthatoz/Atoz/common/standard/transform.jsp?requestURI=/healthatoz/Atoz/ency/starvation.jsp. On the environment at Jamestown, see Carville V. Earle, "Environment, Disease, and Mortality in Early Virginia," in *The Chesapeake in the Seventeenth Century: Essays on Anglo-American Society*, ed. Thad W. Tate and David L. Ammerman (Chapel Hill: University of North Carolina Press, 1979), 96–125; Karen Ordahl Kupperman, "Apathy and Death in Early Jamestown," *Journal of American History* 66 (June 1979); and Darrett and Anita Rutman, "Of Agues and Fevers: Malaria in the Early Chesapeake," *William and Mary Quarterly*, 3rd ser., 23 (January 1976): 31–60.

47. Kelso, *Jamestown: The Buried Truth*, 164–66; Bernhard, "'Men, Women, and Children' at Jamestown." For other accounts of early Jamestown, see Horn,

A Land as God Made It (see chap. 1, n. 21); David A. Price, *Love and Hate in Jamestown* (New York: Alfred A. Knopf, 2003); and Connie Lapallo, *Dark Enough to See the Stars in a Jamestown Sky* (Coral Gables, Fla.: Lumina Stars, 2006).

48. Broadside, quoted in Barbour, *Three Worlds,* 288 (see chap. 2, n. 4). See also Brown, *Genesis of the United States,* 1:354.

49. Council of Virginia, *True and Sincere Declaration,* 339 (see chap. 1, n. 30).

50. Ibid., 344, 343; Van Meteren, *Historical Commentaries,* 2:270.

51. Council of Virginia, *True and Sincere Declaration,* 347.

52. Ibid., 346, 347, 351, 350.

53. Percy, "A Trewe Relacyon," 1100, 1097.

54. Ibid., 1100–1101.

55. Ibid., 1101.

56. http://www.healthatoz.com/healthatoz/Atoz/common/standard/transform.jsp?requestURI=/healthatoz/Atoz/ency/starvation.jsp.

57. Percy, "A Trewe Relacyon," 1101.

5. Deliverance

1. Strachey, "A true reportory," 1008 (see chap. 1, n. 29).

2. Ibid., 1010.

3. Ibid., 1011.

4. Barbour, *Three Worlds,* 294 (see chap. 2, n. 4).

5. Strachey, "A true reportory," 1008; Butler, *Historye of the Bermudaes,* 14 (see chap. 1, n. 19).

6. Ivor Noel Hume, "The Mystery of Sir George Somers and His Bermuda Triangle," in *1607: Jamestown and the New World* (New York: Colonial Williamsburg Foundation and Rowan and Littlefield, 2007), 86–93.

7. Strachey, "A true reportory," 1008.

8. Jourdain, *A discovery of the Barmudas,* 1:20 (see chap. 1, n. 47).

9. Strachey, "A true reportory," 1012.

10. Ibid.

11. Ibid.

12. Ibid.

13. Percy, "A Trewe Relacyon," 1101 (see chap. 2, n. 63).

14. Strachey, "A true reportory," 1014.

15. Percy, "A Trewe Relacyon," 1101–2. In the 1922 transcription, the word *anotannes* was rendered "anatomies," as if Percy had meant to describe the starving survivors as skeletons. But describing them as "anotannes," with flesh hanging on their thin frames, is more precise.

16. Strachey, "A true reportory," 1014.

17. Ibid.

18. Ibid.

19. Ibid.

20. All quotations here are in Percy, "A Trewe Relacyon," 1102.

21. Strachey, "A true reportory," 1021.

22. Kelso, *Jamestown: The Buried Truth*, 89–91 (see chap. 1, n. 10).

23. Strachey, "A true reportory," 1021.

24. De La Warr, "Letter to Salisbury, rec'd September 1610," in *Jamestown Narratives*, ed. Haile, 467 (see chap. 1, n. 26).

25. Strachey, "A true reportory," 1007.

26. Percy, "A Trewe Relacyon," 1102.

27. De La Warr and Virginia Council, "Letter to the Virginia Company of London, 7 July 1610," in *Jamestown Narratives*, ed. Haile, 454.

28. Somers, "Letter to Salisbury, 15 June 1610," ibid., 445; Strachey, "A true reportory," 1022.

29. William Crashaw, "Epistle Dedicatory," in Alexander Whitaker, *Good News from Virginia*, in *Jamestown Narratives*, ed. Haile, 702. See also *A Plaine Description of the Barmudas now called Sommer Ilands . . .* (London, 1613), reprinted in Peter Force, *Tracts and Other Papers, Relating Principally to the Origin, Settlement, and Progress of the Colonies in North America*, 4 vols. (Washington, D.C., 1836–1846), vol. 1.

30. Smith, *Generall Historie*, 2:234–35 (see chap. 1, n. 18).

31. Strachey, "A true reportory," 1027.

32. The story of Strachey's manuscript and Shakespeare's *Tempest* has been recently told in Hobson Woodward's *Brave Vessel*, 147–80 (see introduction, n. 1).

33. Strachey, "A true reportory," 1028.

34. Somers to Salisbury, June 15, 1610, in *Jamestown Narratives*, ed. Haile, 446; Butler, *Historye of the Bermudaes*, 15 (see chap. 1, n. 19).

35. Strachey, "A true reportory," 1029.

36. De La Warr, "Letter to Salisbury," September 1610, in *Jamestown Narratives*, ed. Haile, 466–67.

37. Strachey, "A true reportory," 1036, 1029.

38. Ibid., 1034.

39. De La Warr, "Letter to Salisbury," 455.

40. Strachey, "A true reportory," 1029.

41. Ibid., 1030.

42. Ibid.

43. Percy, "A Trewe Relacyon," 1103.

44. Ibid., 1104.

45. Ibid., 1104, 1105.

46. "Letter to the Virginia Company," in *Jamestown Narratives*, ed. Haile, 463.

47. Zuñiga, "Letter of June 10, 1610," in *Genesis of the United States*, by Brown, 1:392 (see chap. 1, n. 2).

6. A Tale of Two Colonies

1. Butler, *Historye of the Bermudaes*, 110 (see chap. 1, n. 19); Ralph Hamor, *A True Discourse of the Present Estate of Virginia, and the successe of the affaires there till the 18 of June, 1614...*, in *Captain John Smith*, ed. Horn, 1130 (see chap. 1, n. 29).

2. Velasco to Philip III, September 30, 1610, in *Genesis of the United States*, by Brown, 1:418–19 (see chap. 1, n. 2). The Spanish were right: things were not going well in Virginia. See J. Frederick Fausz, "An 'Abundance of Blood Shed on Both Sides': England's First Indian War, 1609–1614," *Virginia Magazine of History and Biography* 98, no. 1 (1990), 3–56.

3. "Report of Francis Magnel's Relation of the first Voyage and the Beginnings of the Virginia Colony," July 1, 1610, in *Jamestown Voyages*, ed. Barbour, 1:155 (see chap. 1, n. 7). Francis Magnel was an Irishman, and it is likely that his name was Maguel or McGill.

4. Robert Rich, "News from Virginia. The lost flock triumphant...," in *Jamestown Narratives*, ed. Haile, 377 (see chap. 1, n. 26); Strachey, "A true reportory," 1016 (see chap. 1, n. 29); Somers, "Letter to Salisbury," in *Jamestown Narratives*, ed. Haile, 446.

5. Council of Virginia, *A True Declaration of the estate of the colony in Virginia, with a confutation of such scandalous reports . . .*, in *Jamestown Narratives*, ed. Haile, 473–74.

6. Butler, *Historye of the Bermudaes*, 15.

7. Smith, *Generall Historie*, 2:350–51 (see chap. 1, n. 18).

8. John Stowe, *Annales or Generael Chronicles of England* (London, 1615), quoted in Brown, *Genesis of the United States*, 2:750.

9. Butler, *Historye of the Bermudaes*, 16.

10. Ibid., 175, 306.

11. Letter of Don Francisco de Varte Caron, May 24, 1611, in "Spanish Intentions for Bermuda," ed. Wilkinson, 52, 53 (see chap. 1, n. 6).

12. De La Warr, "Letter to Salisbury, 22 June 1611," in *Jamestown Narratives*, ed. Haile, 526.

13. William Box's account of De La Warr's voyage in Smith, *Generall Historie*, 2:237.

14. De La Warr, "A Short Relation to the Council of Virginea," in *Jamestown Narratives*, ed. Haile, 529.

15. Velasco to Philip II, August 22, 1611, in *Genesis of the United States*, by Brown, 1:495.

16. Woodward, *Brave Vessel*, 7 (see introduction, n. 1).

17. Rowse, *Expansion of Elizabethan England*, 160 (see chap. 2, n. 1). Hobson Woodward's *Brave Vessel* (147–56) offers a well-reasoned account of Strachey's connection to *The Tempest*. For an analysis of the arguments surrounding this literary mystery, see Alden T. Vaughan, "William Strachey's 'True Reportory' and Shakespeare: A Closer Look at the Evidence," *Shakespeare Quarterly* 59, no. 3 (2008): 245–73.

18. Charles Richard Sanders, "William Strachey, the Virginia Colony, and Shakespeare," *Virginia Magazine of History and Biography* 57, no. 2 (1949): 122.

19. David Kathman, introduction to *Dating "The Tempest,"* http://shakespeareauthorship.com/tempest.html. See also Charles Boyce, *Shakespeare A to Z: The Essential Reference to His Plays, His Poems, His Life and Times, and More* (Oxford and New York: Roundtable Press, 1990); and Avery Kolb, "*The Tempest,*" *American Heritage* 34, no. 3 (1983): 26–35.

20. Strachey, "A true reportory," 984–85.

21. Virginia Mason Vaughan and Alden T. Vaughan, eds., *The Tempest,* Arden Shakespeare Critical Edition (Walton-on-Thames, England: Thomas Nelson and Sons, 1999), 6, 287.

22. William Strachey, *For the Colony in Virginea Britannia. Lawes Divine, Morall and Martiall, &c.,* in "First-Hand Accounts from Virginia, 1575–1705," http://etext.lib.virginia.edu/etcbin/jamestown-browse?id=J1056, 8–9.

23. On the history of *A Map of Virginia,* see Barbour, *Complete Works of John Smith,* 1:121–26 (see chap. 1, n. 13).

24. Culliford, *William Strachey, 1571–1621,* 133 (see chap. 1, n. 27).

25. Ibid., 140.

26. Kelso, *Jamestown: The Buried Truth,* 189 (see chap. 1, n. 10).

27. Edmund Morgan, *American Slavery/American Freedom: The Ordeal of Colonial Virginia* (New York: W. W. Norton, 1975), 80ff.

28. Vaughan, *American Genesis,* 79 (see chap. 2, n. 6). On Thomas Dale, see Darrett Rutman, "The Historian and the Marshal: A Note on the Background of Sir Thomas Dale," *Virginia Magazine of History and Biography* 68 (July 1960).

29. Percy, "A Trewe Relacyon," 1110 (see chap. 2, n. 63); "Declaration of the Englishman in Virginia, 1611," in *Jamestown Narratives,* ed. Haile, 545.

30. Velasco to Philip III, December 24, 1610, in *Genesis of the United States,* by Brown, 2:531–32; Percy, "A Trewe Relacyon," 1111.

31. Thomas Dale, "Letter to Salisbury, 17 August 1611," in *Jamestown Narratives,* ed. Haile, 557.

32. Velasco to Philip III, December 31, 1610, in *Genesis of the United States,* by Brown, 1:443.

33. John Chamberlain to Dudley Carleton, February 12, 1612, in *The Letters of John Chamberlain,* ed. Norman Egbert McClure, 2 vols. (Philadelphia: American Philosophical Society, 1939), 1:334.

34. Wilkinson, "Spanish Intentions for Bermuda," 69.

35. Velasco to Philip III, June 18, 1612, in *Genesis of the United States,* by Brown, 2:560.

36. Ibid.

37. Smith, *Generall Historie,* 2:353; Lefroy, *Memorials,* 1:66 (see chap. 1, n. 47).

38. "An addition sent home by the last ships from our Colonies in the Barmudas," in *Memorials,* by Lefroy, 1:65–72. A long report by an unknown writer who may have been in Virginia as well (69n1).

39. Butler, *Historye of the Bermudaes,* 20.

40. Henry, Earl of Northampton, to James I, quoted in Lefroy, *Memorials,* 1:65.

41. John Chamberlain to Sir Dudley Carleton, July 9, 1612, in *Letters of John Chamberlain,* ed. McClure, 1:367.

42. Barbour, *Jamestown Voyages,* 2:322.

43. Smith, *Generall Historie,* 2:351–52; Butler, *Historye of the Bermudaes,* 18–19.

44. Wilkinson, *Adventurers of Bermuda,* 67 (see chap. 1, n. 32).

45. Smith, *Generall Historie,* 2:354.

46. Ibid.

47. Wilkinson, *Adventurers of Bermuda,* 2.

48. Diego de Molina, "Letter [to Don Alonso de Velasco], 28 May 1613," in *Jamestown Narratives,* ed. Haile, 748; Chamberlain to Carleton, October 27, 1613, in *Letters of John Chamberlain,* ed. McClure, 1:483.

49. Smith, *Generall Historie,* 2:354.

50. Harris, *Bermuda Forts, 1612–1957,* 46n9 (see chap. 3, n. 30).

51. Butler, *Historye of the Bermudaes,* 26, 33–34.

52. Ralph Hamor, quoted in Michael Leroy Oberg, *Dominion and Civility: English Imperialism and Native America* (Ithaca: Cornell University Press, 1999), 64. See also Morgan, *American Slavery,* 82; and Lefroy, *Memorials,* 1:228.

53. Acuña to Philip, October 5, 1613, in "Spanish Intentions for Bermuda," ed. Wilkinson, 75.

54. John Clark, "Confession of the English Pilot of Virginia, 18 February 1613," in *Jamestown Narratives,* ed. Haile, 693, 694; "John Clark of the *Mayflower,*" *Massachusetts Historical Society Proceedings,* 3rd ser., 54 (1920): 61–77.

55. Digby to James I, February 18, 1613, in *Genesis of the United States,* by Brown, 2:606–7.

56. Digby to James I, March 5, August 15, 1613, ibid., 609, 656; Wilkinson, "Spanish Intentions for Bermuda," 64.

57. Velasco to Philip III, May 30, 1613, in *Genesis of the United States,* by Brown, 2:634; Don Diego de Molina, "Letter [to Don Alonso de Velasco], 28 May 1613," in *Jamestown Narratives,* ed. Haile, 751.

58. Molina, "Letter [to Velasco], 28 May 1613," in *Jamestown Narratives,* ed. Haile, 746, 747, 748, 749.

59. The portrait is reproduced in Haile, *Jamestown Narratives,* 788.

60. Biographical sketch, in *Genesis of the United States,* by Brown, 2:899–901.

61. Wilkinson, "Spanish Intentions for Bermuda," 61, 62, 64, 65.

62. Ibid., 68, 69.

63. Ibid., 73.

64. Acuña to Philip III, October 5, 1613, in *Genesis of the United States,* by Brown, 2:660.

65. Acuña to Philip III, March 17, 1614, ibid., 680–81, 683.

66. Wilkinson, "Spanish Intentions for Bermuda," 74.

67. Crashaw, "Epistle Dedicatory," 702 (see chap. 5, n. 29).

68. Chamberlain to Carleton, August 1, 1613, in *Letters of John Chamberlain,* ed. McClure, 1:468.

69. Rolfe's letters in Ralph Hamor, *A True Discourse of the present estate of Virginia,* 1164, 1165; in Horn, *Captain John Smith,* 1115–68 (quotes on 1164, 1165). On Pocahontas, see Robert S. Tilton, *Pocahontas: The Evolution of an American Narrative* (Cambridge: Cambridge University Press, 1994); and Camilla Townsend, *Pocahontas and the Powhatan Dilemma* (New York: Hill and Wang, 2004).

70. Horn, *Captain John Smith,* 1166.

71. Hamor's visit to Powhatan is in Smith, *Generall Historie,* 2:249–50.

72. Ibid., 248.

73. Butler, *Historye of the Bermudaes,* 31. Ulivari's visit to Bermuda is in Wilkinson, "Spanish Intentions for Bermuda," 84–85.

74. Lewis Hughes quoted in Lefroy, *Memorials,* 1:77; W. F. Craven and Walter Hayward, eds., *Journal of Richard Norwood* (Ann Arbor: Scholars' Facsimiles and Reprints, 1945), lxxvii; Wilkinson, *Adventurers of Bermuda,* 82–88.

75. Horn, *Captain John Smith,* 1115–68.

76. Ibid., 1134–35.

7. THE CONFLUENCE OF THREE CULTURES

1. Lefroy, *Memorials,* 1:116 (see chap. 1, n. 47).

2. Butler, *Historye of the Bermudaes,* 78, 84 (quote) (see chap. 1, n. 19).

3. Wilkinson, "Spanish Intentions for Bermuda," 57 (see chap. 1, n. 6).

4. Winthrop Jordan's *White over Black: American Attitudes towards the Negro, 1550–1812* (Chapel Hill: University of North Carolina Press, 1968) shaped slavery studies for a generation.

5. Virginia Bernhard, *Slaves and Slaveholders in Bermuda, 1616–1782* (Columbia: University of Missouri Press, 1999), 19.

6. J. H. Elliott, "The Iberian Atlantic and Virginia," in *Atlantic World and Virginia,* ed. Mancall, 555 (see chap. 1, n. 1).

7. Kelso, *Jamestown: The Buried Truth,* 87–89 (see chap. 1, n. 10).

8. James I, *A Counterblaste to Tobacco* (London, 1604; reprint, 1616).

9. Butler, *Historye of the Bermudaes,* 29.

10. Smith, *Generall Historie,* 2:262 (see chap. 1, n. 18).

11. Philip Alexander Bruce, *An Economic History of Virginia in the Seventeenth Century* (New York: Macmillan, 1907), 263; Virginia Bernhard, "Bermuda and Virginia in the Seventeenth Century: A Comparative View," *Journal of Social History* 1 (September 1985): 61; Butler, *Historye of the Bermudaes,* 110.

12. For a portrait and biographical sketch, see Vernon A. Ives, ed., *The Rich*

Papers: Letters from Bermuda, 1615–1646: Eyewitness Accounts Sent by the Early Colonists to Sir Nathaniel Rich (Toronto: University of Toronto Press, 1984), 390, 391.

13. Wesley Frank Craven, *Dissolution of the Virginia Company of London: The Failure of a Colonial Experiment* (New York: Oxford University Press, 1932), 126.

14. Ibid., 128.

15. Robert Rich to Nathaniel Rich, in *Rich Papers,* ed. Ives, 25.

16. Robert Rich to Nathaniel Rich, February 22, 1617/18, ibid., 59.

17. John Rolfe to Sir Edwin Sandys, letter of January 1619/20, in *The Records of the Virginia Company of London,* ed. Susan Myra Kingsbury, 4 vols. (Washington, D.C.: Government Printing Office, 1933), 3:243.

18. Brown, *First Republic,* 327 (see chap. 4, n. 7). Scholars have puzzled for decades over the arrival of the first Africans in Virginia. See, for example, Wesley Frank Craven, "Twenty Negroes to Jamestown in 1619?" *Virginia Quarterly Review* 47 (Summer 1971): 416–20; and Alden T. Vaughan, "Blacks in Virginia: A Note on the First Decade," *William and Mary Quarterly,* 3rd ser., 24 (July 1972): 469–78.

19. William Thorndale, "The Virginia Census of 1619," *Virginia Magazine of Genealogy* 33, no. 3 (1995): 60–161; Martha McCartney, "An Early Virginia Census Reprised," *Quarterly Bulletin of the Archaeological Society of Virginia* 54 (1999): 178–96.

20. Brown, *First Republic,* 327.

21. Thorndale, "Virginia Census of 1619," 168.

22. See Daniel Elfrith, "Guide to the Caribbean, 1631," ed. Stanley Pargellis and Ruth Lapham Butler, *William and Mary Quarterly,* 3rd ser., 1 (1944): 273–316; and Smith, *Generall Historie,* 2:373–74 (quote on 374).

23. Ibid., 266.

24. "Sir Nathaniel Rich's Draft Defending the Earl of Warwick," in *Rich Papers,* ed. Ives, 148.

25. Craven, *Dissolution of the Virginia Company,* 130.

26. Engel Sluiter, "New Light on the '20. and Odd Negroes' Arriving in Virginia, August 1619," *William and Mary Quarterly,* 3rd ser., 54, no. 2 (1997): 397; John Thornton, "The African Experience of the '20. and Odd Negroes' Arriving in Virginia in 1619," *William and Mary Quarterly,* 3rd ser., 55, no. 3 (1998): 421–34.

27. Annie Lash Jester and Martha Woodruff Hiden, *Adventurers of Purse and Person: Virginia, 1607–1625,* ed. Virginia M. Meyer and John Frederick Dorman, 3rd ed. (1956; reprint, Richmond, Va.: Dietz Press, 1987), 140–41, 141n16.

28. Kingsbury, *Records of the Virginia Company,* 3:243.

29. "Sir Nathaniel Rich's Draft," in *Rich Papers,* ed. Ives, 150; Rolfe, letter to Sandys, January 1619/20, in *Records of the Virginia Company,* ed. Kingsbury, 3:243.

30. On the census, see Irene W. D. Hecht, "The Virginia Muster as a Source for Demographic History," *William and Mary Quarterly,* 3rd ser., 30 (January 1973): 65–92. "A List of the Living and the Dead in Virginia," made in February 1623/24,

lists twenty-two Africans. The list is printed in John Camden Hotten, ed., *The Original Lists of Persons of Quality . . . and Others Who Went from Great Britain to the American Plantations, 1600–1700* (London, 1874), 169–89.

31. "Letter of John Pory, 1619," quoted in Sluiter, "New Light," 395.

32. "John Dutton to the Earl of Warwick, 20 January 1619/20," in *Rich Papers,* ed. Ives, 140 (quote), 91, 389.

33. Ibid., 142.

34. "Governor Nathaniel Butler to the Earl of Warwick, 9 October 1620," ibid., 185.

35. "Sir Nathaniel Rich's Draft," ibid., 148.

36. Ibid., 149.

37. Quoted in Brown, *First Republic,* 358.

38. "Sir Nathaniel Rich's Draft," in *Rich Papers,* ed. Ives, 153.

39. Kingsbury, *Records of the Virginia Company,* 1:367.

40. Lyon G. Tyler, ed., *Narratives of Early Virginia, 1606–1625* (New York: Charles Scribner's Sons, 1907), 283; "Governor Nathaniel Butler to Sir Nathaniel Rich, 23 October 1620," in *Rich Papers,* ed. Ives, 196.

41. Butler, *Historye of the Bermudaes,* 120; Craven, *Dissolution of the Virginia Company,* 96; *A Declaration of the State of the Colony and Affairs in Virginia* (1622), reprinted in Force, *Tracts and Other Papers,* vol. 3, no. 5 (see chap. 5, n. 29). See also Craven, *Dissolution of the Virginia Company,* 95n21. Theodore K. Rabb, *Jacobean Gentleman: Sir Edwin Sandys, 1561–1629* (Princeton: Princeton University Press, 1998), 350, says that the *Declaration* was "almost certainly written by Sandys."

42. Rabb, *Jacobean Gentleman,* 326–27.

43. Ibid., 108.

44. Nathaniel Philbrick, *Mayflower* (New York: Viking, 2006), 26. See also Caleb Johnson, "The True Origin of Stephen Hopkins of the *Mayflower,*" *American Genealogist* 73, no. 3 (1998): 161–71.

45. Smith, *Generall Historie,* 2:284, 295, 262.

46. Ibid., 285.

47. Daniel K. Richter, "Tsenacommacah and the Atlantic World," in *Atlantic World,* ed. Mancall, 64–65.

48. Smith, *Generall Historie,* 2:294.

49. Ibid., 298. See also Alden T. Vaughan, "'Expulsion of the Savages': English Policy and the Virginia Massacre of 1622," *William and Mary Quarterly,* 3rd ser., 35 (January 1978), 57–84.

50. Smith, *Generall Historie,* 2:305–6.

51. Butler, *Historye of the Bermudaes,* 11, 129; Smith, *Generall Historie,* 2:320.

52. "The Virginia Planters' Answer to Captain Butler, 1623," in *Narratives of Early Virginia,* ed. Tyler, 414.

53. Brown, *First Republic,* 519–22.

54. "The Answer of the General Assembly in Virginia to 'A Declaration of the

state of the colony in the 12 years of Sir Thomas Smith's government . . . 20 February 1624,'" in *Narratives of Early Virginia,* ed. Tyler, 423.

55. Jester and Hiden, *Adventurers of Purse and Person,* xxv.

56. Butler, *Historye of the Bermudaes,* 144; Lefroy, *Memorials,* 1:281.

57. Ibid., 1:308–9. On Bermuda slavery there are two histories by native Bermudians: Cyril Outerbridge Packwood, *Chained on the Rock: Slavery in Bermuda* (New York: Eliseo Torres and Sons / Bermuda: Baxter's, 1975); and James M. Smith, *Slavery in Bermuda* (New York: Vantage Press, 1976). See also Bernhard, *Slaves and Slaveholders in Bermuda.*

58. There is a voluminous literature on race and slavery in the English colonies. Alden T. Vaughan's *Roots of American Racism: Essays on the Colonial Experience* (New York: Oxford University Press, 1995) is a good place to begin. Ira Berlin's *Many Thousands Gone: The First Two Centuries of Slavery in North America* (Cambridge: Harvard University Press, 1998) has become a classic.

59. "The Muster of the Inhabitants of Virginia 20 January–7 February 1624/25," in *Adventurers of Purse and Person,* by Jester and Hiden, 7–71. The households described in the following paragraphs are on pp. 24–51.

60. The definitive account of Anthony Johnson is Timothy Breen and Stephen Innes, *"Myne Owne Ground": Race and Freedom on Virginia's Eastern Shore, 1640–1676* (New York: Oxford University Press, 1980).

61. The list is printed in *Rich Papers,* ed. Ives, 241–44.

62. On the lives of Francisco and other Africans in Bermuda, see Bernhard, *Slaves and Slaveholders in Bermuda,* 20–21, 23–24.

63. Quoted in Virginia Bernhard, "Beyond the Chesapeake: The Contrasting Status of Blacks in Bermuda, 1616–1663," *Journal of Southern History* 54, no. 4 (1988): 550.

64. "Governor Nathaniel Butler to Sir Nathaniel Rich, 12 January 1620/21," in *Rich Papers,* ed. Ives, 229.

65. See Jack Forbes, *Africans and Native Peoples: The Language of Race and the Evolution of Red-Black Peoples* (Urbana: University of Illinois Press, 1993); and Timothy Hashaw, *The Birth of Black America: The First African Americans and the Pursuit of Freedom at Jamestown* (New York: Carroll and Graf, 2007).

INDEX